PIMPING FICTIONS

PIMPING FICTIONS

African American Crime Literature and the Untold Story of Black Pulp Publishing

JUSTIN GIFFORD

Temple University Press
PHILADELPHIA

Temple University Press
Philadelphia, Pennsylvania 19122
www.temple.edu/tempress

Published 2013

LIBRARY OF CONGRESS CATALOGING-IN-PUBLICATION DATA

Gifford, Justin, 1975–
    Pimping fictions : African American crime literature and the untold story
of Black pulp publishing / Justin Gifford.
        p.   cm.
    Includes bibliographical references and index.
    ISBN 978-1-4399-0810-5 (cloth : alk. paper)
    ISBN 978-1-4399-0811-2 (pbk. : alk. paper)
    ISBN 978-1-4399-0812-9 (e-book)
    1. American fiction—African American authors—History and criticism.
2. Detective and mystery stories, American—History and criticism. 3. Urban fiction,
American—History and criticism. 4. African Americans in literature. 5. Crime in
literature. 6. Pulp literature, American—Publishing—History. 7. Holloway House
Publishing Co.—History. 8. Himes, Chester B., 1909–1984—Criticism and interpretation.
9. Goines, Donald, 1937–1974—Criticism and interpretation. 10. Iceberg Slim, 1918–1992
Pimp. I. Title.
PS374.N4G485   2013
813'.087209896073—dc23
                                                                2012032598

♾ The paper used in this publication meets the requirements of the American
National Standard for Information Sciences—Permanence of Paper for Printed
Library Materials, ANSI Z39.48–1992

Printed in the United States of America

2 4 6 8 9 7 5 3 1

THE
AMERICAN
LITERATURES
INITIATIVE

A book in the American Literatures Initiative (ALI), a collaborative
publishing project of NYU Press, Fordham University Press, Rutgers
University Press, Temple University Press, and the University of Virginia
Press. The Initiative is supported by The Andrew W. Mellon Foundation.
For more information, please visit www.americanliteratures.org.

CONTENTS

Acknowledgments

Every intellectual endeavor is the product of many contributors; this project is no different. I first owe a debt of gratitude to Ross Posnock and Kenneth Warren, early mentors who transformed my understanding of race, literature, and American culture. Many teachers and scholars at the University of Virginia shaped my work and helped me clarify my thinking, including Deborah McDowell, Rita Felski, Marlon Ross, Ian Grandison, and especially Jennifer Wicke, the toughest and fairest critic I have ever encountered. My peers at Virginia, Michael Lundblad, Sarah Hagelin, Andrea Stevens, and Jolie Sheffer, taught me what a supportive intellectual community could be. Many of the arguments in the book were tested at Dartmouth's Futures of American Studies Institute, Harvard's English Institute, and the Cultural Studies Now Conference in London. Special thanks to those who asked probing questions and provided helpful advice in the early stages of developing the project. I am particularly grateful to Eric Lott, the chair of my dissertation committee, whose friendship, guidance, and unflagging support over the years have been a source of inspiration throughout my intellectual journey.

This book would quite simply not exist in its current form without the contributions of a number of people whom I interviewed over the years. Many thanks to Bentley Morriss and Diane Beck, who shared their knowledge of Robert Beck and Holloway House Publishing Company. Thanks to Roland Jefferson, Odie Hawkins, Zola Hawkins, Emory Holmes, and Wanda Coleman, all of whom spent many hours talking with me in interviews and helping me understand the art and business of black crime literature. Their insights were crucial to the development of many of the main arguments of this book. Special thanks to Betty Mae Shue, Camille Beck, and Misty Beck for sharing their memories of Robert Beck in interviews. I owe a particular debt of gratitude to Eddie Allen, who shared with me important primary documents owned by the late Donald Goines. Finally, I would like to thank Jorge Hinojosa and Ice-T, who invited me to participate in their documentary film, *Iceberg Slim: Portrait of a Pimp*, and who provided me access to many primary documents, interviews, and manuscripts.

Furthermore, this project could not have been completed without the help of librarians, private book collectors, and street vendors. The library staff at the Schomburg Center for Research in Black Culture and the Ned Guymon Mystery and Detective Fiction Collection at Occidental College provided me with invaluable assistance. Special thanks to the owners of the Magazine in San Francisco, Black and Nobel Books in Philadelphia, and Black Star Line Music and Video in Harlem for helping me track down rare and out-of-print books and magazines and for sharing their knowledge about the contemporary African American literary scene.

I completed this project with the financial and intellectual support of my home institution, the University of Nevada, Reno. A Junior Faculty Research Grant and several Scholarly and Creative Activities Awards furnished me with the resources to create my database of African American novels and magazines. To my colleagues in the Department of English, I owe thanks for their comradeship and scholarly insight. For their mentorship and critical comments on various drafts of the manuscript, I owe a great deal of thanks to Scott Casper, Eric Rasmussen, Mike Branch, and Jen Hill. I am grateful for all my junior faculty colleagues, whose stimulating and supportive friendship over the years gave me the strength to finish this book. Thanks in particular to Lynda Walsh, whose professionalism has been inspirational to me, and to Cathy Chaput, my friend and ally in the struggle for radical egalitarianism. I want to give special recognition to Erin James, who read and commented on multiple drafts of the complete manuscript and who always asked the right questions.

My students have been an ongoing source of encouragement and research assistance for this project. They have found rare and out-of-print books, helped me construct my database of black crime novels, and challenged my thinking about black popular culture through many exciting conversations. Although there are far too many people on this list to acknowledge, I would like to thank Vanna Nguyen, Linda

Kay Hardie, Jamie Farley, Katie O'Neill, Rachel Baez, Brianna Thompson, and Brad Nelson. I am particularly grateful for my many talented graduate students, as their energetic collegiality and sincere personal investment in literature and cultural politics is what this profession is supposed to be all about. Thanks especially to Josh Culpepper, Tom Hertweck, Sylvan Goldberg, Jessica Fanaselle, and Kyle Bladow, who read drafts of the manuscript and offered insightful comments or who influenced my understanding of African American crime literature through thought-provoking discussion. Special thanks to Emily Katseanas for always serving up realness in our conversations. Additionally, I would like to thank Laurel Griffiths for her exceptional editorial work and for creating the index for this book.

Many thanks to my agent, Matthew Carnicelli, for believing in this project and placing it with a major university press. I would like to thank Temple University Press for its professional treatment of my manuscript. I want to acknowledge the work of my three anonymous readers, who offered a number of insightful comments to help improve the manuscript. I also appreciate the tireless work of my editor, Mick Gusinde-Duffy, who brought this book to completion.

Finally, I would like to dedicate this book to my family and friends. My best friends, Johann Sehmsdorf and Beckett Senter, have been supporters of my writing for over two decades now. Blythe Kladney provided love and encouragement during the most difficult stages of the writing process. I am grateful for the friendship of Rei Magosaki, my co-conspirator and partner in crime for many years. Madeline Chaput, your smiling face has brought magic to the world. Finally, my parents, Larry and Karen, and my sister, Jessica, have been the greatest source of inspiration for my work. Thank you for teaching me how to take joy in fighting the good fight.

Introduction

Late in Ralph Ellison's 1952 classic of African American literature, *Invisible Man*, there is a scene that illustrates the contentious relationship between hip urban styles and black cultural politics that emerged in conversations about racial uplift in the twentieth century. After Invisible Man (IM) witnesses race leader turned sidewalk salesman of Sambo puppets Tod Clifton gunned down by a police officer, he wanders to a subway platform, where he contemplates the meaning of Clifton's death. Because IM is still committed to the communist organization known as the Brotherhood, he cannot comprehend Clifton's seeming betrayal of the party—his decision, as IM puts it, "to plunge into nothingness, into the void of faceless faces, of soundless voices, lying outside history."[1] It is at this moment that IM spots three young men wearing zoot suits entering the subway platform. Sporting conked hair, identical felt hats, ballooning trousers, and "too-hot-for-summer suits," these hipsters display a "severe formality," which reminds IM of an African statue, "distorted in the interest of a design."[2] Fascinated by these codes he cannot quite decipher, IM follows the zoot suiters onto the subway, where he watches them read comic books. Here IM has a realization about the limits of the Brotherhood's model for comprehending the complexities of black urban culture in relationship to political organization: "Then I saw the cover of the comic book and thought, Clifton would have known them better than I. He knew them all the time. I studied them closely until they left the train, their shoulders rocking, their heavy heel plates, clicking remote cryptic messages in the brief silence of the train's stop."[3] Both figuratively and literally transmitting secret codes known only to the hip with their chic outfits, the zoot suiters cause IM to reflect on his own political arrogance of assuming the role of race leader.

Although this moment only takes up a few pages in Ellison's lengthy novel, it is a powerful illustration of one of the unresolved problems posed by African American literature in the twentieth century, namely, the relationships among postures of cool, black culture politics, and the literary marketplace. As consumers of mass-market fiction as well as bearers of edgy popular style, the zoot suiters highlight the cultural and class divides among urban African Americans in mid-twentieth-century America. Furthermore, the scene calls into question the black middle class's presumption of race leadership, given that the culture of the black urban working class remains illegible to them. Although IM starts off the novel thinking of himself as an exemplar of black leadership, a Booker T. Washington–type of figure responsible for the uplift of the black masses, this confrontation with the hipsters leads him to wonder if there might be something politically valuable hidden in the folds of the zoot suit. "But who knew," he asks himself, "who knew but that they were the saviors, the true leaders, the bearers of something precious?"[4] Even as this nagging question remains unanswered throughout the novel, it provides a useful starting point for the following examination of the most popular black literature of the twentieth and twenty-first centuries: African American crime fiction. As a genre and culture industry that dramatizes the contradictory relationship between stylish urban outlaws and black struggles for social and political freedom, African American crime literature stages a charged dialogue about the historical significance of black popular fiction in American political and social life.

Pimping Fictions investigates the black crime fiction tradition and marketplace that has grown over the past fifty years. I use *black crime fiction* here as an umbrella term that encompasses the paperback novels written by African American criminals and prisoners in the years after World War II. This study examines the work of pioneering prison author Chester Himes, the so-called "black experience" novelists published by Holloway House Publishing Company in the 1960s and 1970s, and the popular "street literature" writers that have invented a new African American literary scene in the past decade. As the title of the book indicates, *Pimping Fictions* focuses on the quasi-autobiographical tales of pimps, players, and sex workers, as well as the fictionalized exploits of street hustlers, drug dealers, and political revolutionaries. It traces the development of a black literary tradition that includes some of the most widely read black American authors in history, including Chester Himes, Robert Beck (a.k.a. Iceberg Slim), Donald Goines, Joseph Nazel, Odie Hawkins, Wanda Coleman, Vickie Stringer, Sister Souljah, and Nikki Turner. Their popular novels feature stories of black criminals who attempt to escape the confined spaces of modern America—prisons, housing projects, and ghetto streets. Against the backdrop of these white-constructed spaces of containment and surveillance, the criminal characters of this genre become outlaws as a radical stance against systemic white racism.

As a secondary meaning of the title suggests, *Pimping Fictions* also investigates the relationship of the black pulp writer to the paperback publishing industry. While pimping and prostitution are often the subject matter of the novels in this genre, they also operate as apt metaphors for understanding the modes of production of black crime literature. As a number of scholars of African American literature have shown, pimping can be a useful symbolic system for comprehending the black artist's precarious position in the commercial marketplace.[5] This is particularly useful in the study of black crime fiction, which has been promoted as a sensationalist exposé of America's seedy underbelly, especially following the establishment of Holloway House Publishing Company, a white-operated niche publisher of paperback novels in the late 1960s. The constraints created by the pulp publishing industry have placed black crime novelists in a particularly vulnerable position in the literary marketplace, as they have fought to strike a balance among commercial, political, and artistic imperatives. Tracing this twin development in black crime fiction—the story of the black criminal against the backdrop of the American ghetto, and the struggles of the black crime writer in the literary marketplace—*Pimping Fictions* investigates black pulp publishing's advance as a coherent body of literature and as a cultural movement worthy of scholarly attention.

The organizing argument of this study is that black crime fiction developed as a literary and political response to white-sponsored methods of containment created in the years following World War II. Urban renewal policies, Federal Housing Authority–supported white flight in every American major city with a sizable black population, and the mass incarceration of black men and women in state and federal prisons have all constituted very real geographical and social divisions in America. To borrow from Michel Foucault, the regulated spaces of the ghetto street, the prison, and the project are "heterotopias of deviation," disciplinary spaces that regulate the behavior of people who are considered outside the perceived social norm.[6] Over the course of the twentieth century, white Americans created a range of institutional and individual methods to contain African Americans in ghetto neighborhoods and prisons. This study examines the transforming modes of representation in popular black literature as an artistic and political response to these material and symbolic spaces of racial containment. In this way, my work departs from other examinations of black crime literature, such as Jerry H. Bryant's *Born in a Mighty Bad Land* and Jonathan Munby's *Under a Bad Sign.*[7] While these works take seriously the study of black criminal self-representation, they tend to view the pimp, the hustler, and other black criminal characters as more recent literary expressions of the "bad man" character, an African American antihero that can be traced back to the ballads of Stagolee. While this kind of "vernacular criticism" no doubt has merit as a way of identifying a coherent African American cultural tradition, it also has the limitation of treating the black criminal figure as a transhistorical archetype that transcends time and place.[8] *Pimping Fictions* looks to contextualize the popular representations of black criminals by examining the literature as a creative collective response to the repressive racial regimes of Jim Crow modernity. In this way, this study builds on the recent investigations into the relationship among African American literature, the spaces of urban modernity, and cultural politics, such as Madhu Dubey's *Signs and Cities: Black Literary Postmodernism* and Carlo Rotella's *October Cities: The Redevelopment of Urban Literature.*[9] However, I shift attention away from black naturalist, modernist, and postmodernist works in order to look at how the black crime fiction genre and marketplace have been shaped by America's carceral spaces and how this literature has in turn shaped these spaces.

One of the features of black crime literature that makes it so complex is that it is saturated by contradictions in its stance toward the allure of criminal posturing as well as the respectability of the middle class. All the major innovators of the genre—Chester Himes, Robert Beck, Donald Goines, Joseph Nazel, Wanda Coleman, Vickie Stringer, and Sister Souljah—had contentious relationships with their black middle-class backgrounds, and their works illustrate a sincere ambivalence toward criminal life as a radical stance against white racism and a politically ineffectual black bourgeoisie. Many of them viewed black crime literature as a compelling, though ultimately compromised, mode of resistance to a racist society. By exploring this combination of celebration and exploitation of criminal characters that constitutes black crime fiction—what Eric Lott in another context calls "love and theft"—we gain a better understanding of the contradictory impulses, the unstable modes of representation, and the diverse range of expressions in this genre.[10] The cross-class romances, the tales of frustrated upward mobility, and the narratives of failed revolution are as much mediations on the intraracial class conflict in African American urban life as they are critiques of white racism. By looking at black crime literature in this way—that the criminal life is a seductive stance taken up in response to a racist society and the black bourgeoisie's assumptions of cultural hegemony—the study links together a diverse range of texts, from Chester Himes's antidetective novel to the pimp autobiography of Robert Beck, from the black revolution novels of Donald Goines to the ghettopia fantasies of Joseph Nazel. In a range of complicated and contradictory ways, black crime fiction displays deeply conflicted feeling about the styles and ethos of the criminal underworld as well as about middle-class discipline and respectability. By tracing these incongruous impulses, I hope to provide a clearer understanding of African American crime literature as a paradoxical expression of black popular culture.

At one level, my discussion of black crime fiction adds to histories of African American cultural and literary movements. Although there have been a number of significant literary and cultural histories of American and African American detective fiction, including Stephen Soitos's *The Blues Detective*, Erin Smith's *Hard-Boiled*, and Sean McCann's *Gumshoe America* among many others, there has been virtually no critical attention paid to black crime writing or the culture industry that supports it.[11] The untold story of black pulp publishing and black crime literature represents an important missing chapter in the history of popular literature and African American cultural production. As a literary and cultural history of popular black crime fiction, this book looks to expand the fields of American and African American literature, popular culture, and critical race studies. In particular, this study seeks to enlarge the conversation about black cultural production by contextualizing black crime literature's creation as part of a larger history of contentious alliances between black artists and liberal white patrons. This dynamic can be seen in histories of the creation of the slave narratives, the patronage of Harlem Renaissance writers, the creation of the so-called "race records" in the 1920s, the funding of midcentury "protest" fiction, and the commercialization of hip hop.[12] I draw from a wide range of research materials collected over the past decade—including interviews with publishers, authors, and editors; unpublished letters and manuscripts;

and book contracts and other records—in order to reveal the similarly multifaceted racial history of black crime literature's production.

Pimping Fiction also looks to deepen the conversation about the relationship among black popular culture, African American political and economic freedom, and class division. Black popular culture's role in the quest for equality has been a central concern for artists, race leaders, and intellectuals at least since the formation of the Fisk Jubilee Singers in the middle of the nineteenth century, and especially following the Harlem Renaissance of the 1920s. For instance, Langston Hughes argues in his seminal essay "The Negro Artist and the Racial Mountain" that black popular forms such as the blues could provide much-needed cultural energy and authority for black intellectuals interested in the project of racial uplift and democratic equality. He writes, "Let the blare of Negro jazz bands and the bellowing voice of Bessie Smith singing the blues penetrate the closed ears of the colored near-intellectuals until they listen and perhaps understand."[13] About a decade later, Richard Wright makes a similar argument in his polemic essay "The Blueprint for Negro Writing." He positions his own work as a rejection of Harlem Renaissance writing, claiming that "Negro writing in the past has been confined to humble novels, poems, and plays, prim and decorous ambassadors who went a-begging to white America." However, Wright also states that black folklore could aid the black novelist in the struggle to "create values by which his race is to struggle, live, and die."[14] Ralph Ellison, in both his novel and his essays, again and again looks to black popular culture as the necessary starting point of any broad-based political movement. For instance, responding to the Zoot Suit Riots of 1943, in which white police officers and servicemen roamed the streets of Los Angeles, beating up black and Chicano youths wearing the sharkskin garments, Ellison writes, "Much in Negro life remains a mystery; perhaps the zoot suit conceals profound political meaning; perhaps the symmetrical frenzy of the Lindy Hop conceals clues to great potential power—if only Negro leaders would solve this riddle. For without this knowledge, leadership, no matter how correct its program, will fail."[15] Ellison's statement about the potential political meaning of the zoot suit encapsulates what a number of radically egalitarian African American thinkers contemplated over the course of the twentieth century: black popular culture must be at the core of the project of black art and cultural politics. As a body of work that has essentially translated the urban styles and vernacular of the hip into a mode of literary expression that has been read widely among large numbers of black people, black crime fiction can play a significant role in discussions of the past, present, and future of black cultural politics.

By providing an analysis of the poetics and politics, as well as the production and consumption, of black crime literature, I borrow from the critical frameworks provided by recent scholars of mass-market literature. Informed by the methodologies and practices of the Birmingham School of Cultural Studies, the burgeoning study of genre literature has significantly altered the way we think about romances, dime novels, pulp magazines, hard-boiled detective literature, and domestic fiction. It has also changed the way we conceptualize readers of this fiction.[16] Responding to the classic culture-industry-as-form-of-domination thesis of Frankfurt School Marxists Theodor Adorno and Max Horkheimer, and building on the work of Cultural Studies pioneers Raymond Williams and Stuart Hall, critics such as Janice Radway, Michael Denning, and Fredric Jameson have argued that mass-market books such as romances and dime novels require a distinct mode of analysis because of their unique position as commodity and bearer of cultural ideology.[17] Black crime fiction requires similar attention, as many critics have traditionally passed over this genre despite its enormous popularity among fans and its far larger cultural influence. These critics have assumed incorrectly—simply by their neglect of the genre in toto—that these books are formulaic and that their individual differences are insignificant in the face of their negative ideological effect. This view of mass culture as a form of domination is deeply problematic, as it does not account for the significant differences between individual authors of the genre, nor does it take seriously that readers are anything other than passive dupes. If we are truly invested in American and African American literary traditions and their larger relationships to cultural politics, popular movements, and social change, then black crime fiction presents us with a unique opportunity to redraw the very boundaries of what counts as the American canon and even cultural knowledge. We can no longer afford to ignore this genre of literature, if for no other reason than its complex history and modes of representation challenge our commonsense understandings of freedom and incarceration; race, class, and gender identity; and the connections between high and low culture. Furthermore, as the "other" of the African American literary tradition—a body of work that has been actively repressed in the canon-building project of the past four decades—black crime fiction has been a shadow companion to the more well-received works of Ralph Ellison, Toni Morrison, and James Baldwin. By revealing some of the unsuspected connections between these literary traditions, as well as the unique aesthetics of black crime literature, this study seeks to begin a conversation about the meaning and significance of this genre.

Of course, a more thorough cultural analysis of black crime fiction must be aware of the complex and contradictory ideologies transmitted in these books, while remaining attentive to the style, artistry, and influence of individual authors. While on the surface, these novels appear to be generic pulp fiction, there is significant diversity among them, especially among fans of and writers of the genre. Certain texts have gone through dozens of reprints, and they have sold millions of copies, such as Robert Beck's *Pimp: The Story of My Life* (1967) and Donald Goines's *Whoreson* (1971), thus achieving the status of "classics" among readers. The representations of black masculinity promoted in these books have influenced everything from blaxploitation films to gangsta rap to contemporary African American literature. In the analysis that follows, *Pimping Fictions* negotiates a discussion of black crime fiction that treats it as a distinct expression of a particular African American literary and cultural tradition, while remaining attentive to its position as a mass-market commodity in the literary marketplace.

One of the main imperatives for understanding the roots of black crime literature is that it is now one of the driving forces of the African American literary market. On any given day, all along 125th Street in Harlem and Fulton Avenue in Brooklyn, dozens of tables overflow with the latest street literature titles from hundreds of aspiring African American authors. Also known as "hip hop fiction" as well as "urban literature," so-called "street literature" features contemporary stories of pimps, prisoners, and female hustlers. This newest incarnation of the genre has unexpectedly emerged as one of the most significant recent developments in African American literature and cultural production. By some estimates, modern street literature constitutes anywhere between 50 and 70 percent of total sales at many black bookstores around the country. Studying the history of black crime literature now can provide context for the emerging popularity of street literature and the controversies that have attended it. With such titles as *A Hustler's Wife*, *Thugs and the Women Who Love Them*, *Gangsta*, *Dime Piece*, and *Dirty Red*, these popular novels have generated much public debate over their explicit representations of violence, their literary merits, and their status as a commodity in a rapidly changing literary marketplace. They are often written in the gritty vernacular of the streets, and they document the struggles, victories, and defeats of black working-class men and women embroiled in lives of urban crime. These books are often self-published by amateur authors or produced by independent black-owned imprints, and they are read widely by African Americans in inner-city communities and by inmates in America's rapidly expanding city, state, and federal prisons. As a literary form and a literary marketplace, street literature shares connections with earlier African American cultural movements and popular literature markets, but it also represents a brand-new mode of literary expression that has its own unique brand of aesthetics, politics, writers, and readers. A mixture of utopian fantasy and urban realism, street literature is undoubtedly the literary successor to hip hop music in expressing the popular consciousness of the black underclass. However, its roots can also be found in the best-selling pimp autobiographies and ghetto action novels of novelists Robert Beck and Donald Goines. *Pimping Fictions* delineates a literary tradition of black crime literature by outlining the themes, poetics, and politics of publishing, from the works of these early pioneers to the modern novels of street literature authors.

Chapter Breakdown

Each of the six chapters explores the development of the black crime fiction genre by investigating a particular figure within a space of containment as well as the position of the black writer in the commercial space of the literary marketplace. Chapter 1 spells out the relationship between black crime fiction and emerging forms of white containment through an examination of the groundbreaking author Chester Himes. Although Himes's Harlem Domestic novels that feature his black detective duo Coffin Ed Johnson and Gravedigger Jones have received considerable academic attention in recent years, his prison stories and the detective farce *Run Man Run* have been mostly overlooked. This chapter rethinks Himes's location in the American and African American literary canon as the forerunner to today's black crime novelist. Critical attention usually places Himes at the end of the hard-boiled detective tradition that includes figures such as Dashiell Hammett and Raymond Chandler. However, I reposition Himes as more of a transitional figure who marks a transformation in American popular literature from white-authored detective novels to black crime novels. Focusing on Himes's *Run Man Run* (1959), I read the novel as his clearest articulation of the limits of detective fiction as an aesthetic and political form for black novelists. By privileging the perspective of the black criminal over that of the white detective, *Run Man Run* operates as a harbinger of an emerging literary marketplace that would cater to popular black audiences and showcase the power of black voices. I also read Himes's representation of the criminal on the run as a reflection of the author's own negotiation of the emerging crime fiction marketplace. Working within the confines of a publishing industry that did not yet market black-authored books to black audiences, Himes made do with genre conventions and literary forms that were inapt to the needs of black crime novelists.

Chapter 2 investigates *Pimp: The Story of My Life* by Robert Beck, a.k.a. Iceberg Slim. The book's publication announced the emergence of a new niche of black mass-market publishing by focusing on the first-person narrative of an urban pimp. This chapter illustrates how Beck's best-selling autobiography established the narrative forms, urban vernacular, and criminal character that came to influence hundreds of subsequent black experience novels, hip hop music, and contemporary street fiction. In *Pimp*, Beck invents a figure whose postures of black cool offer a radical critique of forms of white containment, while simultaneously reproducing a naturalized oppression of women as the very basis for his freedom. Employing hip masculinity as a way of handling the containment of urban ghettoization in the American city, the pimp of Beck's narrative operates as a radical departure from of the black-criminal-as-victim represented in Himes. However, the power of the pimp depends on the expansion of ideologies of victimization of women. This chapter explores this paradoxical mix of liberation and containment as it is represented in *Pimp: The Story of My Life*. Furthermore, it outlines Beck's difficult position in the pulp marketplace, underwritten by white corporate patronage. Beck essentially created a national black audience with *Pimp*'s publication by teaming up with the white-owned mass-market paperback publisher Holloway House. Drawing on interviews with Beck's publisher, Bentley Morriss, and many others involved in the process of publishing *Pimp*, I show how Beck himself was pimped by the industry of black pulp publishing.

Chapter 3 builds the case for black crime fiction's unexpected political efficacy by examining the novels of Robert Beck's most important literary protégé, Donald Goines. Perhaps an even more influential literary figure than Beck among contemporary black street fiction writers, Goines expanded on the pimp autobiography in a variety of ways. Between 1971 and his murder in 1974, he wrote fourteen novels (and sixteen if we include those novels published posthumously) that feature the stories of pimps, pushers, prostitutes, hit men, and heist artists. He essentially established the parameters of the popular genre, creating a blueprint for black crime writing that solidified Holloway House as the premier publisher of the black experience novel. However, by the end of his career, Goines replaced the stories of hustler heroes with narratives of underground black revolution, thereby exhibiting the radical potential of the genre. Examining the trajectory of Goines's short literary career, this chapter outlines how the exploitative practices and methods of commercial containment of pulp publishing paradoxically helped produce a radical form of race- and class-consciousness in the black crime novel.

Chapter 4 surveys the vast body of literature published by Holloway House in the second half of the 1970s, following the death of Goines and the decline in Beck's literary production. Writers such as Odie Hawkins, Joseph Nazel, Amos Brooke, Charlie Harris, and Omar Fletcher—inspired by the works of Goines and Beck—expanded the pimp-autobiography and black-revolutionary novels in keys ways. The most significant shift in the genre is that most of these later novels feature utopian solutions and happy endings. In the novels of Beck and Goines, the pimp and revolutionary enjoy momentary freedom from spaces of white containment only to be captured or killed at the novel's end. By contrast, in the books of the post-Goines era, the black protagonists escape from oppressive ghetto spaces, and they dismantle figures of white power. This chapter shows how such fantastical solutions reflect the degree to which methods of white containment in the form of ghettos, prisons, and economic stratification had calcified by the mid-1970s. In the face of such overwhelming political, racial, and spatial oppressions, the utopian crime novel provided black urban readers with entertainment and temporary escape from these conditions of everyday life.

Chapter 5 provides a cultural history of *Players* magazine, an unlikely offshoot of the black experience novel and the first commercially successful men's magazine aimed at a black audience. Started in 1973 by Holloway House's owners as a supplement to and advertising vehicle for its black experience novels, *Players* attempted to capitalize on the emerging fascination with the pimp and hustler invented in the pages of the novels. However, the black editors used the form of the men's magazine to expand the representation of the "player" in unexpected directions. Writers such as Wanda Coleman, Stanley Crouch, Joseph Nazel, and Emory Holmes took advantage of the interest in the figures of the pimp, the hustler, and the revolutionary by infusing these figures with more high-minded intellectual interests. They co-opted this character of the street for the purposes of promoting a populist political agenda under the guise of a "titty" magazine. The player represented in the pages of this magazine was intellectually savvy and a politically aware figure, one versed in literature, art, and contemporary black social issues. Additionally, the history of *Players* in many ways mirrors that of the black experience novel with regard to its creation, production, and eventual degradation. *Players* was originally an avant-garde publication that featured one of the most impressive collections of criticism, art, and entertainment found in any black American magazine. During its prime in the mid-to-late 1970s, *Players* introduced the editorial work of now-famous poet Wanda Coleman, essays by Stanley Crouch, nude photos of Pam Grier and Zuedi Araya, fiction by Ishmael Reed and James Baldwin, and celebrity interviews with countless black personalities, including Gil Scott Heron, Maya Angelou, Sam Greenlee, Don King, Dizzy Gillespie, and others. But just like the novels published by Holloway House, *Players* suffered in quality from the white owners' focus on profits, and it eventually devolved into just another pornographic magazine as black editors and writers were increasingly forced out of the company. This chapter adds to our understanding of the genre of black crime literature by examining the expansion of the figures of the pimp, the hustler, and the player in the sphere of mass-market magazine culture.

Chapter 6 surveys the contemporary African American literary scene by investigating the popular emergence of street literature, the latest manifestation of the black crime novel. With the publication of Sister Souljah's *The Coldest Winter Ever* in 1999, Vickie Stringer's *Let That Be the Reason* in 2001, and Nikki Turner's *A Hustler's Wife* in 2003, black crime fiction has enjoyed a resurgence in popularity, garnering new audiences, particularly women. Many of the most popular and successful authors of this genre are now women, and this chapter reveals how authors such as Souljah, Stringer, and Turner have rewritten the narratives of Beck and Goines from a female perspective and for a female audience. Specifically, it looks at how the stories of the pimp, the revolutionary, and the utopian romance have been hijacked by female authors in order to reverse the exploitative gender dynamics of the black crime novel. It also investigates the rise of the self-publishing marketplace and the creation of the independent black publishing house, both of which have largely displaced companies such as Holloway House. Black crime fiction began as an expression of a largely disregarded black urban subculture in the 1960s and 1970s, published by virtually one niche publisher; however, with the materialization of self-publishing as a viable commercial and literary enterprise, black crime literature has emerged as a driving force of the African American literature market. This book concludes with a discussion of the complex race, class, and gender politics of this new publishing industry, paying particular attention to the relationships between black-owned imprints and the large black prison population that has come to support such industries as both writers and readers. In this contemporary literary marketplace, the female entrepreneur represents a new direction in black pulp publishing, as a number of female authors-turned-publishers have figured out how to transform the mass incarceration of African America into an organized literary and commercial enterprise. As the African American prison population now approaches one million people, and as African American women represent the fastest-growing incarcerated group in the country, street literature has come to reflect the social conditions and collective wishes of a carceral society. The development of a prison-industrial-literary complex represents the most logical expansion of the entrepreneurial ethos that has always been intertwined with the development of black crime fiction. Ultimately, *Pimping Fictions*' overarching aim is to trace this relationship between developing forms of racial, social, and geographical containment and the coherent literary tradition of black crime fiction in the twentieth and twenty-first centuries.

1 / "He Jerked His Pistol Free and Fired It at the Pavement": Chester Himes and the Transformation of American Crime Literature

In 1903, W. E. B. Du Bois predicted in his seminal *The Souls of Black Folk* that, "the problem of the twentieth century is the problem of the color line."[1] In doing so, he was anticipating a social and spatial crisis that came to define urban race relations in the United States. Indeed, we might characterize the twentieth century as the era of developing strategies—political, economic, ideological, and individual—for the management of apparently encroaching black populations into America's urban spaces. As African Americans migrated to cities en masse during World War I and then in even larger numbers following World War II, there emerged a growing perception among whites that their neighborhoods were being invaded. "Discourses of decline," as urban historian Robert Beauregard has called them, materialized that began to link black neighborhoods to vice, crime, and moral decay.[2] In the first few decades of the twentieth century in cities all over America, whites employed various methods of intimidation, including block restrictions, neighborhood associations, and even bombings in order to force African Americans into the city's worst housing stock.[3] Following World War II, nonwhite racial identity and declining property values were conjoined in the national imaginary in a kind of discursive and symbolic unity. Under the auspices of "urban renewal," more systematic methods of containment were adopted to restrict the growing black urban population, including the Federal Housing Authority–sponsored suburbanization, the construction of segregated housing projects, and increasingly, in the final decades of the twentieth century, the criminalization and incarceration of the black urban poor.[4] Between 1950 and 1970, an estimated seven million whites fled American cities, while at the same time five million African Americans came to occupy those abandoned spaces left behind.[5] This American apartheid, a spatial/racial divide between white suburbs and the black inner city, became one of the defining characteristics of racial identity throughout the course of the twentieth century.[6] It is this bureaucratized arrangement of racialized space that forms the material basis for the development of black crime literature.

Over this same period, black crime fiction—that is, African American–authored literature written from the perspective of the criminal or prisoner—increasingly became a figurative theater where these problems of incarceration, containment, and ghettoization were dramatized.[7] As a genre of literature focused on urban streets, spaces of surveillance, criminal exploits, and confrontations with white authority, black crime fiction has been employed by black writers as a mode of populist protest against institutional and individual forms of white control. Although hundreds of black crime writers have come to populate the literary marketplace in the twenty-first century, the first black crime writer of major importance in the twentieth century was Chester Himes. Himes is best known for his so-called "Harlem Domestic" novels, nine books that popularized the first black detective team in American literature, Coffin Ed Johnson and Grave Digger Jones.[8] But Himes started as a writer of prison stories while incarcerated at the Ohio State Penitentiary in the early 1930s. In his earliest works—published in black publications such as *Abbott's Monthly* and *Atlanta Daily World*, as well as the general men's magazine *Esquire*—Himes explored the theme that came to define the genre of black crime literature in the twentieth century: the criminal's response to methods of white containment and silencing. For example, as early as his story "To What Red Hell" (1934), Himes introduces a figure that was to appear in a variety of guises throughout his career, the figure of the criminal who goes on the run in order to contest spaces of containment.[9]

While this figure of the criminal on the run reappears as a central character in a number of Himes's works, including his full-length prison novel *Cast the First Stone* (1952) and his first detective novel, *For the Love of Imabelle* (1957), his most articulated version of this character appears in his *Run Man Run*. Written in France at the height of his popularity in 1959 and then published in the United States in 1966, *Run Man Run* is the only one of Himes's detective novels that does not feature his black detectives Coffin Ed Johnson and Gravedigger Jones. A dramatic departure from Himes's more famously farcical novels, *Run Man Run* is instead the grim story of white detective Matt Walker who hunts down a black porter named Jimmy Johnson after Johnson witnesses Walker's murder of two fellow porters. Mostly ignored by the public at the time of its U.S. publication and by critics in the years since then, *Run Man Run* is generally passed over as the anomaly of Himes's otherwise successful career as a detective novelist.[10] Michael Denning, representative of critics who dismiss the novel, writes, "This is not in the least comic and is very different from the Grave Digger/Coffin Ed series. It becomes a sort of belated version of *Native Son* and, without the naturalistic detail, is largely unsuccessful."[11]

Going against the grain of contemporary scholarship in literary and cultural studies, I view *Run Man Run* as a significant text for rethinking Himes's contribution to the tradition of American literature as well as the marketplace of black pulp fiction. While scholars have passed over it in favor of studying Himes's comical racial carnivals, attention to *Run Man Run* reveals its unsuspected importance for rethinking African American crime literature's relationship to the intersecting issues of race, urban space, and the literary marketplace in America. At one level, *Run Man Run* is a hybrid detective/crime novel that self-consciously reverses the hard-boiled tradition created by Dashiell Hammett and Raymond Chandler, by shifting reader sympathy to the black criminal away from the apparently heroic detective figure. The hard-boiled detective has been described by critic and detective fiction enthusiast William F. Nolan as a "wary, wisecracking knight of the .45, an often violent, always unpredictable urban vigilante fashioned in the rugged frontier tradition of the western gunfighter."[12] In the traditional detective stories and novels of Hammett and Chandler, lone male heroes such as the Continental Op or Detective Marlowe struggle against the overwhelming technical, economic, social, and spatial forces of the modern city, represented variously by gangsters, pimps, femme fatales, corrupt cops, and wealthy capitalists. By contrast, Himes's story of a white detective who murders black workers and then relentlessly chases one black witness across Manhattan to silence him shifts the focus of the detective novel to dramatize the black population's struggle against the urban geographies of white design. *Run Man Run* parodies detective fiction tropes and showcases how the literary form and marketplace of detective fiction were ill suited to the needs of the black literary artist as well as the black populations he or she attempts to represent. *Run Man Run* illustrates the dual concerns of the criminal in the city and the black writer in the popular literature marketplace, both of which are central to understanding black crime fiction.

As a number of recent scholars have shown, since the earliest detective stories of Edgar Allan Poe, American crime and detective fiction has promoted racial ideologies of white superiority as well the policing of racial/spatial boundaries.[13] This chapter expands on this scholarship by positioning Himes as the first of many black novelists to employ the crime fiction form to critique the dominant cultural and racial ideologies of twentieth-century American society, ideologies that promoted urban segregation and the exploitation of black populations. In Himes's story, the criminal character Jimmy is not a criminal at all but rather a Columbia law student who is the victim of a deranged system. He is ultimately drawn into Harlem's criminal underworld as a tactical response to violent racism embodied by the detective. Himes's novel anticipates many of the black crime novels of the latter half of the twentieth century through the story of members of the black middle class who are drawn to the criminal underworld as a radical stance against white racism. Although Himes is usually regarded in academic circles as the most important heir to the detective tradition of Dashiell Hammett and Raymond Chandler, my analysis invites us to rethink Himes as a more intermediary literary figure, bridging the hard-boiled detective literature of the early twentieth century to the popular African American crime literature that has emerged in the past four decades. Himes accomplished this by working within the genre and literary marketplace of white-authored detective literature, while shifting narrative focus from the white detective hero onto the usually scapegoated black criminals who populate these stories.

The remainder of this chapter is divided into two sections. Each section explores the relationship between racial containment and American crime and detective literature. In the first section, I examine how Raymond Chandler's 1940 classic hard-boiled detective novel *Farewell, My Lovely* promoted the policing of urban racial boundaries in the middle of the twentieth century. By contextualizing the representation of *Farewell, My Lovely*'s imaginary landscape against the backdrop of the historical developments of white containment, I provide a clearer picture of detective fiction's collusive relationship with discourses and policies that equate black migration to urban decline. As a white author who helped pioneer hard-boiled detective literature, Chandler operates as an important literary foil to Himes. The second part of the chapter reads *Run Man Run* as Himes's revision of Chandler's detective story as well as a creative indictment of the effects of white racism on black populations in urban spaces. Unlike Chandler's novel, which features the white detective as the mediator of knowledge, *Run Man Run* employs a narrator who reports on the perspective of the detective *and* the criminal he chases. This double-consciousness not only undermines the authority of the white detective, but it also reimagines the black criminal as a competing hero in the novel, a form of representation which will be developed more fully in the works of Robert Beck and Donald Goines. I conclude with a discussion of how *Run Man Run*'s treatment of detective tropes and criminal figures offers a meta-commentary on the black writer's vulnerable position in the literary marketplace of pulp publishing.

"I Had the Place to Myself": Raymond Chandler and the Fictions of Urban Decline

In Raymond Chandler's early short story "Noon Street Nemesis," published in *Detective Fiction Weekly* in 1936, there is a moment that provides a telling illustration of white anxieties about encroaching black populations into America's urban spaces. At the opening of the story, undercover narcotics detective Pete Anglich awakens in his flophouse hotel room in Los Angeles's Central Avenue district, one of the city's emerging African American neighborhoods. Stepping from his shower, the detective sees that a black thief named the Smiler, dressed in a "purple suit and Panama hat" and sporting "shiny, slicked-down hair," has broken into his room, stolen his Colt .45, and is in the process of robbing him. After a brief exchange of banter with the Smiler, and armed only with a wet towel, the naked detective overpowers and kills the criminal:

> Pete Anglich flipped the wet end of the bathtowel straight at the Smiler's eyes.
> The Smiler reeled and yelled with pain. Then Pete Anglich held the Smiler's gun wrist in his hard left hand. He twisted up, around. His hand started to slide down the Smiler's hand, over the gun. The gun turned inward and touched the Smiler's side.
> A hard knee kicked vigorously at Pete Anglich's abdomen. He gagged, and his finger tightened convulsively on the Smiler's trigger finger.
> The shot was dull, muffled against the purple cloth of the suit. The Smiler's eyes rolled whitely and his narrow jaw fell slack.[14]

The entire scene only spans a few pages at the beginning of the lengthy story about the detective's investigation of underworld grifters and Hollywood con men. However, Anglich's violent encounter with the Smiler provides a graphic picture of the role that black characters play in the construction of white-guy heroism in American hard-boiled literature. The purple-suited Smiler occupies the position of a ready-made criminal, whose confrontation with Anglich establishes the white detective as the protagonist of the story. Anglich, with his dead-eye aim, disarms the Smiler by first blinding the criminal with his towel, symbolically castrating him. Then, with his "hard left hand" the hypermasculine detective takes possession of the Colt .45 and shoots the Smiler through the purple cloth of his suit. That Chandler describes the Smiler's ostentatious zoot-like outfit as the target of the detective's violence is especially important insofar as it reveals the white fears about emerging black urban subcultures. In fact, this passage—with its focus on a white detective policing stylishly dressed black criminals—eerily anticipates the so-called Zoot Suit Riots of 1943, in which police officers and servicemen roamed Los Angeles streets accosting black and Mexican youths caught wearing the sharkskin suits. Here, one of Chandler's earliest stories shows how detective fiction reflects and helps further produce white ideologies that African American urban migration was tantamount to a criminal invasion and that heroic white violence is a justifiable response.

Such a story is pretty standard fare for the pulp detective magazines that were popular from the 1920s to the early 1950s. As a number of critics have noted, in terms of the production, consumption, and subject matter of the pulp magazines, they were the domain of white men. Like pulp magazines' nineteenth-century predecessor, the dime novel, they were targeted emphatically toward men, especially marginally white ethnic immigrants and working-class men clustered in American cities.[15] Although H. L. Menken and George Jean Nathan had considered the possibility of making a pulp magazine targeted at a black audience before creating *Black Mask* (which, despite its name, was not actually aimed at blacks), they decided that there was not enough money in the African American community to support it.[16] The authors of detective fiction, too, were integral to the atmosphere of white manliness that pervaded the pulps. Paid by the word instead of the work, the authors of pulp fiction often identified themselves with the white industrial working class. For Hammett, Chandler, and the rest of the *Black Mask* writers, the culture industry of pulp fiction provided a community where, through the mechanized production of literature about excessively masculine white guys, writers could imagine a cross-class identification with the white industrial workers to whom the stories were marketed. As detective literature critic Erin Smith sums it up, "Hard-boiled writing culture created an all-male imagined community that included writers, readers, and the he-manly heroes of this fiction."[17]

Although unapologetic racism pervades much of Chandler's work, this is not the point here.[18] For Chandler's representation of the detective in "Noon-Street Nemesis" illustrates a complex engagement with and policing of black bodies and dark spaces. According to Toni Morrison's influential formulation in her work of literary criticism *Playing in the Dark*, black characters from the fiction of Edgar Allan Poe to Ernest Hemingway serve the interests of white authors by offering themselves up as scapegoats and victims to be variously captured, castrated, and killed.[19] Although these characters appear to be immaterial to the story as a whole, according to Morrison, they lubricate the plot and aid in the architecture of the new white man by operating as sites of projection and intense self-reflection. To use her words, white American literature is often populated by images of "impenetrable whiteness," images that "function as both antidote for and meditation on the shadow that is a companion to this whiteness—a dark and abiding presence that moves the hearts and texts of American literature with fear and longing."[20] To return to "Noon Street Nemesis," the naked white detective operates as an image of this "impenetrable whiteness." His identity as urban hero is established through a confrontation with and defeat of the Smiler, who is the detective's shadow and the embodiment of an emerging black urban culture in mid-twentieth-century America.

Additionally, the emerging black neighborhood operates in detective literature as a symbolic proving ground for the constitution of white masculine identity. In Chandler's seminal essay "The Simple Art of Murder," he provides what was to become one of the most enduring definitions of the American hard-boiled detective: "But down these mean streets a man must go who is himself not mean, who is neither tarnished nor afraid. The detective in this kind of story must be such a man. He is a hero; he is everything. He must be a complete man and a common man and yet an unusual man. He must be, to use a rather weathered phrase, a man of honor."[21] In this oft-cited definition of the hard-boiled detective, Chandler fashions the figure as "a man of honor" of America's "mean streets." While many critics have pointed to Chandler's poetic, if insistent, repetition of the word "man" as the essential feature of his definition, there is a racial valence to the characterization of the detective as "neither tarnished nor afraid" as well. For if we keep in mind that the "mean streets" of Chandler's literary imagination were based on the developing African American neighborhood of Watts, then his characterization of the detective as not "tarnished" highlights that his moral decency is connected to his racial visage.[22] Simply put, the detective's whiteness is synonymous with honor and uprightness, while the criminal's blackness implicates him as disgraceful and degraded. In this world, the black urban neighborhood operates as a spatial extension of this binary. Black urban geographies are the repositories for the abject qualities of American life that the detective must maneuver if he is to emerge as a cultural hero.

Although Chandler explores the detective's relationship to the mean streets of Central Avenue in his early stories "Noon Street Nemesis" (1936) and "Try the Girl" (1937), his most elaborated and complex examination of this dynamic takes place in his second novel, *Farewell, My Lovely*. At the opening of the novel, Chandler's venerable private eye, Philip Marlowe, visits a section of Central Avenue that is in the midst of racial transition: whites are moving out as blacks are moving in. It is this transition that Marlowe represents in his opening lines: "It was one of the mixed blocks over on Central Avenue, the blocks that are not yet all Negro. I had just come out of a three-chair barber shop where an agency thought a relief barber named Dimitrios Aleidis might be working. It was a small matter. His wife said she was willing to spend a little money to have him come home. I never found him, but Mrs. Aleidis never paid me any money either."[23] At the start of *Farewell, My Lovely*, Chandler begins with an image of the man of the mean streets that he characterizes as the fundamental feature of hard-boiled detective literature. Although Marlowe insists "it was a small matter," with his swift, deliberate narration and his self-deflating humor, his story about a vanishing barber hints at deeper white anxieties about the changing racial character of the city. The disappearance of the marginally white (probably Greek) Dimitrios Aleidis from one of the racially mixed blocks in South Central Los Angeles is a parable for urban succession as a whole. Ethnic whiteness is giving way to blackness, and although the block is "not yet all Negro" in this increasingly African American neighborhood, Marlowe insinuates that it will be soon. It is Marlowe's use of the word "yet" that signals the larger societal unease over the changing composition of the urban neighborhood. Although he does not explicitly state it, in Marlowe's estimation, there is something inexplicably threatening in the neighborhood inevitably turning "all Negro," a reflection of the white worries that the emergence of black neighborhoods was a signal of urban decline.

But even though Marlowe gives voice here to white public worries about black trespassing of urban spaces, the fact is that throughout the twentieth century, whites had developed a number of individual and institutional strategies for containing African Americans in restricted ghettos. During the first decades of the twentieth century, the Central Avenue corridor had been Los Angeles's most ethnically diverse neighborhood, composed of blacks, Italians, Asians, Latinos, whites, and immigrants from southern and eastern Europe who had all come to find work in L.A.'s burgeoning industrial economy. As the African American population increased during the 1920s and 1930s with the First Great Migration, however, whites employed formal and informal methods of intimidation, including violence, block restrictions, and neighborhood associations to create a racially divided city. According to Los Angeles historian Mike Davis, through these methods, "95 percent of the city's housing stock in the 1920s was effectively put off limits to Blacks and Asians," creating what he calls a "white wall" around Central Avenue.[24] This "white wall" that kept blacks confined to the Central Avenue corridor was one of the spatial features that defined American race relations in Los Angeles through the first half of the twentieth century.

Understanding the systematic ways in which whites attempted to contain black populations along Los Angeles's Central Avenue and in many other American cities helps us understand more clearly Chandler's representation of the detective's negotiation of the city. To borrow again from Morrison's formulation, Chandler's novel raises the specter of the black neighborhood in order to posit the white detective as an image of "impenetrable whiteness" as an antidote for the "dark and abiding presence" that is the Central Avenue black neighborhood. The way that the novel accomplishes this is more complex than in the early story "Noon Street Nemesis." For one thing, race is spatialized more explicitly in the novel; the struggle between the white hero and his black nemesis is expanded to a larger contestation over symbolic control of the neighborhood. Additionally, the detective in *Farewell, My Lovely* enlists a white ethnic character by the name of Moose Malloy to do the detective's dirty work for him. Immediately after Marlowe gives up on the Aleidis case, he spots Moose Malloy, a former resident of the neighborhood who has just been released from prison after eight years: "I stood outside the barber shop looking up at the jutting neon sign of a second floor dine and dice emporium called Florian's. A man was looking up at the sign too.

He was looking up at the dusty windows with a sort of ecstatic fixity of expression, like a hunky immigrant catching his first sight of the Statue of Liberty."[25] Here, facing a racially darkening Central Avenue, Marlowe casts the white ethnic Malloy in romantic terms, a kind of ideal immigrant. As a diminutive of *Hungarian*, *hunky* was a slang term of the early twentieth century used generically to describe a variety of immigrants from Hungary, Poland, Romania, Czechoslovakia, and other southern and eastern European countries who were arriving in droves to American cities. These immigrants came by the millions to provide a deskilled labor force for the burgeoning Fordist economy of the early twentieth century. By the time of Chandler's novel, however, due to the nativist backlash of the 1920s, the Depression of the 1930s, and the impending world war, immigration had slowed considerably, and European immigrants of this type were becoming a kind of vanishing American.

Chandler's novel reaches back to an image of this idealized immigrant American in the figure of Malloy to act as an imaginary fortification against racial succession. When Malloy returns to Central Avenue to find his old flame, a former nightclub singer named Velma Valento, he becomes enraged when he discovers that the bar Florian's, where she used to work, has transformed into a "dinge joint."[26] Originally opened by Mike Florian as a place of entertainment for working-class ethnic whites, in the time that Malloy has been away in prison, it has become a bar owned by African Americans. Malloy is outraged by this transformation of the neighborhood, and he goes on a violent rampage, maiming and murdering occupants of the bar. In fact, Malloy's first victim looks suspiciously like the purple-suited Smiler from "Noon Street Nemesis"; however, in this version of the story, the detective does not commit the violence but rather watches it with a kind of amused neutrality. As the burly Malloy tosses the Smiler figure in a gutter, the detective records this violence in terms that further dehumanize the black victim:

Something sailed across the sidewalk and landed in the gutter between two parked cars. It landed on its hands and knees and made a high keening noise like a cornered rat. It got up slowly, retrieved a hat and stepped back onto the sidewalk. It was a thin narrow-shouldered brown youth in a lilac colored suit and a carnation. It had slick black hair. It kept its mouth open and whined for a moment. People stared at it vaguely. Then it settled its hat jauntily, sidled over to the wall and walked silently splay-footed off along the block.[27]

As in "Noon Street Nemesis," the black figure in the purple suit and slick black hair in *Farewell, My Lovely* operates as an embodiment of black urban culture that is silenced and contained to pacify white fears about black encroachment. However, the detective does not manhandle the Smiler figure himself but rather excuses and repeats the violence through his dehumanizing representation of the victim. By calling the youth "it" seven times in as many sentences, Marlowe sanctions Malloy's brutality while retaining a clinical distance from it. Whereas in "Noon Street Nemesis" the detective and the Smiler engage in witty banter before their fight, the Smiler figure here has no voice at all but can only whine and make "high keening noise like a cornered rat." In this passage, the threat of black intrusion that the Smiler figure represents is totally contained through the combination of Malloy's physical violence and Marlowe's description of him as a silenced, animalized object.

These themes of the containment and silencing of black urban populations are most fully articulated when Marlowe and Malloy enter Florian's. When Malloy drags the detective into the bar in search of Valento, they together encounter a black presence that is silent and to their white eyes indecipherable: "There was a sudden silence as heavy as a water-logged boat. Eyes looked at us, chestnut colored eyes, set in faces that ranged from gray to deep black. Heads turned slowly and the eyes in them glistened and stared in the dead alien silence of another race."[28] Here, visible racial difference—what Marlowe describes as ranging from "gray to deep black"—symbolizes an Other so utterly alien that communication is impossible. When no one can tell Malloy about Valento's whereabouts, he charges into the owner's office, murders him, and flees the scene. Having related this incident with apparent detachment, Marlowe finishes the story with a curious remark: "When the prowl car boys stamped up the stairs, the bouncer and the barman had disappeared and I had the place to myself."[29] Marlowe deploys this statement as a dry denouement, a disavowal of the violence he has just witnessed. However, in the context of the novel's preoccupation with issues of racial and urban succession, his statement "I had the place to myself" also reads like a smug reclamation of rightfully white territory. With Malloy providing the expulsion of the black people who have taken over Florian's, Marlowe is free to claim the emptied black business without being directly implicated in the violence to which he has been party. Chandler erects this elaborate scene of racial confrontation in order to provide an imaginary resolution to the apparent crisis of the black invasion. In *Farewell, My Lovely*, Marlowe the detective becomes the symbolic master of the dark city by representing through denial and deferral the violence he witnesses but in which he does not participate, at least not directly. No longer dirtying his hands with the actual labor of policing black bodies, Marlowe achieves his heroic status by gazing on and writing the expulsion of the black criminal body without having to perform it. Marlowe's indirect violence toward black people here mirrors the strategies developed by whites to contain black urban populations on the eve of World War II. After the first few decades of the twentieth century, whites shifted from individual acts of violence to more distant and coordinated acts of social violence, such as housing covenants and block associations. With the emergence of public housing high-rises, increased white flight, and organized slum clearance, these containment strategies became even more institutionalized and bureaucratic. It is to these strategies that we now turn through an analysis of Chester Himes's response to *Farewell, My Lovely*: *Run Man Run*.

Chester Himes and the Invention of Black Crime Fiction

At about the same time that Raymond Chandler was publishing his early detective stories in *Black Mask* magazine, Chester Himes was writing his own first narratives from behind the prison walls at Ohio State Penitentiary. Himes was an avid reader of *Black Mask*, the premier detective fiction magazine, and he tried his hand at creating his own hard-boiled stories. Significantly, his early work focuses less on the figure of the detective and more on the detective's nemesis, the criminal. One of Himes's most interesting stories about the criminal is "To What Red Hell," a story about a prison fire, published in the men's magazine *Esquire* in 1934. It was based on an actual incident Himes witnessed in which over three hundred convicts were killed by an inferno that consumed Ohio State Penitentiary, and it showcases what was to become a central concern in Himes's work throughout his career, namely, the criminal protagonist's response to forms of violent containment. "To What Red Hell" is the tale of a convict named Jimmy who runs frantically from one grotesque spectacle to the next across the burning landscape of the prison yard after convicts start a fire in order to cover their escape attempt. Surrounded on all sides by the "big gray face of solid stone" that encloses the prison, Jimmy dashes from spectacles as varied and horrifying as the charred, vomit-covered remains of his fellow inmates to prisoners picking the pockets of the dead.[30] Jimmy takes flight over and over again in an attempt to avoid the disturbing scenes before him, only to find that escape is illusory: "There was an eternity in which he ran, running and gasping and shouting and shoving and running and cursing and striking out blindly with clenched fists and slipping and falling and getting up and running again, in which he seemed to be standing still while the chaos rushed past him, pulling at him, clutching his sleeves, choking him."[31] Because he is trapped behind the prison walls, Jimmy cannot in fact evade the horrible scenes of death and violence. He can only run around in a circle due to the containment structure of the prison. Actual escape from these displays of grotesque carnage is forever suspended, and running becomes a compensatory tactic used to confront the absurdity of the moment, a tactic that is reflected in the narrator's galloping, fast-paced prose. While Chandler's early work—like much of detective fiction—focuses on the containment of criminal bodies, Himes's first stories essentially reverse this dynamic, focusing instead on the criminal's resistance to surveillance and control. Himes's representation of the criminal on the run represents his most significant challenge to the ideologies of white violence embodied in the work of Chandler and detective literature more broadly.[32]

Run Man Run offers the most developed articulation of Himes's figure of the criminal on the run. Written twenty-five years after "To What Red Hell," *Run Man Run* expands the space of enclosure from the prison yard to the city itself. This allows Himes the opportunity to explore the potentialities for the criminal-on-the-run figure as a critique of urban containment practices and American race relations. It also directly challenges the representations of African Americans paraded in the pages of *Farewell, My Lovely*. Critics have not traditionally read *Run Man Run* as a creative revision of *Farewell, My Lovely*. However, a well-known moment in Himes's interview with John A. Williams offers some insight on Himes's disapproval of Chandler's representations of black neighborhoods.[33] Commenting on the opening of *Farewell, My Lovely*, in which Marlowe visits Central Avenue, Himes remarks that the novel's representations of black Los Angeles illustrate the implicit prejudices of white-authored hard-boiled literature: "You know, they didn't open those night clubs and restaurants on Central Avenue until Thursday. [Williams interjects: "Maid's day off?"] Yeah, they were closed. Because you know, some of Raymond Chandler's crap out there, he writes in *Farewell, My Lovely*, he has this joker ride about in the Central Avenue section. Some of that's very authentic—it was like that. A black man in Los Angeles, he was a servant."[34] Here Himes's colloquial statement to Williams reveals the extent to which detective novels such as *Farewell, My Lovely* produce a racist representation of the black neighborhood. Showing off his own skills as a detective, Himes reads the opening of Chandler's novel as dependent on a fantasy of the availability of black nightclubs and restaurants on Central Avenue for white use. While granting that some of Chandler's depictions of Central Avenue are indeed "authentic," his larger point is that the portrayal of black Los Angeles in the novel is "crap" and that Marlowe is a "joker," a tourist of Watts. For Himes, Marlowe's expedition to Los Angeles's dark underworld does not so much reveal something about the black neighborhood as it exposes the detective figure's dependence on the black neighborhood and its inhabitants for the constitution of his own identity. Therefore, when Himes concludes his comments with the statement "A black man in Los Angeles, he was a servant," he anticipates Morrison's idea that in American literature, black characters and neighborhoods provide serviceable rhetorical devices for white authors to construct narratives about white masculine heroism.[35]

The narrative of *Run Man Run* directly undercuts the heroism of the white hard-boiled detective. *Run Man Run* accomplishes this by restaging the opening scene of racial conflict between the white detective and serviceable black characters that we witness in *Farewell, My Lovely*. In effect, it recasts the white detective as a definitively more sinister character in the literary imaginary. At the opening, the novel's antagonist, Detective Matt Walker, stumbles drunkenly through midtown Manhattan searching for his missing car. Like Chandler's Marlowe, Himes's Walker gazes on the city before him. However, in his drunken state, he is unable to read its meaning clearly: "When he came to 37th Street he sensed that something had changed since he'd passed before. How long before he couldn't remember. He glanced at his watch to see if the time would give him a clue. The time was 4:38 A.M. No wonder the street was deserted, he thought. Every one with any sense was home in bed, snuggled up to some fine hot woman."[36] Shifting from the usual first-person narrative of the hard-boiled detective story to a third-person omniscient narrative, Himes employs a voice that collapses the authority of the detective figure. The illusion of intimacy that is produced by the detective's autobiographical address is replaced here by a third-person omniscient narrator, which treats the detective's perspective as just part of the story rather than the voice that relates the totality of meaning. Walker's inexplicable anxiety that "something had changed since he'd passed before" suddenly transforms into a familiar narrative of black criminality when he spots a black porter named Luke taking out the trash at a fast-food restaurant. Although Walker has only forgotten where he has parked his car, the porter provides a site/sight on which he can project his fantasy that a black man has stolen his vehicle: "He knew immediately that the Negro was a porter. But the sight of a Negro made him think that his car had been stolen instead of lost. He couldn't have said why, but he was suddenly sure of it."[37] Walker has no material evidence that Luke is responsible for the theft of his car; in this racially determined landscape, however, the "sight of a Negro" provides all the evidence that the detective needs to launch his own investigation.

Following this hunch, Walker questions Luke and then heads to the kitchen to interrogate the mopping porter named Fat Sam. As he questions Fat Sam, Walker's general feelings of unease coalesce into the proverbial reconstruction of events in which the porter becomes part of an elaborate car-jacking racket: "'I'll tell you how you did it,' the detective said in a blurred uncertain voice. 'You came back here from out front and used that telephone by the street door. Your buddy was working and he didn't notice.' By now the detective had got his eyes focused on Fat Sam's face and they looked dangerous. 'You telephoned up to Harlem to a car thief and told him to come down and lift it. That's right, ain't it, wise guy?'"[38] Himes reveals how the detective's narrative solution to the crime is actually little more than a fantasy about black criminality. At one level, this is a lampoon of *Farewell, My Lovely*. While Marlowe's knowledge of black neighborhoods at the opening of *Farewell, My Lovely* is a crucial indicator of his prowess as a detective, Walker's racist projections actually end up becoming the source of the crime itself. Pursuing his own line of thinking to its logical conclusion, Walker murders both Luke and Sam. Himes deflates white authority by unveiling it as the fabrication of a racist subconscious. He suggests that the art of ratiocination is little more than an elaborately reasoned justification for racial violence.

What further distinguishes *Run Man Run* from the traditional hard-boiled detective novel is that Himes provides the voices and perspectives of both the detective and the detective's usually silenced black victims. Himes's use of the third-person omniscient narrator, then, not only collapses the authority of the detective but uses it to create a more polyphonic text. When Walker accuses Fat Sam of stealing his car, Sam does not cower or sit silently before these allegations. Much like Himes in his interview with Williams, Sam mocks the detective's conflation of blackness and criminality as an anachronistic rhetorical device. After listening to Walker's wild accusations, Fat Sam replies, "Here you is, a detective like Sherlock Holmes, pride of the New York City police force, and you've gone and got so full of holiday cheer you've let some punk steal your car. Haw-haw-haw! So you set out and light on the first colored man you see. Haw-haw-haw! Now, chief, that crap's gone out of style with the flapper girl."[39] Fat Sam openly ridicules Walker's powers of deductive reasoning by sarcastically comparing him to Sir Conan Doyle's genteel detective Sherlock Holmes, the popular successor to Edgar Allan Poe's C. Auguste Dupin. Acting as a mouthpiece for Himes, Fat Sam further states that the detective's projection of criminality onto black bodies is a tired contrivance, invented in the pages of pulp magazines during the 1920s.

But as Himes's novel illustrates, having a voice is not so much a source of protection for the black characters of the novel as it is a dangerous liability. Walker is infuriated by Fat Sam's irreverence, and, still half believing his own suspicions that the porters have stolen his car, he murders Fat Sam and Luke and hides their bodies in the company refrigerator. Himes does not conceal Walker's murder of the two porters behind the clipped, hard-boiled prose employed by Chandler but instead forces the reader to confront the monstrous spectacle. Describing Fat Sam's death, the narrator says, "He fell forward, pulling the tray from the rack along with him. Thick, cold, three-day-old turkey gravy poured over his kinky head as he landed, curled up like a fetus, between a five-gallon can of whipping cream and three wooden crates of iceberg lettuce."[40] While the terse writing style of white detective fiction authors often serves to cover over the horror of racial violence—as in the case of Chandler's representation of Anglich's murder of the Smiler—Himes refuses to sanitize these moments by placing the denigrated black body in full view of the reading audience. Sam is quite literally squeezed between cans of whipping cream and crates of lettuce, an image of grotesque containment, as the restaurant porter is reduced to the food over which he labors each day. In this scene, Walker emerges not as a detective hero but as a butcher whose position as an officer of the law sanctions disturbing acts of racial violence. But what is stylistically distinct about Himes's representation of the black-man-as-victim-of-racism trope is that he retains an edge of dark humor to offset the absurd horror of the violence.[41] "Poor bastard," Walker thinks after he has killed Fat Sam. "Dead in the gravy he loved so well."[42] While exposing the detective to be the source of violence against blacks, something that Chandler's text skillfully denies, Himes's novel nevertheless invites the reader to laugh at these moments of obscene bloodshed. Moving beyond the protest literature of Wright's *Native Son* (1940) and even his own early works, such as *If He Hollers, Let Him Go* (1945) and *Lonely Crusade* (1947), Himes creates a mode of representation that is not quite naturalist and not quite slapstick. He combines the pro-test and the popular in this text by using racist humor to draw attention to the very violence that the text denounces.[43]

Run Man Run also utilizes detective fiction tropes in order to cri-tique the updated urban containment strategies of black populations of Himes's own historical moment. Written nearly twenty years after *Fare-well, My Lovely*, and shifting the topography of violence from Los Ange-les to New York, *Run Man Run* critiques the policies of urban renewal that had been developed in the post–World War II period as a method for containing urban minorities. This movement from west to east is a movement that calls attention to the specific urban renewal strategies that had been developed in places such as New York in the second half of the twentieth century. Detective Walker is quite literally the embodi-ment of postwar white mobility in *Run Man Run*: after retrieving his lost car, he spends much of the novel driving through the city in search of Jimmy, and at one moment late in the book, he even drives out to his sister's house in the white suburbs of Westchester County. However, the scene that makes explicit Walker's connection to modes of white mobil-ity is in the middle of the novel, a scene in which he cruises through Harlem in search of Jimmy. In a moment that looks very much like the opening of *Farewell, My Lovely*, Detective Walker surveys the city before him and notices its changing racial character:

> When he came out he noticed how the neighborhood had changed since his school days at City College. Colored people were mov-ing in and it was getting noisy. Already Harlem had taken over the other side of the street. This side, toward the river was still white, but there was nothing to stop the colored people from walking across the street. . . . South of 145th street the Puerto Ricans were taking over, crowding out the Germans and the French, who'd got-ten there first. It was like a dark cloud moving over Manhattan, he thought. But it wasn't his problem; he'd leave it to the city planners, to Commissioner Moses and his men.[44]

Here Himes draws on the familiar image of the apparently disinterested detective looking out at the city in order to highlight the social crisis of ghettoization that was brewing in midcentury America. Observing Har-lem in racial transition, Detective Walker characterizes the migration of African Americans and Puerto Ricans into urban America as a danger-ous encroachment. Although Walker worries at first that there is "noth-ing to stop colored people from walking across the street"—a reflection of typical white anxieties about minority in-migration that dominated public discourse throughout the twentieth century—he consoles himself with the thought that Commissioner Moses and his men will contain the racial menace through city planning. What is particularly striking here is that whereas in *Farewell, My Lovely* Marlowe relies on the unorganized violence of the embittered white ethnic Moose Malloy to restrain the African American urban presence, Detective Walker relies on the bureaucratic power of Robert Moses, a real historical figure who infamously destroyed the fabric of many New York neighborhoods with his urban renewal programs and highway construction projects. By casting Moses as the figure that will do the racial policing that the detective cannot accomplish, Himes makes an explicit connection between detective literature's violence against black characters and Moses's midcentury management of urban populations. *Run Man Run* unmasks the figures of ostensible rationalism as conspiring agents of Jim Crow modernity by positing that the implicit agenda of both Moses and the white detective is actually to contain black communities.

While Chandler's novel excuses those early white strategies of containing urban minorities—specifically, white ethnic violence against black populations—Himes's novel interrogates those strategies for containment that were developed after World War II. This is why Himes's linkage of the detective and Moses is an important one. More than any other single figure of the twentieth century, Robert Moses was responsible for creating modern America's racially divided landscape. Before he was ousted from his position as chairman of the Mayor's Committee on Slum Clearance for New York in 1968, Moses led the nation's largest slum clearance program. A proponent of the superblock solution, he viewed slums as a spreading cancer that needed to be flattened and replaced by homogeneous high-rise housing projects. In the decades following World War II, these Le Corbusier–inspired facilities were constructed in New York and then in Chicago, St. Louis, Baltimore, Detroit, and many other American cities during Moses's influential reign. However, the "projects," as they are widely known, now have become virtual prisons for poor African Americans and other minorities almost since the very moment of their construction. Moses further promoted white flight and black ghettoization with the construction of the modern expressway system, which allowed whites fleeing the city to populate the developing suburbs. For instance, dynamiting his way through the Bronx to make room for the Cross-Bronx Expressway, Moses displaced some sixty thousand working-class New Yorkers and transformed that neighborhood into an international symbol of urban blight.[45] Robert Caro estimates in his Pulitzer Prize–winning book on Moses that over the course of his career, the "power broker" evicted somewhere around a half a million people from their homes, a disproportionate number of them black and Puerto Rican.[46] Although attempts have been made in recent scholarship to rethink Moses's contribution to the creation of the modern American city, he no doubt institutionalized the model for a more systematic, policy-based containment of urban minorities.[47]

In the face of the violent racism of the white detective, *Run Man Run* posits the criminal on the run named Jimmy Johnson as the true protagonist of the novel. Sharing the same first name as the criminal from Himes's story "To What Red Hell," Jimmy in *Run Man Run* is not actually guilty of any crime. Jimmy is the only witness to Walker's murder of Luke and Sam, and he is therefore a liability whom Walker needs to silence in order to cover his other killings. Graduating with honors from North Carolina College, Jimmy is a law student at Columbia University and works at the Schmidt and Schindler automat to support his education. He is described as someone so upstanding that "there's hardly a white student in Harvard who wouldn't envy [his] clean record."[48] Because no one will believe Jimmy that the detective is a murderer, and because Walker continues to pursue him throughout the novel, Jimmy is increasingly drawn to the criminal underworld of Harlem as a response to the racism he faces. Putting this kind of black "criminal" on the run at the center of the novel allows Himes to show the allure of criminal posturing as a response to racist authority, even as he remains ambivalent about its effectiveness.

Toward the novel's conclusion, after Jimmy has been on the run and been unable to convince anyone that Walker is trying to murder him, he goes to Harlem in search of an illegal gun in order to defend himself. Jimmy's search for a firearm provides Himes an opportunity to showcase black neighborhoods as sites of cultural empowerment and not, as Chandler would have it, mean streets. In a scene that again mirrors the opening of *Farewell, My Lovely*, where Marlowe encounters the city in racial transition, Jimmy observes the changing character of Harlem. However, his reaction to the transformation is decidedly different. In Himes's story, it is the arrival the corporate restaurant, rather than the so-called dinge joint, that serves as the barometer of decline in the black neighborhood for the black protagonist: "He'd always heard that one could find anything and everything in Harlem, from purple Cadillacs to underwear made of unbleached flour sacks. But he hadn't found anything good to eat. The big chain cafeterias had come in and put the little restaurants out of business. All you could get in one of them was grilled chops and French fried potatoes. . . . He was tired of eating Schmidt and Schindler food, luncheonette-style food, no matter how good it was supposed to be."[49] Reversing the dynamic of Chandler's novel, in which the dinge joint signals the decline of the formerly white neighborhood, Himes's text postulates that it is in fact the fast-food restaurant with its white-bread tastes, systematized order, and displacement of black businesses that marks decline in Harlem.

This is partly why Himes's novel shifts the sites of violence from a black-owned dinge joint to Schmidt and Schindler's, a fictional chain restaurant based on the Horn and Hardart automat. In mid-twentieth-century America, the Horn and Hardart automat was one of the main precursors to fast-food restaurants like Burger King and McDonalds, dispensing coffee, buns, and sandwiches through tiny glass-door compartments. First started around the turn of the twentieth century, Horn and Hardart reached the height of its popularity in the 1950s, with about a hundred locations throughout New York and Philadelphia serving over a quarter of a million people a day.[50]

The corporate restaurant, with its emphasis on sterilized, rationalized regulation, operates as Himes's metonym for Moses's postwar city as a whole. After Walker has gotten away with murder, the superintendents restore order to Schmidt and Schindler's by removing all traces of the bodies. This process is described in detail by the omniscient narrator: "The wooden, ribbed floor where the bodies had lain were scraped, scrubbed, and washed down with scalding water spurting from a plastic hose. It was as though they were trying to wash away the deed itself. . . . By eleven A.M. the murder had been expertized, efficiently, unemotionally, thoroughly, and as far as was discernable, the slight pin-prick on the city had closed and congealed."[51] Here Himes uses the perfectly expressive word "expertized" to describe the process of removing both the murdered black bodies and all evidence of the murder itself. In this way, the removal of the bodies mimics the process of urban renewal itself, in which entire neighborhoods were bulldozed to make way for expressways and housing projects. Like the automat restaurant, which emphasized the importance of sanitation, orderliness, and a modernist aesthetic, Moses's postwar city privileged large-scale building projects that disregarded the violent impact on individual citizens. The elimination of Luke's and Fat Sam's bodies from Schmidt and Schindler's functions as Himes's allegory for the violence visited on populations of working-class urban minorities in postwar America.

Himes ends the novel with Jimmy eating soul food to prepare himself for the final confrontation with the detective. At the conclusion of *Run Man Run*, Himes uncouples the symbolic conflation of black neighborhoods and mean streets evidenced in Chandler by recasting Harlem and its locally owned businesses as Jimmy's only protection in a dangerous white world. In fact, Himes represents a dingy restaurant as a site of temporary rescue for Jimmy. After passing up the fast-food cafeteria, Jimmy stumbles on a soul food restaurant sitting inconspicuously on the same block: "He came to a dingy plate-glass, curtained-off storefront which held a sign reading: HOME COOKING. It looked like a letter from home. He went inside and sat at one of the five empty tables covered with blue-and-white checked oilcloth. To one side a coal fire burned in a potbellied stove. It was hot enough in there to give a white man a suntan."[52] The soul food restaurant, with its dingy and curtained-off window, is a symbol of black shelter in the novel, as it has the capacity to hide Jimmy momentarily from the pursuing detective. It is a stark contrast to the fast-food corporation, as the restaurant is humorously inhospitable to whites, even emitting enough heat to literally darken whiteness. Furthermore, the restaurant nourishes Jimmy. Unlike at the Schmidt and Schindler's, where porters like Fat Sam are reduced to the very food they serve, the soul food joint provides Jimmy a feast, which provides him with a moment of temporary empowerment: "He chose hog maws and turnip greens with a side dish of speckled peas. He splashed it with a hot sauce made from the seeds of chili peppers. The hot dish with the hot sauce scorched the inside of his mouth and burned his gullet as it went down. Sweat ran down his face and dripped from his chin. But after he'd finished, he felt a hundred percent better. He felt mean and dangerous and unafraid; he felt as if he could take the killer by his head and twist it off."[53] Himes provides his readers here with one of his rare expressions of how black cultural institutions such as the soul food restaurant could provide a bulwark against a violent white world. By consuming African American delicacies, such as hot-sauce-drenched hog maws, Jimmy is literally internalizing black cultural identity, an identity that gives him courage to face the detective. Whereas for Chandler, the black neighborhood and the dinge joint are an imaginary staging ground where Marlowe can make a brief journey into the urban exotic, for Himes, the black community and its local businesses provide for his black protagonist a space of temporary security and empowerment.

Himes's most explicit celebration of black cultural institutions occurs when Jimmy stops in front of the window of a black bookstore. The bookstore has on display, among other titles, James Weldon Johnson's *The Autobiography of an Ex-Colored Man*, Wallace Thurman's *The Blacker the Berry*, George Schuyler's satiric *Black No More*, Richard Wright's autobiography *Black Boy*, and St. Clair Drake and Horace Cayton's *Black Metropolis*. At this moment, Jimmy is seduced into believing that he is safe from the violent detective: "Suddenly he felt safe. There, in the heart of the Negro community, he was lulled into a sense of absolute security. He was surrounded by black people who talked his language and thought his thoughts; he was served by black people in businesses catering to black people; he was presented with the literature of black people. *Black* was a big word in Harlem. No wonder so many people desired their own neighborhoods, he thought. They felt safe; there was safety in numbers."[54] Himes reveals here that the very ghettos created by ideologies of white power also provide a space of black solidarity and resistance. Rather than operating as a symbol of invasion—what Walker characterizes as a "dark cloud moving over Manhattan"—the black community in Jimmy's mind is a space of safety and security. In this way, Himes's representation of the ghetto embodies Michel Foucault's idea of the heterotopia. It is a space where white disciplinary power is exerted but also where resistance to that power necessarily follows. Following these moments of black empowerment, Jimmy goes to the Apollo Theater, where he buys an illegal gun in anticipation of his final confrontation with Walker.

However, even as Himes spends the penultimate pages of the novel showcasing Harlem's bookstores, soul food restaurants, theaters, and barber shops, he reveals how these institutions are unequal to the task of protecting black citizens against the totalizing and omnipresent violence of urban renewal and ghettoization. In fact, Jimmy is not actually protected by Harlem but rather is "*lulled* into a sense of absolute security" (my emphasis) by it. In the novel's last pages, Jimmy heads into the Harlem streets to confront Matt Walker in a final duel. The expected showdown between the two characters does not materialize, as Jimmy's act of masculine courage proves ineffectual in the face of Walker's surveillance: "[Jimmy] couldn't hear the shots and didn't know what direction they were coming from. He felt the tearing of the bullet's trajectory inside him. He tried to call for help but didn't have the breath. Nothing came from his mouth but blood. With one last desperate effort he jerked his pistol free and fired it at the pavement."[55] In one of the most powerful images of the novel, Walker silences Jimmy by shooting him from a space of concealment, a metaphor for larger silencing of urban minorities at the hands of urban renewal policies. Although Jimmy survives the shooting and Walker later dies at the hands of the police, Jimmy's desperate final clash with the detective provides a more apt expression of the novel's meaning than the tacked-on happy ending would imply. For while Himes himself escaped from America to France in 1955, the image of Jimmy being gunned down in the streets without seeing or hearing his attacker operates as a potent symbol for the containment that the majority of urban blacks faced in postwar America. Jimmy's final desperate act of firing his gun at the pavement dramatizes that individual armed resistance to the systemic violence that Walker represents is about as effective as shooting the street itself. Even as Walker himself is killed at the novel's conclusion, as this moment reveals, he is not the ultimate danger to urban blacks. It is the street itself that is ultimately the black protagonist's nemesis, as it is the urban ghetto created by white bureaucrats that is the true culprit of racist containment in the postwar decades. For the disappearing detective was to be revenged by other white policymakers such as Robert Moses, who imposed urban renewal on urban minorities in the form of slum clearance, high-rise housing projects, and low-wage service-sector employment in the postwar decades. The image of Jimmy shooting at the sidewalk dramatizes that the Moses-constructed streets are the real target of Himes's critique, as these streets are symbolic of urban segregation in the second half of the twentieth century.

"I Just Wanted to Take It Away from the White Man If Only in My Books": Raymond Chandler, Chester Himes, and the Literary Marketplace

As the dissenting novel of his Harlem Domestic series, a novel that has been subsumable by neither commercial nor critical interests, *Run Man Run* represents a central concern of Himes's literary imagination. It explores the possibilities and liabilities of postures of black criminality in a society where systematic white racism is an overwhelming reality. But another way we can think about the ultimate significance of *Run Man Run* is that it illustrates Himes's precarious position in a literary marketplace run by white publishers. These publishers further contained black writers through marketing strategies that were designed to sell the works of white authors. In other words, as Himes himself encroached on the popular literary marketplace dominated by white pulp writers, publishers devised ways of neutralizing the racial message of his black-sympathetic work. For example, the American version of *Run Man Run* was advertised by the paperback publishing company Dell as the story of a black female nightclub singer: "A girl named Linda Lou, grew up in the streets of Harlem. Singing was her racket but men were her trade . . . she never discriminated." Responding to this blatant misrepresentation of the novel, Himes wrote in a letter to John A. Williams, "Who are they talking about? I wrote a book about a psychopathic white detective killing two brothers and trying to kill a third. And here they go putting down this shit about some black sister out of her mind."[56] As Himes's response here clearly indicates, American publishers were unable to conceive of Himes's novel as a story of racial critique, even though this is the clear focus of the book. This is an issue that plagued Himes's works from the publication of his earliest stories in *Esquire.*[57] By advertising *Run Man Run* as the story of a gold-digging female con artist, the publishers were following a strategy of selling that had been successful with the earlier pulp writers such as Hammett and Chandler. Although this makes commercial sense, given the formulaic approach to marketing pulp fiction, it does show the fact that publishers did not have black audiences in mind when marketing the book, due to the shape of book markets at this time.

Before the emergence of Holloway House Publishing Company in the late 1960s, a subject to which we will turn in chapter 2, the producers of popular American literature simply assumed that a black reading audience did not exist. Therefore, Himes's revisions of the tropes of white-authored detective fiction and his development of the criminal-on-the-run figure in *Run Man Run* can be understood as more than just a challenge to the racial status quo of detective literature and a critique of white urban containment strategies. His fusion of the detective and criminal stories in *Run Man Run* also represents a careful negotiation of a literary market that did not yet recognize black popular writers or an audience of African American readers. Or, to state this in another way, *Run Man Run* is a literary product that reflects a marketplace that attempted to contain African American writers within white-friendly marketing constructs. This containment of Himes's work is also evident in the emerging critical history of his literature, particularly in casting Himes as a successor to Chandler.[58] But there are some problems with this characterization. This narrative of Himes as a successor to Chandler is one that dovetails too neatly with the story of America's racial succession in urban spaces. Just as African Americans came to occupy those urban spaces left behind in the abandonment of America's cities in the postwar years, so the story goes, so too did Himes come to occupy a liter-ary form abandoned by white authors such as Chandler. It is simply not true that Himes came *after* Chandler; he was rather more like a literary foil. Although Himes was certainly an admirer of Hammett, he pub-lished his first prison stories as early as 1933, the same year that Chandler published his first detective story in *Black Mask*. This means that Himes was not so much Chandler's successor as he was a potential rival in the field of literary production. Even though Himes wrote many of his detec-tive novels in the years when Chandler's work was in decline, the two authors nevertheless started publishing at the same moment. From the beginning of each of their careers, both Chandler and Himes employed the popular forms of the detective and criminal story, respectively, in order to engage issues of racial migration and containment. But whereas Chandler's work celebrates figures of heroic whiteness that police and silence black urban bodies, Himes's work consistently attempts to repre-sent the effects of racism.

Rather than thinking of Himes as simply a more authentic transcriber of black experiences and neighborhoods, then, we might think of him instead as a writer negotiating a field of literary production in which he was not recognized. "I had been as much of a tourist as a white man from downtown changing his luck," Himes once wrote of his relation-ship to Harlem. "The Harlem of my books was never meant to be real; I never called it real; I just wanted to take it away from the white man if only in my books."[59] Recalling the interview with Williams in which he discusses Chandler's opening to *Farewell, My Lovely*, Himes in this moment admits that his own representations of the black neighborhood are no more real than anyone else's. However, by saying that he wants to take Harlem away from "the white man if only in my books," Himes suggests that the popular novel was an important site for challenging white representations of African American spaces. Even if Moses and others did succeed in containing African Americans in ghettos, Himes indicates here that literature could remain vital in the battle over the representation of such spaces. In the fight over the material and political organization of black communities, Himes saw that detective and crime literature was a critical site to fight the ideological and cultural confron-tation connected to it.

Himes was an innovative literary artist in hijacking the popular form of the detective novel in order to stage a critique of white ideologies of racial containment. However, he was writing at a moment when white publishers did not yet recognize the commercial possibilities of black popular fiction of this type. Although Himes's Coffin Ed Johnson and Grave Digger Jones novels were republished in the United States in cheap paperback format, they were marketed to the same class of white readers who followed Chandler and Mickey Spillane. Not until the pimp autobiographies and hustler novels of Robert Beck and Donald Goines were published in the late 1960s and early 1970s by Holloway House Publishing Company were black audiences actively courted and African American writers encouraged to create free from the containment of white-targeted marketing. As the first black-authored crime novels to hit the paperback market in the late 1950s, the books of Himes are clear forerunners to the literary phenomenon of black-authored pulp fiction in their concern for street themes, issues of crime and containment, and problems of authorship in a popular market. By pushing the narrative of the white detective chasing a black criminal to its absurd but logical conclusion, Himes's novel offers insight on the ideological and artistic limitations of the hard-boiled American detective story. In *Run Man Run*, he essentially dramatizes its inability to give voice to a black urban population, and he thereby implicitly makes a case for new modes of African American popular literature to be written. As a precursor to the crime novels of Holloway House authors, *Run Man Run* represents a significant transitional novel that bridges the detective literature of figures such as Hammett and Chandler to more contemporary novelists such as Donald Goines and Robert Beck. Years before African American crime fiction gained popularity among black readers, Himes mobilized the popular form of the detective story to engage the issues of racial succession, urbanization, and black popular culture in midcentury America.

2 / Pimping Fictions: Iceberg Slim and the Invention of Pimp Literature

In the final pages of *Pimp: The Story of My Life* (1967), the narrator Iceberg Slim details his escape from the confines of a "steel casket," a solitary confinement cell in the basement of the Cook County House of Corrections where he has been incarcerated for ten months. Having confessed the graphic details of his twenty-five-year career as a Chicago pimp, in this penultimate chapter, Iceberg Slim redeploys his linguistic skills to challenge the book's chief figuration of racist white authority, the warden. When the warden threatens to keep Slim in solitary confinement a month longer than his official release date, he constructs a legal-sounding appeal to secure his freedom: "I wrote a paper based on what I believed were the legal grounds for my release at the expiration of ten months. It had subtle muscle in it too. I memorized the paper. I rehearsed it in the cell. Finally I had the necessary dramatic inflection and fluid delivery."[1] Signaling a new political consciousness in the book, this moment also dramatizes one of the fundamental themes in pimp fiction: that the fluency and verbal style of pimping can be harnessed to challenge white-constructed spaces of containment. At the climax of *Pimp*, Iceberg Slim faces off with the warden and delivers the following speech:

> Sir, I realize that the urgent press of your duties has perhaps contributed to your neglect of my urgent request for an interview. I have come here to discuss the vital issue of my legal discharge date.
> Wild rumors are circulating to the effect that you are not a fair man, that you are a bigot, who hates Negroes. I discounted them

immediately when I heard them. I am almost dogmatic in my belief that a man of your civic stature and intellect could ill afford or embrace such prejudice.

In the spirit of fair play, I am going to be brutally frank. If I am not released the day after tomorrow, a certain agent of mine here in the city is going to set in motion a process that will not only free me, but will possibly in addition throw a revealing spotlight on certain not too legal, not too pleasant activities carried on daily behind these walls.

I have been caged here like an animal for almost ten months. Like an animal, my sensitivity of seeing and hearing has been enhanced. I only want what is legally mine. My contention is that if your Captain of guards, who is legally your agent, had arrested me and confined me on such an unlikely place as the moon for thirty days, technically and legally I would be in the custody of this institution. Sir, the point is unassailable. Frankly, I don't doubt that my release will occur on legal schedule. Thank you, Sir, for the interview.[2]

Employing a combination of feigned deference, veiled threats, and off-beat humor, Iceberg Slim wins his legal release date in the last pages of the autobiography. This moment dramatizes the possibilities that an adapted pimp language could offer black men who are caged like animals in the American prison system. By equating literacy and freedom in this way, Slim exhibits one of the enduring tropes in the African American auto-biography from the slave narrative of Frederick Douglass to *The Autobiography of Malcolm X*.[3] But Iceberg Slim's autobiography also burlesques these stories of literacy and courageous manhood by featuring the misogynist pimp as the organizing figure of the text. Whereas Himes's criminal on the run is silenced by the modes of white containment at the conclusion of *Run Man Run*, Iceberg Slim confronts systematic meth-ods of white violence through his own oppression of women. *Pimp: The Story of My Life* manages these contradictory subversive and conserva-tive energies through a pimp poetics, and it presents an aesthetic stance that maintains a troubled relationship to African American cultural and political movements.

Robert Maupin Beck—the real name of Iceberg Slim—is one of the most influential black American authors that most people have never heard of. After publishing *Pimp: The Story of My Life* in 1967, Beck went on to author four published novels, *Trick Baby* (1967), *Mama Black*

Widow (1969), *Death Wish* (1977), and *Long White Con* (1977); an essay collection, *The Naked Soul of Iceberg Slim* (1971); a collection of short stories, *Airtight Willie and Me* (1979); an album of pimp "toasts" titled *Reflections* (1976); and one novel he never published, titled *Night Train to Sugar Hill*.[4] Taken together, Beck's published works have made him one of the best-selling black American authors of all time. By official counts, he had sold six million books at the time of his death in 1992.[5] Additionally, Beck's books have had a tremendous effect on contemporary black popular culture, inspiring blaxploitation films as well as gangsta rap.[6] Both Tracy "Ice-T" Marrow and O'Shay "Ice Cube" Jackson fashioned their stage monikers from Iceberg Slim's name, and they helped pioneer gangsta rap by transforming Slim's narratives into hip hop songs with mainstream crossover appeal. As Ice-T explains it, "When rap music came along it hit me: the same way he could take his experiences and put them on the page, I could take mine and bring them to the mic. So by the same method he became a writer, I became a rapper."[7] Inspired by Robert Beck's stylized representations of black life in America's urban spaces, gangster rappers such as Ice-T, Ice Cube, and many others essentially transposed a popular literary art into a popular musical form. The hypercool black masculine personas, the stories of ghetto life, and the inventive uses of black urban vernacular that we now associate with hip hop music can be traced directly back to the literature of Robert Beck. We can deepen our understanding of gangsta rap and hip hop culture by decoding *Pimp: The Story of My Life* and the genre of black crime literature that it inspired.

Although the pimp figure had been represented in American literature before—Jerco in Claude McKay's *Home to Harlem* (1928), Boots Smith in Ann Petry's *The Street* (1946), Rinehart in Ralph Ellison's *Invisible Man* (1952), and Norman Mailer's hipster persona in his essay "The White Negro" (1957) are just a few examples of the pimp's presence in the American literary imagination—Beck made the pimp the organizing figure of the African American autobiography. Beck altered the representation of the pimp by constructing a figure of heroic black masculinity whose verbal style and posture of criminal cool could offer tactical challenges to white racism. Of course, outlaw figures such as gunfighters, bank robbers, and tramps had been popular literary heroes for working-class readers from the time of dime novels of the nineteenth century.[8] Furthermore, as a number of scholars have shown, representations of criminal violence have political potential in the African American literary works of Richard Wright and Chester Himes.[9] Beck's first book

FIGURE 2.1. *Pimp: The Story of My Life* (1967) by Robert Beck (Iceberg Slim).

expanded the literary representation of the outlaw hero by creating a popular portrait of the pimp in the emerging literary marketplace of paperback books directed specifically toward black consumers. Beck was an original voice in American literature in that he redirected his skills as a master street linguist to create a mass-market literary product for African Americans. As Beck once put it in an interview,

> What I did with my first book, I simply made a transfer. I knew that in presenting ideas to whores, or to anybody else, that one had to create a certain kind of situation. In other words, it had to be entertaining. Like when you're talking to a whore, you have to fascinate her. I also knew that you had to be logical. I also knew that it had to be tied up in a neat package—that is, no loose ends. And, you had to answer, just as you do the whore, all of the questions before they are asked. And, you can't be heavy-handed with it. You have to do it in a casual way. But, I didn't know this was what they call painless exposition that the writing craft speaks about. For every principle that I used in "Pimp," there's a literary name.[10]

As Beck suggests in this quote, a lifetime of pimping provided him more than just the kernel for his story; it also provided him with an approach to creating an entertaining, compelling, and highly crafted literary product. By suggesting that the art of exposition is critical to both pimping and the craft of writing, Beck exemplifies one of the central concerns of this study implied in the title, *Pimping Fictions*. In terms of content, Beck provided his audience with pimp fiction, insider narratives of his twenty-five-year career as a sexual exploiter of women. But Beck also pimped his fictions, that is, refashioned his linguistic skills to create engaging literary products for a mass-market audience.

In the early 1970s, as blaxploitation films became part of the public conversation about black popular culture, Robert Beck was the subject of a number of sensationalist pieces on pimps in *Sepia*, the *Washington Post*, and the *Los Angeles Free Press*.[11] However, there has been very little academic scholarship on Beck, despite his sizable contributions to African American literary traditions and American popular culture.[12] One reason that he is overlooked is because his work is often misread as unselfconsciously capitulating to white norms of power. As one representative critic has claimed, "the pimp is essentially a capitalist" who exploits the labor of prostitutes in the pursuit of flashy clothes, diamond jewelry, and Cadillacs. There is no radical potential in pimp literatures, the critic argues, because "these are the stuff of bourgeois consciousness."[13] Such readings, which interpret the pimp figure as a straightforward imitation of white bourgeois norms, fail to understand how black style is both a self-conscious adoption of hegemonic power and a form of tactical resistance against systematic racial oppression. Without downplaying the violence against women in the text, my analysis of Beck's *Pimp* expands on recent cultural studies approaches to understanding black urban style. These approaches read black cultural expressions of cool such as the zoot suit, bebop music, and hipster speech as stylistic answers to the social contradictions of twentieth-century race relations. As a figure who organizes the oppositional style of the zoot suit and the hermeneutic of hipster talk into an economic system of sexual exploitation, the pimp has been read as icon of black masculine working-class heroism.[14] My reading of Beck's narrative expands on these approaches by examining how *Pimp* promotes an ethos of composure as a response to the conditions of twentieth-century ghettoization. Beck invented a foundational narrative of modern black masculinity designed to handle the conditions of Jim Crow modernity, using the newly emerging mass market of fiction as a site to create a form of literary protest against urban containment.

Any analysis of pimp literature must be attentive to the gender politics that inform these excessively masculine narratives. In *Pimp*, Slim creates his own form of gender oppression in order to combat racial injustice. As his narrative consistently reveals, the tactical warfare against white racism is underwritten by the oppression of black women. This dualism of resistance and domination is at the very heart of pimp literature. As the ur-text of modern representations of the pimp in popular and literary culture, *Pimp: The Story of My Life* defines an image of defiant black masculinity born out of a struggle with spatial and racial containments of Jim Crow that further reproduces these violences along gender lines. The pimp in Iceberg Slim's narrative, therefore, is a deeply flawed literary hero at best. As Stuart Hall, one of the key architects of cultural studies, reminds us, popular culture is neither wholly subversive nor a form of total domination but a site of struggle, containing both seditious and hegemonic energies. As he states it in one of his essays on black popular culture, "certain ways in which black men continue to live out their counter-identities as black masculinities and replay those fantasies of black masculinities in the theaters of popular culture are, when viewed from along other axes of difference, the very masculine identities that are oppressive to women, that claim visibility for their hardness only at the expense of the vulnerability of black women and the feminization of gay black men."[15] Slim's autobiography repeatedly dramatizes this very structure, as the oppositional masculine identity of the black pimp is always dependent on the exploitation of vulnerable black women and gay men.

One further circumstance that complicates the production of pimp literature is that Beck created his work in the literary marketplace of black paperback publishing. In the first section of this chapter, I provide a cultural history of *Pimp*'s publication at Holloway House Publishing Company in order to outline the forms of representational containment that Robert Beck the author faced in the commercial space of pulp publishing. Investigating how Beck was marketed by commercially minded white publishers, I show that his fictions were in many ways pimped by the industry that sensationalized and thus neutralized the radical potential of his work. I read the emergence of pimp literature against the backdrop of the growing literary marketplace of black pulp publishing in order to reveal how the pioneering text of the genre was created at the intersection of various cross-racial alliances, commercial imperatives, and strategies of confinement. In the second section of the chapter, I outline how Beck's autobiography negotiates these various constraints. While the pimp identity provides the black narrator freedom from white containment in ways unavailable to Chester Himes's characters, he gains this freedom at the cost of victimizing the very same people who are themselves at the social and political margin of American society. It is this central dynamic which defines *Pimp*, and I delineate the self-conscious ways in which Slim's story uses strategies of gender oppression in order to contest racial ones. Operating outside normative spheres of production and consumption, the pimp reaches his full (if fraught) potential through the strategic use of linguistic style backed by violence. This epitomizes a new representational strategy in the world of black crime literature, and it expands on the literary model created by Himes. Beck's autobiography not only models the linguistic powers of the pimp, but it explores the pimp's use value as a potent symbol of black politics. In the final section of the chapter, I investigate the multiple ways in which pimp poetics ultimately fails to provide Iceberg Slim an escape from the many economic, spatial, and racial forms of containment he faces. *Pimp* represents a development of an aesthetic strategy created in Himes; however, Iceberg Slim illustrates that a pimp's criminal posturing is also ultimately unequal to the problem of white containment.

Pimping the Pimp: The Literary Marketplace
and the Invention of Iceberg Slim

First, a genealogy of the black pulp literary marketplace. While Iceberg Slim is able to pimp his way to freedom at the conclusion of *Pimp: The Story of My Life*, Robert Beck, the author, faced a wide range of constraints in the commercial space of black pulp publishing at Holloway House Publishing Company. The creation of this genre of literature involved a new set of contentious relationships between the black writer and the literary marketplace. Orchestrated by white publicists from Hollywood, the publication of Beck's *Pimp: The Story of My Life* represents at once the beginning of a literary renaissance of black popular literature and a further marginalization of black literary talent. Beck may have been providing pimp fiction in the content of his stories, but his white publishers were also pimping the fictions of black authors such as Beck, who were at the very fringe of society and the African American literary scene. The publishers who promoted Beck provided an innovative commercial space for him and other black writers to expand the representation of African American culture in the public sphere. However, they did so within a very narrowly conceived field of literary production, one that sought to contain the representations as sensationalist exoticism. Just as Iceberg Slim the narrator finds it difficult to negotiate the spaces of urban containment in *Pimp: The Story of My Life*, so too did Robert Beck find it challenging to negotiate the commercial space of black pulp publishing as established by the white-owned Holloway House.

Beck's publisher, Holloway House, was originally created in 1959 by two white Hollywood publicists, Bentley Morriss and Ralph Weinstock. They initially imagined the company as a literary supplement for their soft-core nude magazines aimed at a white male audience, *Adam* and *Knight*. Throughout the early 1960s, Morriss and Weinstock had dabbled on the border between tawdry and legitimate fictions. They at first published a seemingly random collection of titles, including the first paperback biography of Ernest Hemingway as well as a transcript of the Adolph Eichmann trial. As Hollywood copywriters, Morriss and Weinstock focused most of their efforts on publishing sensationalist Hollywood biographies, including Barbara Payton's *I Am Not Ashamed* (1963), *Jayne Mansfield's Wild Wild World* (1964), and *My Name Is Leona Gage, Will Somebody Please Help Me?* (1965). Except for the odd legitimate work such as the writings of the Marquis de Sade, in these early years, Holloway House's output included publicity-grabbing Hollywood biographies, literary erotica, pseudoscientific sex surveys, and sex-worker confessionals.

In the midst of the Civil Rights Movement, and especially following the 1965 Watts riot, Morriss and Weinstock began publishing black-authored literature, reflecting—and indeed helping to produce—a social transformation in which ghetto residents were being recognized by corporate America as a cultural force of consumers. As Morriss makes clear in an interview, this transformation of the company was always motivated by commercial imperatives, not political ones: "These were the early sixties. We really hadn't been involved in the Civil Rights Movement, although both Ralph and myself and other people in the company had certain social inclinations and social responsibilities to the rest of the world. We felt it would be kind of cool to do books—black literature, of which there was really very little. And so we felt that it would be kind of personally rewarding, and let's see if we can make some money at it."[16] As Morriss suggests here, the decision to begin publishing black books was only tangentially connected to the Civil Rights Movement. Of greater significance was the fact that the black masses represented at this time a largely disregarded market of readers. Again, as Morriss describes it, "We didn't do it to emancipate a community. We did it because we felt it was economically viable. There were some rewards and pats on the back after that, for which we were grateful. We do this because it is a commodity that will sell."[17] Forthcoming about his motivations for getting into the business of selling black books, Morriss makes clear here the baldly economic origins of black crime literature. From the very beginning, the publication of black crime literature was less about black freedom struggles and more about expanding commodity production into new racial markets that had been overlooked or outright ignored by mainstream publishers.

The publication of Robert Beck's *Pimp* helped ignite a literary renaissance of black crime fiction at Holloway House in the early 1970s. Writers such as Donald Goines, Joseph Nazel, Odie Hawkins, Omar Fletcher, Charlie Harris, and many others published their own Beck-inspired narratives of pimps, junkies, sex workers, hit men, and ghetto revolutionaries with Holloway House. In this, they were assisted by the owners of Holloway House, who recognized that America's black urban working class represented a disregarded market of readers. They sold their books at liquor stores, barber shops, and newsstands in inner-city communities across America. They created an entirely new niche market of black readers by building literary cultures in state and federal prison libraries and on military bases. Holloway House targeted black readers that had never before been targeted, by distributing their books through nontraditional bookselling channels. Pioneering this form of distribution, Holloway House made pimp and hustler novels into underground best-sellers in the years following the Civil Rights Movement. Following on *Pimp*'s unprecedented commercial success, Holloway House over the period of four decades published hundreds of titles by dozens of unknown authors, creating a new genre it christened "the black experience novel."[18]

Publishing and distributing the novels on a large scale turned out to be a challenging task, as Holloway House encountered racism at almost every level of production and circulation. Shut out of mainstream channels of distribution, Morriss and Weinstock turned to local distributors in black communities in the South and in urban centers across the nation in order to get *Pimp* and other black-authored books out to consumers. At first, Morriss found it difficult to convince distributors that there was a market for literature among working-class black men. According to Morriss, the main problem he faced was an entrenched cultural stereotype that African Americans had neither the money nor the desire to buy books: "Distributors would say to me off the record, 'Come on, man. Blacks don't read. They don't have the money to buy books.' Which, of course, was just stupid. We convinced them that they could make some money, and that was the common denominator. It was a slow and deliberate process."[19] Facing a marketplace that presumed the lack of a literary culture among urban African Americans, Morriss succeeded in getting books out to the black consumer by appealing to distributors' respect for the bottom line. This marks a crucial shift from the age of *Black Mask* magazine as well as the publication of Himes's novels, as Morriss the publisher was able to recognize and capitalize on a critical mass of black readers. The very conditions that produced America's confined ghetto spaces also created a culture of readers desiring to read commercial narratives that represented black heroes who were contesting those very same spaces. The spaces of white domination and surveillance produced the very resistance to those sites, and mass-market black crime literature became an important commodity in giving voice to that resistance.

Robert Beck was the first commercially successful black writer to publish his story with Holloway House. After Beck appeared on a number of television talk shows to promote the autobiography, the book caused a local commotion in Los Angeles and became a best-seller. Holloway House used sensationalist advertising to attract an audience rather than linking Beck to a tradition of African American letters, thereby creating a new commercially driven black literary marketplace. On the day after Beck appeared on the Joe Pyne show, the popularity of *Pimp* exploded, securing both Beck's and Holloway House's reputation. As Morriss remembers it, "Half a dozen bookstores in Hollywood and Los Angeles had people waiting in line around the block to buy the book. And when they called and told me that, I didn't believe them, so I drove down to Hollywood Boulevard to see it. And it was a sight. It was like they were giving away something."[20] *Pimp* was not reviewed in any major publications, and the *New York Times* refused to run an advertisement for it because of the title. However, as Morriss describes it, the book nonetheless garnered a popular following through alternative methods of promotion. By booking Beck on television programs and as a speaker on college campuses, and by selling his book at newspaper stands, liquor stores, and other nontraditional book venues, Holloway House was able to constitute an audience for *Pimp* and, later, for a growing list of black-authored books.

Therefore, even as Robert Beck created a new literary product by sublimating his skills as a pimp into a first-person narration of his life, this act of creation needs to be contextualized within the larger commercial enterprise promoted by Holloway House. In certain ways, *Pimp* is actually not all that different in form and content from many of the other sex confessionals published by Holloway House at this moment, including *Point Your Tail in the Right Direction* (1966), a Playboy bunny autobiography; *Some Like It Dark* (1966), the confessions of an African American call girl; *Nine Holes of Jade* (1967), the memoir of a Hong Kong prostitute; and *Honeyman* (1968), the story of a brothel owner. Whatever the individual stylistic merits of Beck's book, it is still an artifact created within the confines of a mass-market literary marketplace that privileged sexy sensationalism over literary merit. Read in this way, Beck's *Pimp* is neither an exposé of what "really happened" during his tenure as pimp nor entirely a self-consciously constructed literary product. It is part of a growing literary market that transformed multicultural perspectives into popular literary products through sexualized advertising strategies.

As a commercial artifact of this type, *Pimp* can be understood as an arena where a variety of competing representations of black identity are on display. For example, consider the difference between Iceberg Slim's statement that opens the autobiography and the ad copy promoting the novel. In the book's preface, Slim tells his audience that the purpose of his confession is a didactic one: "In this book I will take you the reader with me into the secret inner world of the pimp. I will lay bare my life and thoughts as a pimp. The account of my brutality and cunning as a pimp will fill many of you with revulsion, however if one intelligent valuable young man or woman can be saved from the destructive slime then the displeasure I have given will have been outweighed by that individual's use of his potential in a socially constructive manner."[21] Adopting a confessional posture as old as St. Augustine's *Confessions* and part of the English literary tradition dating back to Daniel Defoe, Slim promises to reveal his sordid pimp past as a warning to black youth intent on pursuing a criminal life. By contrast, the back cover of every Holloway House edition of *Pimp* that has been sold in the past four decades reads, "No other book comes anywhere near this one in its description of the raw, brutal reality of the jungle that lurks beneath the surface of every city. Nobody but a pimp could tell this story, and none ever has . . . until Iceberg Slim." While both author and publisher promise an insider look at pimp life, Slim's statement and the ad copy illustrate their differing agendas. As Slim's pronouncement suggests, his ultimate intention in revealing the details of his pimp past is to steer young black men and women away from the Life. By point of comparison, Holloway House's representation of Slim's narrative as an insider's account of the inner-city "jungle" reflects twentieth-century racial ideologies that view black neighborhoods as the site of dangerous but titillating exotic spectacle. In this way, Holloway House's marketing strategy actually serves to uphold the white containment of urban spaces, while at the same time offering a peek into those ghetto spaces that have been cordoned off by strategies of white control. These competing aims—those of the author and those of the publisher—reveal that in the emerging literary marketplace of black pulp literature, Beck was working against forms of representational containment as much as he was introducing new modes of literary expression. Holloway House's sensationalized marketing of *Pimp* served to contain Beck's work in the commercial space of the pulp marketplace in much the same way that confined urban spaces contain Iceberg Slim in the symbolic space of the novel.

Ultimately, we need to understand pimp literature both as an innovative cultural expression drawn from the popular energies of street life and as a literary commodity encoded by the constraints of a commercial literary market. In interviews, Beck himself seemed aware of these constraints. When asked once if he might ever write a book of philosophy, he admitted, "I haven't done the prerequisite reading that one must do so that one will have the shape and form for that kind of writing. I've been forced to write commercial stuff. That luxury has been denied me. To even think about it . . ."[22] Here Beck expresses that while he is attracted to the idea of writing philosophy (later in the interview, he cites James Baldwin as a major influence), this type of writing is so distant from his field of literary production that he cannot even finish his thought. Like many of the writers who would eventually work under the Holloway House imprint, Beck turned to writing pimp/criminal confessionals to escape from a former life of crime. However, as a writer producing commercial materials, he was unable to make very much money from his writing. According to his contracts and royalty statements, he was paid a fifteen-hundred-dollar advance for *Pimp* and received about 5 percent of gross sales in royalties.[23] While this is not an insignificant amount of money, Beck's financial compensation was modest compared with other authors publishing with mainstream houses, especially because Holloway House titles at this time went for the low price of ninety-five cents. The high sales of Beck's books made Holloway House commercially successful and helped lay the groundwork for the company's ascendency as a niche publisher of black crime literature. Neither Beck nor any of his literary protégés earned much literary fame or a sizable income from this arrangement. When Beck died on the eve of the Rodney King riots in 1992, he was penniless, despite the fact that his books had sold millions of copies. One way to view this is that Beck, the former pimp, ended up being pimped by the industry of pulp publication. In Holloway House's financial practices and advertising strategies, it no doubt created the conditions for an underground literary movement and new culture industry. But at the same time, it limited Beck from achieving mainstream recognition or financial independence. In this scenario, pimping turns out to be a useful symbolic system for understanding the position of "black experience" writers. When Beck was asked in an interview if he himself were a whore, he replied, "We all are, if you live under capitalism."[24] With Holloway House taking on the symbolic position of the pimp, the company was in fact structured like a "stable," with writers such as Robert Beck occupying the vulnerable position of sex workers in the literary market of white-owned paperback publishing.

The Invention of Pimp Fiction

At the midpoint in *Pimp: The Story of My Life*, there is a moment which dramatizes the power of pimping to subvert momentarily forms of white containment in mid-twentieth-century Chicago. While still learning the art of pimpology, Iceberg Slim attends a party thrown by Sweet Jones, the book's legendary pimp patriarch, who makes money pimping off white women, an important sign of his high stature. Sweet lives in the penthouse apartment of a "snow-white apartment building" in an exclusive white suburban neighborhood that even employs a white doorman. Stepping out onto Sweet's balcony that overlooks the city, Slim contemplates how pimping has provided his mentor a way out of the oppressive conditions of the South and the northern urban ghetto: "He came out of the white man's cotton fields. He's pimped himself up to this. He's living high in the sky like a black God in heaven with the white people. He ain't no Nigger doctor. He ain't no hot-sheet Nigger preacher, but he's here. He pimped up his scratch passport. That barbed-wire stockade is a million miles away."[25] Here, standing momentarily with a privileged perspective both above and outside the "barbed-wire stockade" of the urban ghetto, Slim sees pimping as affording a means of access into the world of economic, spatial, and racial freedom. Sweet Jones, who wears a white satin smoking jacket and seats himself on a white velour couch, is the narrative's model for black mobility, as he has generated enough money to literally enshroud himself in whiteness. Furthermore, Sweet Jones is "no Nigger doctor" or "hot-sheet Nigger preacher"; he has escaped to the white world without becoming a member of the black middle class. As an oppositional figure to both white racists and the black bourgeoisie, Sweet Jones is black masculine heroism incarnate in *Pimp*. Not only is he wealthy, but he has achieved black mobility without capitulating to the tastes and manners of the vacuous middle class. From the lofty perspective of Sweet's penthouse, Slim decides that pimping is also the only way he can make it out of the ghetto: "I don't wanta be a stickup man or a dope peddler. I sure as hell won't be a porter or dishwasher. I just wanta pimp that's all. It's not too bad, because whores are rotten. Besides I ain't going to croak them or drive them crazy. I'm just going to pimp some real white-type living out of them."[26]

Refusing to submit to the same fate as the porter Jimmy in *Run Man Run*, Slim chooses pimping as the method of creating for himself a "scratch passport," a monetary means of escaping the ghetto. Whereas in Himes's novel, Jimmy is overwhelmed by the city streets, Slim's story presents the pimp as a figure who can negotiate these spatial oppressions by mastering the codes, styles, and language of the pimp game. However, as Slim's decision to pimp also reveals, such mobility also depends on both literal and symbolic gender oppression. In providing a justification for becoming a pimp, Slim characterizes women as "rotten," lifeless, decaying objects. It is this tension—pimping as a form of freedom from white constraint and pimping as a form of gender oppression—that is the distinguishing feature of *Pimp: The Story of My Life*.

By adopting the stylistic postures and linguistic strategies of the pimp, Iceberg Slim is able to negotiate spaces of white confinement in ways unavailable to the black characters of Himes's novel. In *Pimp*, Slim rejects the alienating systems of service labor, the spatial confines of white containment, and a pathway to black bourgeoisie respectability— for instance, early in the book, Slim is expelled from Booker T. Washington's Tuskegee Institute. Instead, Slim chooses a path of criminal self-education in the form of learning the codes of the street and the language of the hip. As cultural studies scholars have recently argued, such postures of cool combined "expressive style with public composure" and operated as tactical responses to public censure and white violence in the context of the African American migration to the urban north.[27] As fashion statements in the extreme, donning sharkskin suits and conking one's hair were expressions of calculated hostility, or as Eric Lott has put it, "a politics of style beyond protest, focusing the struggles of its moment in a live and irreverent art."[28] Practicing a politics of opposition in everyday life, zoot suiters, cool cats, and mack men worked on the level of fashion, language, and posture what could not be expressed directly in the political avenues then open to them in Jim Crow America. These "race rebels," as Robin Kelley has called them, opened up new artistic visions and occupied new stances in the world, creating a form of black populist modernism.[29] Beck's autobiography can be understood as part of this tradition of displaying a politics of style. Told almost entirely in the rarified vernacular of the street pimp, *Pimp* transposed an African American oral tradition of street rap onto the literary form of the autobiography. In fact, because the editors at Holloway House "at first didn't understand what the hell he was talking about," they insisted Beck create a glossary for the back of the book.[30] Containing terms such as "hog" (Cadillac), "gangster" (marijuana), and "girl" (cocaine), the glossary reflects the degree to which Slim's vocabulary and style represented an entirely new cultural expression to the majority of Americans.

In *Pimp*, Iceberg Slim adopts the styles and criminal behaviors of the pimp as a tactical response to the racial and spatial oppressions of the urban North. Chicago, where historically the majority of Slim's narrative of his pimping occurs, exemplifies the developing white strategies of containment that were deployed throughout the twentieth century in the American city. As sociologist Horace Cayton and anthropologist St. Clair Drake argue in their seminal study of black Chicago, *Black*

Metropolis: A Study of Negro Life in a Northern City, the segregation of African Americans in the South Side of Chicago's African American ghetto, known as the Black Belt, was directly the product of white racism: "The persistence of a Black Belt, whose inhabitants can neither scatter as individuals nor expand as a group, is no accident. It is primarily the result of white people's attitudes toward having Negroes as neighbors."[31] Noting that white ethnics had moved into various neighborhoods after a process of acculturation, so-called "undesirable" Negroes were actively kept from "invading" white neighborhoods through bombings, homeowners associations, and housing covenants. For instance, in midst of the First Great Migration of African Americans to Chicago from the South, between July 1917 and March 1921, fifty-eight black homes were bombed, an average of one every twenty days.[32] As African Americans migrated to Chicago in larger numbers, more institutional methods were devised to circumscribe the boundaries of the Black Belt, including the use of restrictive covenants, an agreement—often put in writing in the deed to property or a lease contract—among property owners not to rent or sell to blacks. Following the Supreme Court's abolishment of racially restrictive covenants in *Shelley v. Kraemer* in 1948, the government itself helped extend the status quo of racial segregation in Chicago and other American cities in new ways, sponsoring Federal Housing Authority–supported white flight to the suburbs and creating the intensive centralization of high-rise housing projects in black neighborhoods. For example, Chicago's Robert Taylor Homes, upon its completion in 1962, became the largest public housing project in the world. Bordered by the physical boundaries of train tracks on one side and the Dan Ryan Expressway on the other, the twenty-eight-building complex housed some twenty-seven thousand occupants, nearly all of whom were poor and black. This project became a central symbol of what urban historian Arnold Hirsch has called America's "second ghetto."[33]

Iceberg Slim's narrative reflects these conditions of white urban containment and dramatizes how pimp cool is adopted as a tactical posture of defense against them. The autobiography spans from his first memory of being sexually abused by his babysitter in 1921 at the age of three to his release from prison in 1961, precisely the years during which white containment strategies were aggressively developed. Although Beck's autobiography never once mentions the Civil Rights Movement, the urban riots, or any of the other social upheavals of his contemporary moment, his narrative about pimping for survival presents an ethos of coolness as a pathway to freedom in modern America's segregated

landscape. Throughout the narrative, Slim characterizes the black neighborhood variously as a "high walled white world," a "black stockade," a
"barbed-wired stockade," and even a "black concentration camp," and he
sees that corrupt and corrupting women must be brought under control
in order to facilitate his escape from these spaces of containment.[34] For
example, when at the age of seventeen, Slim convinces his first girlfriend,
named June, to sleep with an old neighborhood gambler for five dollars, he views it as an opportunity for mobility: "She turned him in less
than five minutes. My seventeen-year-old brain reeled. I could get rich
with this girl and drive a big white Packard."[35] From the very beginning
of Slim's criminal career, pimping for him is synonymous with wealth,
whiteness, and mobility. Slim conceptualizes his escape from the "black
stockade" through mobility afforded by purchasing the Packard. It is no
accident that the Packard that Slim dreams of buying is white. It is this
color that most readily symbolizes affluence in the book. Later, when
Slim enlists his first prostitute, he suddenly has a vision that pimping is
a way out of the economic and spatial constraints of Jim Crow America:
"I shuddered when I thought, what if I hadn't kept my ears flapping back
there in the joint. I would be a boot black or porter for the rest of my
life in the high walled white world. My black whore was a cinch to get
piles of white scratch from that forbidden white world."[36] Having picked
up some of the essential pimp lines from fellow prisoners while serving
his first bits in prison, Slim is able to secure his first prostitute who will
earn him the money to access white spaces. This is a significant shift
from Himes in that this pimp protagonist can circumvent the vulnerable
position of boot black or porter and negotiate dangerous urban spaces by
mastering the linguistic skills and abusive behavior of the pimp. Willing
to exploit his fellow ghetto citizens in ways that Himes's protagonist is
not, and employing the language of the streets in order to accomplish
his ends, Iceberg Slim represents a deeply flawed new hero of the black
urban scene.

Importantly, Slim's economic and spatial mobility requires victims to
become the objects of urban violence, and those victims are often the
women who populate the spaces with him. Representations of violence
against women abound in *Pimp: The Story of My Life*. Women are variously beaten, whipped with wire hangers, verbally abused, raped, and
shot. Slim provides narrative justification for these actions through a
convenient symbolic structure in which the pimp protagonist is the primary victim of sexualized violence and parental failure. In this setup,
pimp masculinity becomes a compensatory identity to be staged as a

defense against dangerous women. Drawing on Beck's extensive reading of psychoanalysis, especially Freud and Jung, he represents the pimp as a psychologically complex figure with a troubled relationship to his past.[37] The opening line of the autobiography provides a portrait of this dynamic which motivates the pimp protagonist: "Her name was Maude and she Georgied me around 1921. I was only three years old. Mama told me about it, and always when she did her rage and indignation would be as strong and as emotional perhaps as at the time when she had surprised her, panting and moaning at the point of orgasm with my tiny head wedged between her ebony thighs, her massive hands vise-like around my head."[38] Literally caught between a sexually predatory babysitter and an enraged mother—another image of containment—the protagonist turns to organized sexual aggression as a way of reclaiming his threatened masculinity. Significantly, the pronouns "she" and "her" that Slim uses to describe the babysitter and his mother become willfully confused in these sentences. From the beginning of the narrative, women are not individually distinguished from one another but rather are an undifferentiated threat that must be renounced or contained for the pimp to achieve mastery over his environment.

This representation of the pimp appears to endorse straightforwardly the dominant discourses about the "pathology" of the black family that emerged in the mid-1960s, represented most notably by Daniel Patrick Moynihan's "tangle of pathology" thesis.[39] As critics Hortense Spillers, Michelle Wallace, and Phillip Brian Harper, among others, have argued, the notion of wounded black masculinity caused by the dreaded "female-headed household" is one of the most damaging cultural myths of America modernity.[40] As these critics claim, such a myth functions to obscure the very real structural racism and processes of urban segregation that gave rise to black poverty in the first place by scapegoating the figure of the overbearing black mother. Slim's narrative collaborates with this mythology of black women and then suggests that becoming an agent of sexualized violence is a compensatory strategy to cope with them. By the conclusion of the first chapter, the protagonist has reversed his position from victim of sexual violence to a victimizer: "Dangerously," he writes in the final lines of the chapter, "I was frantic to sock it into every young girl weak enough to go for it. I had to run for my life one evening when an enraged father caught me on his back porch punching animal-like astraddle his daughter's head."[41] Here in an image that is a literal reversal of the abuse that Iceberg Slim experiences at the hands of his babysitter: he overcomes the forms of sexual abuse he faces in his childhood by enacting the very sexual violence formerly visited on him. The pimp's confrontation with apparently hazardous women serves to displace the larger social, racial, and spatial concerns onto individualized gender struggles over power.

Beck's representation of the subversive qualities symbolized by the pimp is no doubt an ambiguous one. On the one hand, the pimp is constructed as an oppositional figure to institutional and individual forms of white racism and urban containment. On the other hand, the masculine identity promoted in *Pimp* perpetuates a mythology of women as "bitches" and "whores" who are complicit in keeping black men down. As Patricia Hill Collins has argued in her groundbreaking book *Black Feminist Thought*, the portrayal of black women as stereotypical mammies, matriarchs, whores, and other controlling images has been an essential part to maintaining the ideological status quo of black female oppression. In particular, she argues, "the Jezebel, whore, or sexually aggressive woman . . . is central in this nexus of elite white male image of Black womanhood because efforts to control Black women's sexuality lie at the heart of Black women's oppression."[42] Slim's narrative redeploys these stereotypical images of black female sexuality in the service of constituting a black masculine identity that is successful at negotiating white racism. In this way, Slim's book recapitulates ideologies of gender oppression in order to achieve black masculine power.

Nowhere is this symbolic structure more powerfully illustrated than when Sweet Jones gives Slim an account of the "unwritten book" of pimping:

> There ain't more than six of 'em who are hip to and pimp by the book. You won't find it in the square-Nigger or white history books. The truth is that book was written in the skulls of proud slick Niggers freed from slavery. They wasn't lazy. They was puking sick of picking white man's cotton and kissing his nasty ass. The slave days stuck in their skulls. They went to the cities. They got hip fast.
>
> The conning bastard white man hadn't freed the Niggers. The cities was like the plantations down South. Jeffing Uncle Toms still did all the white man's hard and filthy work.
>
> Those slick Nigger heroes bawled like crumb crushers. They saw the white man ramming it into the finest black broads.
>
> Those broads were stupid squares. They still freaked for free with the white man. They wasn't hip to the scratch in their hot black asses.

> Those first Nigger pimps started hipping the dumb bitches to the gold mines between their legs. They hipped them to stick their mitts out for the white man's scratch. The first Nigger pimps and sure shot gamblers was the only Nigger big shots in the country.[43]

This passage provides a microcosm of the simultaneous rebellious and oppressive energies that define the mythology of the pimp. Furthermore, it illustrates the complex interactions between class, race, and gender politics in pimp fiction. On one level, Sweet's unofficial history historicizes the pimp as a figure coming out of slavery, who rejects the economic exploitation of both the sharecropping South and the industrial North. The pimp achieves freedom from these strictures by mastering linguistic skills and vernacular innovation, and he uses these skills to organize women into a sexual stable. The "pimp book," as he calls it, is the repository of the codes, vernacular, and rules that black men have mastered in order to thrive in the modern city. Such linguistic originality is reflected in the very delivery of Sweet's history itself. Employing the specialized street vernacular invented by pimps—terms such as "crumb crushers" (babies), "hipped" (informed), and "scratch" (money)—and reclaiming the word "Nigger" to refer to black working-class men, Sweet here showcases the power of pimping as an insubordinate posture against white and black respectable society. Read against the context of the Great Migration and the expansion of racial and economic oppression in urban America, the self-made pimp expresses a real defiance against a racist society by refusing to capitulate to urban capitalism's expansion of economic injustice.

But on another level, the pimp's freedom from these strictures depends on real and representational violence to be performed against black women. In Sweet's self-serving history of the pimp's origins, black women are nothing more than "dumb bitches" whose desire to have sex with white men for free is a betrayal of the race, and it is this betrayal that provides the necessary justification for the pimp to exploit them. In a tricky displacement, former slaves and black workers elevate themselves to the status of capitalists and bourgeois subjects (even while rejecting the "square-Nigger" status of the black middle class) at the expense of women who themselves then become the source of alienated labor. All of this is then contained by the stylistic innovations and the cool poses of the pimp. While the pimp's world is bleak and unapologetically misogynist, it is a world that is confronted through a hip posture and pimp poetics that attempt to contain its violences. In other words, in a terrain where brutal capitalists and racist cops rule the landscape, the pimp's style expressed through linguistic innovation is deployed to surmount the brutalities he faces. In the move from the legitimate work of the service economy to the illegitimate work of pimping, verbal innovation in the form of the "pimp book" enables the pimp at least temporary freedom from spaces of white containment in ways unavailable to Himes's criminal on the run. Simultaneously, this freedom is created by victimizing the women who are silenced.

The pimp of Iceberg Slim's autobiography, then, can best be understood as a figure who self-consciously extends the structures of white power, economic exploitation, and gender violence in order to achieve his own radically individualized form of liberty from spaces of containment. As Sweet Jones tells Slim in one of his many teaching sessions about the pimp game, "Slim, a pimp is really a whore who's reversed the game on whores." And while "whores in a stable are like working chumps in the white man's factory," Sweet theorizes, "a good pimp is like a slick white boss." All of this leads Sweet to conclude, "Pimping ain't no sex game. It's a skull game."[44] Disillusioned by the lack of possibility for the political freedom of African American people more broadly, the pimp instead sees that only radically personal achievements of independence are possible, achievements that are purchased by adopting the very apparatuses of white oppression that helped create systematic black inequality in the first place. While this ethos undeniably runs counter to an agenda of large-scale liberty for black people, it nevertheless reflects the dark historical realities of Jim Crow America, in which economic, social, and political freedoms were simply not available to the majority of African Americans. The pimp in Beck's autobiography is a figure who adopts the economic conservatism of capitalism but rejects the leadership and moral uprightness of the black bourgeoisie in the face of a system that is already rigged.

"We Made Iceberg Slim Together": *Pimp* as Domestic Theater

One feature of *Pimp* that prevents it from being just a straightforward endorsement of violence against women or a pornographic fantasy about the verbal and sexual prowess of the black pimp is that Iceberg Slim consistently represents pimping as a compensatory, but inadequate, tactic for overcoming the spatial and racial boundaries of the American city. Told as a series of vignettes over twenty-two chapters, *Pimp* emphasizes the failure of pimping to achieve long-term economic security or permanent spatial mobility. In Slim's story, the narrator never emerges as triumphant. While each of the chapters features Slim obtaining some vital skill from an older mentor in his education in the pimp game, most of these chapters conclude in an ironic reversal. Although Slim leaves prison at the end of the book and settles into a "square" family life with a wife and two children, the remainder of the book features Slim ending up as a casualty of violence, the victim of someone else's con game, or a prisoner heading back to jail. For example, immediately following Slim's enlistment of June, his first would-be sex worker, he lands in jail for the first time when he advertises her services to a friend of June's father. Pages later, when Slim tries to con an old ex-prostitute named Pepper, she double-crosses him and puts him back in prison. Chapter after chapter, just as Slim thinks he has mastered the skills necessary to survive as a pimp, he finds that no amount of pimping expertise can overcome the structural oppression of white racism and urban containment. Even though Slim is able to employ his linguistic skills in order to escape jail at the conclusion of the narrative, throughout the rest of his story, Slim is constantly frustrated in his attempts at mobility.

Nowhere is this lesson illustrated more dramatically than in the chapter titled "Melody Off Key." When Slim meets a wealthy white woman named Melody who is having car trouble in the South Side of Chicago, he sees that romancing her is his opportunity to get out of the ghetto permanently. As they drive out to her house in the suburbs together, Slim looks out at the white neighborhood with its plush houses and tree-lined streets and thinks, "Ain't it a bitch? Ninety-eight percent of the black people back there in Hell will be born and die and never know the joys of this earthly Heaven. There ain't but two passports the white folks honor. A white skin, or a bale of scratch. I sure got to pimp good and cop my scratch passport. Well at least I get a Cinderella crack at Heaven."[45] Characterizing the divide between suburbs and the inner city as equivalent to the divide between heaven and hell, Slim sees wooing Melody as a passport to paradise. As a wealthy white woman who lives in suburbs outside black Chicago, Melody is the pimp's access point to class and geographical mobility. He hopes first to swindle Melody out of her wealth and then to turn her into a prostitute. However, Slim's "Cinderella" story turns out to be a fairy tale indeed. When they arrive at Melody's home and start undressing, Slim realizes that she is actually a he: "I stroked her belly. I felt cloth. I took a close look. A custom flesh-colored jock belt bandled her crotch. I ripped the elastic top down over her round hips. I jumped back. My rear end bounced on the floor. I struggled to my feet. I shouted,

'You stinking sissy sonuvabitch!' His real entasis had popped up pink and stiff. It was a foot long and as thick as the head of a cobra."[46] Here, as in many of the concluding chapters of the book, Slim thinks he has found a way out of the ghetto through the mastery of pimp skills, only to find himself in a position of sexual vulnerability. Through his confrontation with Melody's cobralike "entasis," the pimp's masculine power is deflated and his dream of economic and spatial mobility deferred. At the conclusion of the scene, Slim is portrayed as a pathetic figure, as he steals Melody's piggy bank full of change and wanders the suburbs for an hour before he can find a bus to take him back to Chicago. Slim's autobiography deploys scheming women and ambiguously gendered men to demarcate the boundaries that stand in the way of freedom, and he continually attempts to contain, control, and conquer these character in order to achieve success. While the gender, race, and class politics of *Pimp* are clearly problematic, Slim himself undercuts the pimp's power by consistently illustrating the pimp's failure to achieve domination over these figures. In most every chapter, Slim's prostitutes argue with him, stab him, and repeatedly send him to jail. More than any other chapter of the novel, the Melody chapter dramatizes that while pimping may provide a fantasy of mobility, it is inadequate to the entrenched forms of white power and spatialized containment. Stories of spectacular failure constitute the bulk of *Pimp*, and collectively they serve to highlight the need for a more politicized stance than the pimp cool provides.

Ultimately, Beck does not celebrate the figure of the pimp but uses him as an organizing figure to reflect on the grim realities of spatialized racism in America. Although the story is related through Slim's first-person narrative, *Pimp* is a particularly dialogic book, channeling the unique voices of sex workers, hustlers, aging gamblers, and other figures from the street. For example, a substantial portion of the autobiography features conversations and debates about the merits and motivations of the pimp game between Slim and his main "bottom woman," Phyllis, also known as "the runt." At one point in the narrative, Phyllis provides her own explanation about the racial and gender politics of prostitution from the perspective of black women in the Life: "I know I ain't got no silky hair and white skin. I'm damn sure hip those white men ain't leaving Heaven to come to Hell every night just for the drive. They coming because those cold-ass white broads in Heaven ain't got what these black whores in Hell got between their legs. Black and low as I am, I got secrets with their white men those high-class white bitches ain't hip to."[47] On one level, this speech reveals how Phyllis consents to her own condition of oppression. Even though she is not a simple dupe of Slim's pimp cons, her claiming of her sexual agency in the face of white racism is the very logic that contributes to her exploitation. Phyllis's antagonism toward white women—an antagonism that bespeaks the historical differences of gender oppression facing black women versus white women—is one of the key motivating factors that drives her to prostitution. In saying so, Phyllis articulates that she has her own complex motivations for participating in the pimp game, given the realities of the racial boundary of the ghetto/suburbs divide. Recognizing that the ghettoization of black people has created a white cultural construction of her as "black and low," she also sees that this structural containment simultaneously gives her a certain amount of power as the embodiment of a taboo. This is undeniably a compensatory psychological rationalization that Phyllis creates in order to handle the multiple forms of racial and gender oppression she faces. However, it also illustrates that even the victims of Slim's cons have their own individual voices and agency. These voices do not so much displace the authority of the pimp—especially as these voices are ultimately contained within Slim's larger story of his journey—but they do nonetheless illustrate Beck's attempt to represent the complex identities of men and women from the black underclass.

We can understand *Pimp* as a literary artifact that emerged at the intersection of a variety of commercial, political, aesthetic, and social concerns. Even as the pimp is represented as a stylish figure of black masculine cool, whose oppositional stance presents a challenge to Jim Crow urbanism, his heroism is consistently ironized throughout the text. One final observation about the creation of *Pimp* may shed light on the complex and contradictory impulses of the text. Although in interviews Beck represents the autobiography as a reflection of his experiences, in fact, he created *Pimp* in a collaborative effort with his common-law white wife, Betty Mae Shue. Before her death in 2009, Shue gave a series of interviews with Jorge Hinojosa for the documentary on Beck, titled *Iceberg Slim: Portrait of a Pimp*, interviews which disclose surprising revelations about the creation of *Pimp*.[48] After Beck's release from prison in 1961, he moved to Los Angeles to be with his ailing mother. He met Shue, a waitress, at a hamburger stand in 1962, and following a brief courtship, they moved in together. Beck supported them by working door-to-door as a pest exterminator, and it was at this moment that Shue came up with the idea of writing *Pimp* together. As Shue tells it, "When he got home from canvassing, as he called it, to find other jobs, he'd want to talk. And he would tell me these outrageous things. And I said, 'A woman would go out and sell herself and give the money to a man. You are out of your goddamn mind. Ain't no woman I ever knew or heard of do some shit like that.' It was just incomprehensible. I couldn't believe it. But this is what he told me. And this is what I told him: 'Let's start writing this down.'" Shue reveals here that in addition to occupying the position of original audience for *Pimp*, she also was instrumental in the creation of the book. Even as she voices the frank discomfort with the misogyny of pimping, Shue admits that she recognized at the time that these were stories worth writing down for potential publication.

Starting in the mid-1960s, Beck and Shue developed a collaborative writing process that lasted a dozen years and produced Beck's seven books. Working up a chapter in longhand, Beck would then perform the dialogue with his wife in front of their young children in order to refine it. As Beck's oldest daughter, Camille, recalls, "I remember from the time I was four years old watching this show. We didn't have TV. It was like watching a play. He would act out all the parts and then say to her, 'Okay, now you take this one.' Male or female. It didn't matter."[49] As Camille's testimony suggests, *Pimp* was a kind of morality play created as a form of domestic theater for their kids. *Pimp* was not simply the off-the-cuff remembrances of Beck but the negotiated, consciously constructed product of his domestic alliance with Betty Mae Shue. Even as the book promotes the outlaw individualist as a radical figure of defiance against white racism, the literary representation of the pimp was created out of this familial partnership. "Creating *Pimp* was not a one-person process," Betty remembers, "but a two-person process. We made Iceberg Slim together." As these recent interviews with Beck's family suggest, *Pimp* was surprisingly created in a cross-racial, cross-gender alliance, thereby complicating its status as a literary artifact. Shue's testimony contributes to our understanding of the creation of pimp literature as a shared project. It is not only Robert Beck but Beck and Betty Mae Shue together who should be credited for creating one of the most popular and influential books in African American literary history.

Conclusion

We might understand the significance of Robert Beck's contribution to African American literary production by turning briefly to his final, unpublished novel, *Night Train to Sugar Hill*. Told in the third person, *Night Train to Sugar Hill* is the story of the final days of an aging ghetto philosopher named Baptiste Launreau O'Leary, a thinly veiled representation of Beck himself. At the conclusion of the novel, the seventy-five-year-old Baptiste, determined to take radical action against crack cocaine in South Central, murders Los Angeles's largest distributor of crack cocaine, Ernesto Portillo. Boarding a midnight train to New York City, Baptiste rides cross-country to live out his remaining days with his daughter, Opal. While on the train, Baptiste finishes the conclusion of the autobiography he has been writing over the course of the novel. As the omniscient narrator puts it, "Baptiste sat on the side of his bed polishing the completed manuscript of his autobiography. He had been absolutely candid about the good and bad he had done in his lifetime. He had included a detailed account of Portillo's murder and why. Opal would not submit it to her agent friend for publication until after his death—which was soon, he knew."[50] Baptiste actually dies on the way to New York City, and when Opal arrives at the station to pick him up, all that is left of him is the single copy of his autobiography. Although the police suspect Baptiste of Portillo's murder, they release his autobiography to his daughter, thinking that it does not contain any valuable clues.

Completed only two years before Beck's death, *Night Train to Sugar Hill* is relatively unremarkable compared to his earlier efforts such as *Pimp* and *Trick Baby*. Nevertheless, the metaliterary conclusion provides a striking image of how we might understand Robert Beck's contribution to American literature and African American culture as well as his vulnerable position in the literary marketplace of black publishing. While the authorities dismiss Baptiste's autobiography as insignificant to their investigation, it actually contains the confession to the murder of Portillo that they seek. Thus, although the autobiography appears to lack consequence to official accounts, as a matter of fact, it holds the key to the truth of events.

Even as *Pimp: The Story of My Life* has been largely disregarded as trashy and misogynist, it nonetheless contains a significant but often marginalized perspective on a particular cultural response to twentieth-century racism. To be sure, the pimp's poetics is loaded with problematic representations of gender and sexuality, and as a radically individualized reaction to systems of power, the pimp is a limited tactician at best. Nevertheless, in the post–Civil Rights cultural transformation, pimp literature emerged as a popular literary form. Starting with Beck, subsequent black writers have worked with these tropes, figures, and narratives and formed an uneasy alliance with white Hollywood publicists to create a mass-market literary renaissance of their own. Even within the confines of a largely exploitative Holloway House system, Beck and

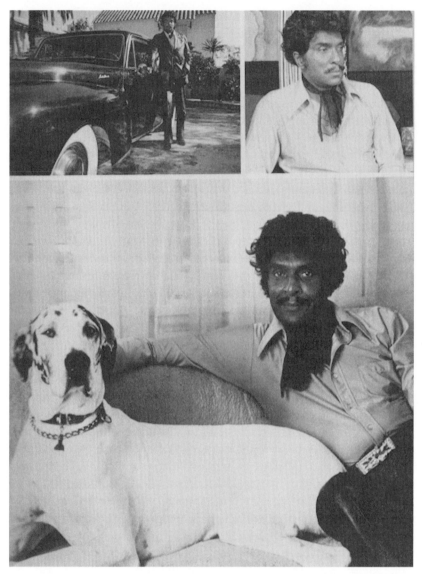

FIGURE 2.2. Photo spread of Robert Beck in a 1977 issue of *Players* magazine.

others managed to create an expression of black cultural politics that attempted to walk a fine line between entertainment for the black masses and the creation of a radically antiestablishment social message. Tied to pulp publishing and members of the criminal underworld, Holloway House literature starting with Beck did not appear to engage directly the communal freedom of black people. But by employing the mass-market paperback to create an image of heroic black masculinity, Beck accomplished what other black authors such as Chester Himes had been unable to accomplish before, that is, to command the attention of a large black reading audience. Beck created popular narratives that provide cathartic fantasies of mastery over urban spaces also unavailable to Himes's characters, fantasies that are ultimately revealed to be insufficient to the discipline of white power. In doing so, Beck invented a literary strategy that dismantles the glorious image of the pimp, and he provided a critical starting point for the further development of aesthetic responses to methods of white containment. Imitating the literary blueprint left behind by Beck, writers such as Donald Goines expanded the black crime novel to feature figures of explicit revolutionary action. The development from an individualized response to systems of white violence to a collective radical one represents one of the main trajectories of the genre, and it is this transformation that is the subject of the next chapter.

3 / The Revolution Will Not Be Televised: Donald Goines, Holloway House Publishing Company, and the Radicalization of Black Crime Literature

Toward the conclusion of Donald Goines's first novel, a fictionalized pimp autobiography titled *Whoreson: The Story of a Ghetto Pimp*, there is a moment that reveals the literary influence of Robert Beck's *Pimp: The Story of My Life*.[1] Having mastered the street arts of "Trickology" from an early age and having risen through the ranks to become one of Detroit's most ruthless pimps, the novel's title character, Whoreson Jones, cons a suburban white woman named Stella into giving him twenty thousand dollars. As they drive out to her suburban home together, Whoreson realizes that his verbal virtuosity gained through pimping and conning skills have bought him passage out of the Detroit ghetto: "When we got to the suburbs, it was like another world to me. No broken-down houses staring you in the face. Everything neat and clean, the streets unlittered with tricks accosting every woman that walked past. Yes, Stella, you're going to pave the way so that I'll never have to live in another slum again."[2] Recalling the "Melody Off Key" chapter of Iceberg Slim's narrative, this moment crystallizes the way in which pimping is imagined in "black experience" fiction as a potential escape from forms of white containment. In this version of the story, too, the title character discovers that the con is an inadequate strategy to contend with systems of white power. Although Whoreson successfully bilks Stella out of her twenty thousand dollars, only a few pages later, he is betrayed by one of his former prostitutes and sent back to prison. As he sits behind bars in the final scene of the book, he reflects, "Mockery was the answer to my stupidity, for what else could I call it? Not cleverness. What could be clever about a man who wasted over ten years of his life behind prison walls? By the time I got out, I'd have over ten years in, and for what? Twenty thousand dollars. A man working at a carwash would make more than that over a ten-year span."[3] As in Iceberg Slim's story, the verbal prowess associated with pimping provides Whoreson temporary transcendence over the spatial containments of the urban ghetto. Yet such mobility is short-lived. In the end, Whoreson merely trades the confined space of the Detroit ghetto for the confined space of the prison cell.

Written by Donald Goines while he was behind bars at Jackson State Penitentiary in 1970 after reading *Pimp: The Story of My Life*, *Whoreson* exemplifies the growth of black crime fiction produced by Holloway House Publishing Company following the commercial success of Robert Beck's works. Although lacking the extensive specialized vernacular that constitutes Beck's pioneering story, *Whoreson* nevertheless marks a significant development of black crime literature. The story dramatizes how the figure of the pimp, the setting of white spatial confinement, and the narrative of frustrated mobility are flexible literary devices that can represent a range of black urban landscapes. For despite the individual differences between American cities with sizable black populations—cities such as New York, Los Angeles, Chicago, Detroit, Baltimore, Cleveland, St. Louis, and Philadelphia—all experienced similar patterns of deindustrialization, white flight, and the concentration of black inner-city poverty in the post–World War II years. Shifting the geography of the pimp autobiography from Chicago to Detroit, Goines illustrates that the black crime genre can be employed to express a national consciousness of black populations contending with forces of white urban containment, the prison-industrial complex, and low-wage service-economy jobs in a number of American places. As Thomas Sugrue argues in his important study of Goines's hometown of Detroit, for example, the city once known as the "arsenal of democracy" had, in the decades following World War II, become a symbol of America's urban crisis. Enacting similar strategies of containment that were prevalent in other major American cities, white Detroiters constructed vast expressways to encourage white flight, formed hundreds of homeowners associations in order to combat the perceived "Negro invasion," performed individual acts of violence against blacks who tried to move out of the narrowly defined geographical boundaries of the ghetto, and concentrated the construction of public housing in black inner-city neighborhoods. According to Sugrue, "White Detroiters invented communities of race in the city they defined spatially. Race in the postwar city was not just a cultural construction. Instead, whiteness, and by implication blackness, assumed a material dimension, imposed onto the geography of the city. Through the drawing of racial boundaries and through the use of systematic violence to maintain those boundaries, whites reinforced their own fragile identity."[4] Like Himes's New York and Beck's Chicago, Goines's Detroit was—and to a large degree, still is—a city in which racial divides were constituted through spatial boundaries, and like these other writers, Goines employed black crime fiction to contend imaginarily with these geographies of confinement.

Goines contributed to the genre of black crime literature by expanding the parameters of Holloway House's black experience novel to engage with these spatial and racial forms of segregation. While it was Robert Beck who invented the figures, tropes, vernacular, and narratives of black fiction at Holloway House with his pimp autobiography, it was Goines who streamlined the process of writing crime novels there, producing fourteen best-selling books (sixteen, if we count the books published posthumously) for the company before his murder in October 1974. He created fast-paced plots about black gangsters, hit men, detectives, junkies, prostitutes, drug dealers, and ghetto revolutionaries, all of whom enjoy temporary escape from spaces of white confinement only to be killed, captured, or otherwise contained at the novel's end. Goines devised a profitable literary formula that appealed to an emerging market of black readers. He provided them with popular stories that offer fantasies of overcoming forces of white oppression combined with realist narrative conclusions that foreclose these possibilities.

In this regard, Goines's most significant contribution to the genre of black crime fiction genre is his four-novel Kenyatta series that he created at the end of his literary career. Replacing the pimp and hustler heroes of his earlier fiction with a ghetto revolutionary named Kenyatta, Goines attempted to move black experience literature beyond the narrow boundaries of the genre that he himself had helped erect—and outside the interests of his white publishing house—in order to create a mode of social critique that also doubled as popular entertainment for black readers. Although the radical black freedom fighter was a figure that had always been embedded in the fiction of Himes and Beck, Goines expanded the mode of literary representation of the black crime novel in order to make such a figure an explicit part of this popular literary landscape. The Kenyatta novels draw from many of the trappings of the pimp autobiography of Robert Beck; however, by staging the narrative of black revolution on the grounds of the black crime novel, Goines introduced altogether new components to the genre. The Kenyatta series is written in the third person, and it emphasizes plotting over stylized language. It therefore reflects both the radical possibilities of the black crime novel as well as the streamlined commodification of the literary form. This expansion of the form also reflects a change in the historical moment as the Black Panthers, the Black Power Movement, and global decolonization movements had become significant social and political currents within black cultural thought. Goines's novels represent imaginative responses attempting to come to grips with these new historical realities.

Additionally, Goines, more than his literary forbearers Himes and Beck, employed the black crime novel in order to comment explicitly on the containment of black crime novelists within the system of white corporate patronage. Like Beck, Goines published his literature in an uneasy partnership with Holloway House; together, they created an economic and artistic relationship that echoed larger white/black cultural and spatial divides. Following the commercial success of Beck's work, Holloway House mechanized its labor process starting with Goines by deskilling its artists and rationalizing black crime narratives into saleable commodities. Holloway House emphasized the ghetto authenticity of authors such as Goines over other artistic and political imperatives, such as connections to other black literary traditions or black radical movements, as this self-authenticating gesture had been a proven commercial strategy for the wide-scale marketing of black crime novels. In Goines's late novel *Never Die Alone*, he shows that he was well aware of this problematic relationship between the black writer and the white publishing industry, as he self-consciously employs the hustler autobiography as a literary device to reflect on the racial politics of black pulp publishing. *Never Die Alone* is the story of how a struggling Jewish novelist uses a first-person autobiographical journal of a black drug dealer to find his literary voice, and therefore *Never Die Alone* simultaneously offers fans a *Pimp*-style narrative of a black outlaw hero at the same time as it subtly interrogates the marketing strategies employed to commodify Goines's own books.

The first section of this chapter continues the story of black pulp publishing's development through an examination of Goines's relationship to Holloway House. Through an investigation of a range of archival materials—including Goines's own unpublished letters, interviews with editors at Holloway House, and advertisements used to promote his work, I reveal how Goines's transformation of the black crime fiction genre was in part motivated by the methods of white containment he faced there.

In the second section of the chapter, I explore Goines's radicalization of the black crime genre by examining his most openly political representation of black heroes trapped in spaces of white containment in the Kenyatta series. More than any earlier black crime novels, the Kenyatta series entertains the emancipatory potential of black crime literature by making black revolutionaries the central protagonists of the novels. In the final section, through an analysis of Goines's novel *Never Die Alone*, I explore how Goines employed the black crime novel to contemplate his difficult position in the literary marketplace of black pulp publishing at Holloway House. As the first of many metaliterary novels in the black crime genre, *Never Die Alone* brings together the figure of the writer in the marketplace and the criminal in the city in ways that explore the parallel forms of containment that they face.

Donald Goines and the Marketplace of Black Pulp Publishing

Even as Goines is celebrated among hip hop artists and modern street literature authors, he remains off the radar of most literary and cultural scholars.[5] While anthologies such as *The Norton Anthology of African American Literature* now include rap lyrics as part of the African American literary tradition, the pioneering crime literature of Goines and Beck continues to be ignored by many in the academy. Even those few critics who do appreciate Goines's work seem ambivalent about it, divided between a disparagement of the mass-culture aspect of his fiction and an appreciation of the ethnographic authenticity of his representations of American street life. As Greg Goode, one of the only critics to analyze Goines's books, writes, "They are offensive to many because of the obscenity, sex, and violence, all well before their time in graphic explicitness. The titles, and in early printings, the naïve bullet-and-blood style cover art, make the books appear to be utter trash. They are poorly written for the most part, in an uneasy mix of Black English and misspelled, ungrammatical Standard English. The descriptions, transitions, plots, and narrative voice are sandpaper rough."[6] Goode goes on to forgive these faults, because he argues Goines's work faithfully reflects the lives of the black underclass. "Nevertheless," he writes, "the Goines corpus is important because it is perhaps the most sustained, realistic, multifaceted, widespread fictional picture ever created by one author of the lives, activities, and frustrations of poor urban blacks."[7] This response is emblematic of the general attitude toward black crime literature more broadly. On the one hand, there is a disdain for the mass-market aspect of the work reflected in the critic's dismissal of the sex and violence, the cover art, and the apparent trashiness of the writing. On the other hand, Goode celebrates the literature as an authentic expression of black people's culture, a fictional distillation of the lives of working-class African Americans.

This approach for understanding Goines in particular and mass-market black literature in general is limiting in that it casts black crime literature as part of an irresolvable dualism: it is either a form of mass-marketed cultural domination administered from above or an expression of collective popular desires emerging from below. However, we might gain a better understanding of this fiction by seeing it as connected to very specific modes of production and consumption. For while the crime novels of Goines helped give literary form to a black urban culture existing at the very margins of society, such literary commodities also regulated and limited the meaning of blackness they purport to describe, especially as these novels were underwritten by white patronage.[8] This relationship between white publishing interests and black storytellers echoes the invisible power dynamics between white figures of authority and black protagonists outlined in Goines's novels themselves. Black crime literature can be understood neither as simply a form of mass entertainment nor as an expression of a genuine people's culture. Rather, the culture industry of black crime literature constituted the very idea of black urban authenticity that it sold to consumers, backed by white investment.

Goines's image as an authentic black crime writer can be understood as primarily the invention of Holloway House. As I outline in the previous chapter, Holloway House established its reputation as the world's leading publisher of black crime novels by selling an image of ghetto authenticity to working-class African Americans. While Holloway House's marketing strategy provided a glimpse into a black subculture that had been underrepresented in American literature before, it also attempted to contain those very representations within a very strict set of discursive principles. Starting first with Beck and then continuing with Goines, Holloway House commodified the criminal experience of black authors as a way of selling its fiction. By the time Goines started publishing with Holloway House in the early 1970s, the company had solidified its marketing approach by publishing almost exclusively black-themed novels. It did so primarily by emphasizing the author's outlaw background as a mode of advertisement. *Dopefiend: The Story of a Black Junkie*, the second novel Goines wrote but the first to hit the shelves, provides a telling example of how Holloway House had standardized its commercialization of black urban authenticity by the early 1970s. On the back of the novel, Holloway House emphasizes *Dopefiend*'s authority by presenting Goines as an insider of America's mean streets and prison facilities: "Donald Goines is a talented new writer who learned his craft and sharpened his skills in the ghetto slums and federal penitentiaries of America. *Dopefiend* is the shocking first novel by this young man who has seen and lived through everything he writes about."[9] This reproduces a marketing formula that had already been successful with Beck's self-authenticating autobiographical work. Holloway House essentially presents Goines's debut novel as a firsthand look at the inner-city ghetto and the American prison system.

However, *Dopefiend: The Story of a Black Junkie* has a misleading title, and the cover provides a misleading description of the book's content. *Dopefiend* is not actually the story of Goines himself or any single heroin addict but rather the interweaving narratives of a number of junkies, who, despite their diverse class, gender, and racial backgrounds, all fall victim to heroin abuse. Like Goines's other works, *Dopefiend* is not a testimonial of one person's real life but a complex literary product that gives expression to a group that needs a voice. As the omniscient narrator sums up at the end of the opening chapter, "The white powder looked innocent lying there in the open, but this was the drug of the damned, the curse of mankind: heroin, what some called 'smack,' others 'junk,' 'snow,' 'poison,' 'horse.' It had different names, but it still had the same effect. To all of its users, it was slow death."[10] *Dopefiend* is not a personal account of Goines's own struggles with heroin addiction; it is instead a novel which explores the effects of addiction on social figures from all aspects of American society, including inner-city drug dealers, down-on-their-luck prostitutes, the black middle class, and even suburban whites. Thus, Goines's representation of the totality of American life is strikingly at odds with the advertisements of the book, which tend to fetishize the black criminal outlaw image.

Tellingly, in more recent editions of *Dopefiend*, the "white powder" quote is printed as an epigraph at the beginning of the novel, with one significant line added by the publisher: "To all of its users—to all the dopefiends in the Detroit ghetto—it was slow death." Here, as in the ad copy for *Pimp*, Holloway House attempts to offer readers a sensational glimpse into the black American underworld, while at the same time maintaining symbolic control over that space. By adding the line "to all the dopefiends in the Detroit ghetto" to the epigraph, the publisher illustrates that the business of staging racial authenticity is motivated as much by a desire for further containment of the Detroit ghetto as a desire for commercially driven exposure. In other words, even though Goines wrote *Dopefiend* as an examination of heroin's effect on a large cross-section of American society, Holloway House's ad copy for the book insists on reducing it to a novel about dopefiends of the Detroit ghetto. This flattening out of the themes and central concerns of the novel is emblematic of the company's approach for pimping fictions to the black reading public.

Goines's brief but productive career at Holloway House coincided with the company's streamlined approach of publishing lower-quality, ghetto-themed literary materials. His tenure at the company is reflective of the systematic exploitation that many black writers faced under the Holloway House system. A small-time criminal who had been to prison over a dozen times, Goines looked to publishing ghetto crime novels as a way to escape his criminal past. And initially, he was successful, publishing such street literature classics as *Dopefiend*, *Black Girl Lost*, *Black Gangster*, and *White Man's Justice, Black Man's Grief* in his first few years as an author.[11] However, after moving to Los Angeles following the publication of his third novel to write full-time for Holloway House, Goines found mass-market publishing to be another kind of prison from which he could not escape. In Los Angeles, Goines was at the most productive point of his career, writing nearly a dozen novels in less than two years. However, he received as little as a seven-hundred-fifty-dollar advance for each novel and seven cents in royalties per book sold. His advances were half of those that Robert Beck received, and Goines had to write as much as a book per month to support his wife and two young daughters as well as an ongoing heroin habit. *Crime Partners*, *Death List*, and *Eldorado Red* were released by Holloway House just weeks apart from one another, and many of the novels Goines produced in the middle of his career are significantly poorer in quality than his first few novels. Much like his literary mentor Robert Beck, Goines became a writer in order to escape the perilous economies of pimping and prostitution, only to end up being pimped by the culture industry of black crime fiction itself.

An examination of Goines's private letters illustrates that while he may have had larger literary aspirations, he was compelled by the Holloway House system to churn out his novels quickly. In a letter found in his briefcase at the site of his murder, titled "Private Thoughts on a Lonely Sunday" and dated September 1973, Goines complains, "I want to write, but there is not much money in paperbacks as we both know, unless the writer turns them out like comic books. I want to write something that you and I would be proud of. I have a novel in mind but it's utterly impossible for me to spend that much time on one book when I can turn out three others in the same length of time."[12] Here Goines's private thoughts (which actually seem to be directed toward his publisher) dramatize the central dilemma of the black crime novelist working at Holloway House. Writing for a market that did not pay much money, the black crime novelist was required to sacrifice craft for a paycheck. As this letter indicates, Goines had a more ambitious novel in mind than the ones he had been hastily producing at Holloway House. The kind of containment that Goines faced as a literary artist in the pulp publishing industry directly mirrored that which his characters encounter in the black experience novels themselves.[13]

Goines's participation in this system may have in fact led directly to his murder. According to onetime editor at Holloway House Wanda Coleman, because Goines was under such intense pressure to write his novels quickly, he would outright steal people's stories and pass them off as his own:

> He would just steal people's material. He'd go, get to know them, go onto the scene, get them talking about themselves, and then he would write their stories. So he told me, "I'm going home to get more stories, Wanda." He believed he was cleverer than his adversaries and would outsmart them. He even told me that (bragged is the word) he deliberately encouraged police arrests so that during incarceration he could milk other inmates to steal more stories. I really flipped when he said that. I was worried about him.[14]

Here Coleman suggests that, while Morriss may have created the conditions of exploitation at Holloway House, Goines was killed because he participated actively in this system. The prison, initially a space of containment and incarceration, in this scenario doubles as a site of literary cooptation. While Morriss has always claimed that he published Goines's later novels under the pseudonym Al Clark because he feared market saturation, Coleman offers a less charitable interpretation of the use of the pen name. In her interpretation, Holloway House employed it to cover their theft of other people's material:

> Whoever killed [Goines] took pictures of him holding his novel, and they sent them to Bentley. It was an obvious message to Goines's publisher that they knew the true identity of "Al Clark,"

the pseudonym Goines was using in his efforts to disguise his rip-
ping off other people's material. These people were letting Holloway
House know that they were not stupid, and furthermore, they could
read through the text to see the writer beneath it. I had warned
Morriss and Weinstock that what they were doing was dangerous,
that they were going to get Goines killed because Goines wasn't a
good enough writer to disguise his style.[15]

Without attempting to resolve debate over the specific cause of Goines's
murder, I do want to point out that this statement illustrates Goines's
problematic position in the literary marketplace. In Coleman's scenario,
both Morriss and Goines underestimated the true danger of mining
materials from America's prisons and streets.[16] While Holloway House
should clearly be held accountable for its role in the exploitation of black-
authored material, Goines's own expropriation of the stories of fellow
inner-city occupants and prisoners further complicates the status of
black crime literature. Goines apparently consented to (by participating
in) the cultural theft that impoverished many black artists who came to
work under the Holloway House imprint, thereby reproducing the system of exploitation that his works in many ways sought to expose.

After Goines's murder, Holloway House unsurprisingly shaped this
event to suit the company's marketing strategies. As Emory Holmes,
another editor at the company, remembers it, the owners used photographs of Goines's dead body as advertisements for the new biography
they were constructing. According to Holmes, "Donald Goines had
been murdered. Ralph Weinstock had flown to Detroit and convinced
Donald Goines's mother that Donald Goines no longer belonged simply
to her family, that he now belonged to the world. So they convinced the
family to let the Holloway House people be with his body for a while.
They open up Donald's dead hands and put one of his books in his
hands and used it as an ad for his next book."[17] These photos accompa-
nied a sensationalist biography written by Eddie Stone, called *Donald
Writes No More*. Stone was the pen name of Carlton Hollander, a white
B-movie screenwriter who also completed Goines's final unfinished
manuscript, *Inner-City Hoodlum*. At the opening of *Donald Writes No
More*, Hollander presents the prototypical image of Goines, an image
that Holloway House has perpetuated to this day: "During his lifetime,
Donald Goines had been a pimp, a numbers runner, a cardshark, a
pool hustler, a whiskey still operator, a thief, and a dope addict. He had
lived and thrived in the teeming ghetto of Detroit. He had made small

fortunes and lost them; had risen from the gutter to the penthouse and fallen back again."[18] Starting with the fiction that Goines "had risen from the gutter" (Goines was, in fact, from a relatively stable middle-class background), Hollander's biography then goes on to create a number of fictions which have since become regarded as fact, including the story that Goines was murdered while sitting at his typewriter.[19] *Donald Writes No More* is less a biography than a myth-making apparatus created by Holloway House. In an interview with *F.E.D.S.* magazine, Goines's sister suggests that the book is "fake, it's bull."[20] Furthermore, Eddie Allen notes in his excellent biography of Goines the peculiar disclaimer that Hollander employs to open the book: "Some characters, places and incidents are either the product of the author's imagination or used fictitiously. Any resemblance to actual locales or persons, living or dead, is entirely coincidental."[21] Sharing the same disclaimer that precedes all of Goines's own fiction, Hollander's biography provides an emblem of how Holloway House collapsed the distinctions between biographical fact and fiction in order to sell more books under the "Donald Goines" trademark.

"He Felt the Pavement Come Up and Smash Him in the Face": Donald Goines's Kenyatta Series

How did Goines respond to these conditions in his work? One of Goines's responses was to transform the black experience novel into a much more openly politicized expression. At the conclusion of Goines's posthumously published *Kenyatta's Last Hit* (1975)—the final novel in Goines's four-book Kenyatta series—there is a point that dramatizes the relationship between radical black politics and spaces of white containment that are central concerns of these novels. Having killed off racist cops and white drug dealers from Detroit to Los Angeles, an underground revolutionary organization attempts to murder Clement Jenkins by sneaking up to his Las Vegas penthouse. Jenkins is the novel's central figuration of white authority. He is a light-bulb manufacturer, industrialist, influential political lobbyist, and the West Coast's largest distributor of heroin. In fact, as a manufacturer of white lights on Las Vegas's garish Strip, Jenkins is quite literally the novel's source of whiteness. Living atop the Sands Hotel in his secluded penthouse, he is the embodiment of invisible surveillance itself. Kenyatta's organization attempts to slip up to Jenkins's penthouse in the service elevators; however, he kills them off before they ever arrive, and the expected final climactic battle between them never materializes:

> One of Clement Jenkins' more lucrative businesses was the devel-
> opment of nerve gases for the United States army. But his mission
> was anything but patriotic. As soon as he developed a newer, more
> lethal gas for the U.S., he would turn around and sell that same
> gas to Russia. CL-809 was the most lethal yet, creating an instant
> spasm of the nervous system, causing instant suffocation through
> strangulation. The beautiful part of CL-809 was that its effects
> lasted for only fifteen seconds. Then it was absorbed into the atmo-
> sphere and became harmless. Neither Stonewall nor any of his men
> inside the elevator ever knew what hit him. In an orgy of convul-
> sions, each man struggled for a split second to retain his life. But
> that had been only a motor reaction and not one from the brain.
> They were all dead before any one of them ever had the opportunity
> to realize that death was coming.[22]

Here, the revolution that has been growing over the course of four novels comes to a sudden, unceremonious halt. This image of Kenyatta's follow-ers being trapped in a crowded service elevator, killed off by the invis-ible white hand of combined military and business interests, operates as a profound symbol of how even Black Power advocates are unequal to the task of infiltrating and overcoming spaces of white containment. Goines's novel—written in the midst of the Cold War—makes explicit how the United States' official policy of "containment" to forestall the spread of Communism abroad is also a strategy used domestically to restrain black revolution. A space of extreme confinement, the service elevator also carries with it connotations of working-class entrapment as well as the confinement of a prison cell. *Kenyatta's Last Hit* does not offer readers catharsis through guns-a-blazing violence but instead ends with an image of impotent struggle. The lethal blow delivered by the invisible gas evaporates into the air, taking on a harmless, innocuous appearance, a form of containment that mirrors the pervasive-yet-imperceptible bureaucracies of white segregation in the postwar moment. The Kenyatta series expands on the imaginary universe of black crime fiction in which pimps, prostitutes, and hustlers as individuals rise up momentarily only to buckle in the end under the system of white capitalist oppression. For as Goines illustrates here, even united freedom fighters cannot finally overcome the spatial oppressions that urban African Americans face. Goines displaces the larger political, economic, and racial struggles of

FIGURE 3.1. Donald Goines's *Kenyatta's Last Hit*, published posthumously in 1975.

black life onto the entrapped space of the service elevator and thus provides a powerful image of how the black crime novel could be developed to engage the social crisis of the American ghetto.

Although the Kenyatta series is a very different literary enterprise than Goines's earlier pimp and hustler novels, it represents his fullest use of the popular black crime novel as a vehicle to express black political and social concerns in the tumultuous period following the Civil Rights era. It features the intertwining stories of a quasi–Black Panther organization, as well as the usual suspects of the crime novel, including a black and white detective duo, pimps, junkies, hit men, drug dealers, and white businessmen. The Kenyatta series represents the genre's most ambitious ghetto epic. Taken together, the novels span over seven hundred pages in total length and capture the social totality of American life from the black criminal perspective in ways only hinted at in earlier books. It is plotted as one long novel and features a revolutionary named Kenyatta as the central protagonist, thereby reflecting Goines's most concerted attempt to write a serious work of political critique from within the popular form of the ghetto action novel. By creating this series, Goines transformed pimp literature into a radically political art form and reimagined the black crime novel as a more expansive literary expression. The popular plot elements of hits, heists, capers, and escapes serve to highlight Goines's growing class and race consciousness in his work. Goines's Kenyatta novels titillate and entertain, but they also frame the social crises of police brutality, class warfare, and urban segregation, thus providing a microcosm of the struggles occupying the lives of working-class blacks in the early 1970s. This attempt to employ popular crime elements to express a radical political consciousness is one of the defining features of these novels.

As a form of popular entertainment for black readers, the Kenyatta series provides figurations of heroic black masculinity capable of dismantling white authority. While a number of black characters figure centrally in the novel (including one of the most fully realized black detectives in African American fiction, Ed Benson), the main representation of black heroism is Kenyatta, a revolutionary from Detroit who over the course of the series builds a militant organization of two thousand black-belt assassins. On one level, the charismatic leader Kenyatta is an expansion of the existing prototype of the pimp. He employs a combination of charm and wit, and he uses his linguistic skills in the service of building a militant organization. Aside from this, Kenyatta also inverts the pimp, employing his magnetism and influence to pull prostitutes *off* the streets, to take apart the white-controlled drug trade, and to create a grass-roots organization capable of transforming the landscape of the American ghetto itself. At an early point in the first Kenyatta novel, *Crime Partners*, Kenyatta convinces two black hit men to join him by promising that his organization will get "rid of dope pushers and race-hatin' cops." Unlike Iceberg Slim's first-person narrative, however, which focuses on the speech of the pimp itself, Goines's streamlined third-person action novel focuses on the effect of the speech. In response to Kenyatta's pledge, one of the hit men, named Billy, decides to join the organization: "'I believe you, brother. When you state it like that I can't help but believe you,' Billy said truthfully. And at the time he did believe. It was one of Kenyatta's strong points, the ability to make people believe in his dream. Whether he could make it true or not, he could make people believe him."²³ Significantly, in Goines's narrative, the emphasis is less focused on Kenyatta's verbal innovations; the narrator simply tells the reader that Kenyatta has the power to make people believe him, rather than showing it through the speech itself. This is a clear departure from something like Sweet Jones's oral history of the origins of the pimp in Iceberg Slim's narrative, in which Jones employs linguistic innovativeness to justify the existence of the pimp. In part, this reflects Goines's differing style in comparison to Beck, as Goines wrote more action-oriented, plot-driven novels. But it also suggests that Goines was creating within the constraints of a more efficient mode of literary expression. At this latter stage of Holloway House's cultural production, the focus is on high output, rather than individualized style. This mode of expression reflects a combination of new stylistic approaches and publishing imperatives. By emphasizing high production, Holloway House increased surplus value while retaining the basic elements of the black crime novel that it had helped create. Thus, although Goines moved the black crime novel into the realm of a more explicitly radically political sensibility, he did so by surrendering stylistic innovation central to the pimp autobiography.

Although the reading audience might not be impressed by Kenyatta's verbal prowess, the masses within the novel are, and they begin joining his organization in order to transform the ghetto landscape: "There was a growing number of young, idealistic blacks who had joined with the tall, bald-headed black man. They had known that the government, the law enforcement agencies, and the supposed poverty programs were not working. Kenyatta had told them that the situation was in their hands, that they were the force behind the ghetto, and that they would be the ones who could make it better for their brothers."²⁴ Kenyatta convinces thousands of blacks to join his organization in an attempt to reform the ghetto itself through the destruction of figures of white power. Significantly, his organization fills a gap left by the failure of the Civil Rights Movement to bring about economic or social equality for the majority of African Americans. The novel promotes the militant organization because it provides a more radical stance than the integrationist ethos adopted by the black middle class. Kenyatta's strategy to combat problems of white containment is to kill off systematically white racist cops and heroin dealers: "My people are trained, and every one of them has only one thought in their mind. Kill the honky. That's our rally cry. Death to Whitey."²⁵

With the goal of ridding the ghetto of white economic and police control, Kenyatta's group performs a stunning series of murders spanning from Detroit to Los Angeles. Goines represents violence as more than the inevitable byproduct of a repressive class- and race-based society; it becomes a regenerative action that can foment revolution through the destruction of white authority. For instance, early in *Crime Partners*, Kenyatta and his people begin their revolutionary cause by murdering a racist white policeman. While scenes of graphic violence are common in all of Goines's literature, the murder of the racist cop is significant for the way that it redirects the frequent black-on-black violence in his other novels toward a recognizable white authority: "A hard blow hit him in the chest and he staggered heavily. As he reeled back against the car, the night seemed to explode with fire. He clawed at his holster, but it was a feeble effort. Another staggering blow sent him down to his knees, and before he could recover he felt the pavement come up and smash him in the face."²⁶ This is an image of the unrelenting brutality of the city itself, and the pavement coming up to smash the policeman in the face signals a new moment in black crime literature. This is a symbolic reversal of the hostile city streets that silence Jimmy in *Run Man Run*. For whereas Jimmy is shot by the white racist cop and he responds by impotently firing a bullet at the pavement itself, here the racist cop is silenced when he is shot by black militants and the city street rushes up to smash his face. This makes the city an active agent in combating racism, whereas before it had simply been a site constructed to contain blacks. Scenes like this occur over and over again in the Kenyatta novels, and the force of these moments come from a literal dismantling of bodies of white power, such as cops and businessmen. The introduction of Kenyatta to the world of black crime literature demonstrates a reversal of the social order in which figures of dangerous white authority are subdued by black rebellion in the urban spaces that they occupy. Goines's final novels reflect his emerging radical consciousness, as they express the sentiment that the viciousness of ghetto life—and the spaces of the ghetto themselves, it seems—can be harnessed to achieve political effects.

In reimagining the black experience novel as a vehicle for a narrative of revolution, Goines attempted to expand black crime fiction to be more attuned to contemporary issues of radical black nationalism as well as the decolonization movements taking place across the globe. Goines is particularly interested in the relationship between violence and the reclamation of black space. He names his central protagonist after Jomo Kenyatta—Kenya's first black president following emancipation from British colonialism—and thus draws an explicit symbolic connection between the conditions of America's ghettos and African colonies. A number of critics had been making such comparisons throughout the 1960s, including Franz Fanon, Kenneth Clark, Harold Cruse, and Stokely Carmichael.[27] For example, according to sociologist Kenneth Clark's 1965 study of the American inner city, *The Dark Ghetto*, "The dark ghetto's invisible walls have been erected by white society, by those who have power, both to confine those who have no power, and to perpetuate their powerlessness. The dark ghettos are social, political, educational and—above all—economic colonies."[28] Much like the elevator scene from *Kenyatta's Last Hit*, which opened this discussion, Clark's analysis also emphasizes both the invisibility of white forms of containment and that these forms of control are specifically linked to America's internal colonization.

Goines's Kenyatta novels attempt to represent these intellectual and political currents in the space of the ghetto crime novel. First of all, Kenyatta supports the use of violence to combat the occupying police force and to reoccupy that contested space—a central tenet of Franz Fanon's influential book on decolonization, *The Wretched of the Earth* (1961). Kenyatta also sees that creating black-owned space outside the ghetto is crucial to the cause of black freedom. Taking a few new recruits to the organization's secluded farm and training facility an hour outside Detroit, Kenyatta explains why this space is so vital to the cause: "You don't have no police harassment, and for a black man that is something in itself. A man can completely forget the color of his skin out here. It don't make no difference if you're black or green. Don't nobody bother you about it. Whereas, back in the city, a black man is constantly on his guard because of the white pigs fuckin' with him."[29] Kenyatta here echoes much of the discourse surrounding the decolonization of

European-controlled African nations during the 1960s by directly connecting the decolonization of the American blacks to both the black ownership of land and the expulsion of the white police presence. Kenyatta's approach to decolonizing the black American ghetto through violence and the recuperation of land in the novel actually repeats what had occurred historically in Kenya, where the militant Mau Mau organization had spurred the nation's independence from British rule through violent expulsion of white settlers. Jomo Kenyatta was imprisoned as one of Mau Mau's leaders, and he later became the president of Kenya following its independence. Goines's Kenyatta series draws from these historical transformations in order to create a mythology of African American life. This fantasy of black-controlled land outside the ghetto is a fantasy that is nonetheless foreclosed by white violence. In Goines's novels, the militant organization provides utopian spaces and momentary freedom from white containment, thereby infusing the project of dismantling imperialism with popular fantasies of spatial escape.

Goines's novels also imagine Kenyatta's organization as an expansion of the radical legacy of the recently neutralized Black Panthers. As the narrator puts it in the final installment of the series, "Kenyatta had learned well from the failures of the Black Panthers in the east. He had studied their operation and had learned where they had made their mistake. Basically, they had been too well organized for their own good. And the government, seeking to destroy their threatening existence, had been able to strike quick and hard at the leaders, thus dismantling the entire operation in a swift powerful strike. Kenyatta would not let the same thing happen to his people."[30] Recalling the recent destruction of the Black Panther Party—in which the FBI's notorious COINTELPRO program had effectively dismantled the radical organization—Goines's novels imagine what might have happened had the Panthers gone completely underground.[31] In part, the black experience novels published by Holloway House were invented as an enjoyable distraction from the social crisis of American race relations. However, in Goines's hands, the black crime novel emerges as a theater to stage the radical possibilities of an organized subversion of white power. These novels focus on collective action over individualized escape as well as imaginary rebellions over historical realities, and they provide readers with imaginary opportunities to contend with forces of white containment. Although the Kenyatta series is marketed as mere fiction, it nevertheless entertains the possibility of black revolution in the space of the ghetto crime novel.

Yet while Goines uses the black crime novel to stage the possibilities of black insurrection in America, he reveals the limits of organized violence to mount any kind of significant challenge to forms of white control. Kenyatta's organization sets out to murder the embodiments of the white power structure by killing only white businessmen, drug dealers, and racist cops. But as the story progresses, innocent people—black police officers, hotel maids, and even children—become the unintended victims of violence whose boundaries cannot be contained. In this way, violence, even revolutionary violence, is finally presented as a limited tactic at best. This represents a definitive shift from the violence represented in the pimp autobiography. In Iceberg Slim's narrative, a variety of mythologies about women are deployed in order to justify the violence against them. In the Kenyatta series, no such justifications are offered. Goines's novels make the point that there are casualties of these policies of containment as well as of the organized response to it, casualties whose only crime is their vulnerability. By refusing to justify the violence against a number of innocent black victims who are caught up in the accident of history, Goines's Kenyatta novels dramatize how the black population itself is at last the victim of white racist strategies of containment.

Nowhere is the limit of violence made more plain than in the third novel of the series, *Kenyatta's Escape*, in which the police converge on Kenyatta's farm and kill most of his followers, first with guns, then with flamethrowers, and finally with tanks. It is at the moment the police attack Kenyatta's people, a moment which is reminiscent of the historical police raids on Black Panther headquarters, that the futility of armed black resistance is made totally clear: "The tank opened fire. Where a near white cabin had been, there was now only ruins. The black people inside didn't stand a chance. Before the other black people in the other cabins could realize what was happening the other tank opened fire. It was now a complete massacre. To the white army men inside the tanks, it was a game, something like maneuvers. They had no thought about the black men and women they were killing."[32] At the beginning of the Kenyatta series, the farm provides a utopian space for blacks to escape the spatial containment of the Detroit ghetto and the violent oppression of a racist police force. But by the conclusion of the series, this too is foreclosed as a possible solution. Anticipating the final image of *Kenyatta's Last Hit*, in which the remainder of Kenyatta's followers are killed off by militarized nerve gas in the enclosed service elevators, the black population here is treated as a hostile occupying force to be destroyed through armed response. Moments such as these in the Kenyatta novels are significant indicators of Goines's literary aesthetic as a whole. They illustrate that even as black freedom fighters might enjoy singular moments of victory over individual white characters, when faced with systemic forms of racism, acts of armed resistance are futile. Goines's final literary project provides black readers with moments of cathartic defeat of figures of white power but also realistic resolutions, in which individual acts of heroism are crushed by forces of institutional white authority.

The black heroes of the Kenyatta series find momentary freedom only to be captured or killed by the militarized white authority. This is similar to Beck's pimp autobiography and Goines's own early work, and it indexes the crime novelist's ambivalence toward the subversive energies symbolized by the black criminal figure. Despite the obvious differences between the pimp and Panther narratives, what is structurally similar between them is that they draw on the antiauthoritarian energies of the Black Power moment. They use the black criminal figure as a mirror to view the persistence of forms of white containment in the form of ghettoization, the concentration of inner-city poverty, and police oppression. But they also highlight the limitations of the outlaw's approach to such violence, as the black criminal can be branded a terrorist and subjected to the full force of the American militarized police force. Nevertheless, by expanding the genre of the black crime novel to contemplate more radical forms of African American resistance, Goines combined popular entertainment and militant black politics in ways unrepresented in American literature before.

"It Made It More Real": *Never Die Alone* and the Racial Politics of Black Pulp Publishing

Donald Goines, more than either Robert Beck or Chester Himes before him, employed the black crime novel as a vehicle to contemplate explicitly the constraints of the black pulp publishing industry. In particular, Goines's 1974 novel *Never Die Alone* explores the dilemmas of creating saleable representations of black criminal authenticity within a white-owned literary marketplace. It features the intersecting stories of Jewish Holocaust survivor Paul Pawlowski's search for his literary voice and black gangster King David's rise to power as a ruthless heroin dealer. *Never Die Alone* is a novel-within-a-novel, with Pawlowski's narrative framing King David's first-person autobiography. When Pawlowski finds King David shot down in the streets by rival drug dealers early in the novel, he delivers him to the hospital, though not in time to save his life. As David dies, he wills his autobiographical novel, "The Life Story of a Born Player," to Pawlowski, and the rest of the novel switches back and forth between Pawlowski's perspective and David's autobiography. Similar to Beck's *Pimp: The Story of My Life*, King David's confessional of his many crimes at one level fulfills the conventions of the black experience novel published by Holloway House. But by employing Pawlowski's story as a narrative frame, Goines also utilizes the black crime novel to contemplate his susceptible position in the black crime fiction marketplace without directly exposing himself to the people who wrote his check. In *Never Die Alone*, Goines expands the aesthetic of the autobiographical pimp/player story by covertly combating forms of representational containment promoted at Holloway House. In doing so, Goines brings together for the first time in the space of the black crime novel two figures facing forms of white containment: the criminal in the street and the figure of the writer in the marketplace.

At the opening of the novel, Goines introduces the figure of Pawlowski, a struggling fiction writer who lives in poverty despite the fact that he regularly publishes paperback books. Notwithstanding obvious racial and ethnic differences, Pawlowski is at one level a thinly veiled representation of Goines the paperback writer himself: "A writer's life was pure hell, he reflected. Sometimes he had a few extra dollars, in March or September when his royalty checks arrived. But the other months were hell, unless the writer happened to be a good money manager. But to find a writer who could manage money was rare, because anyone who was adept at it would also have enough common sense to pick a better livelihood."[33] Here, through the figure of Pawlowski, Goines provides a deflected representation of his own difficult situation in the literary marketplace. He represents the struggling writer as a Jewish Holocaust survivor, an individual who has faced violent containment by the Nazis. In doing so, Goines indirectly critiques the marketplace of paperback production at Holloway House without directly divulging himself to his publishers.

Desperate for income, Pawlowski goes hunting for a job at the *Evening Star*, a sensationalist newspaper that publishes race-baiting stories of interracial rape and murder to a white southern audience. In the novel, the newspaper operates as a deflected representation of Holloway House. It is the confrontational scene between Pawlowski and the newspaper's owner, Mr. Billings, that most clearly illustrates Goines's condemnation of the pulp publishing industry to which he is

of pulp publishing and thus retain the "manhood" he has lost by prostituting his talent to the commercial marketplace.

Pawlowski is the primary focus of the opening of the novel; however, he shares the imaginary space of the book with King David, the novel's central black criminal figure. Immediately after leaving Billings's office, Pawlowski encounters King David, a heroin dealer who has been stabbed and left for dead in the streets by his enemies. Pawlowski delivers David to the hospital, but David dies anyway and leaves Pawlowski his white Cadillac, his jewelry, and his most valuable possession, a diary titled "The Life Story of a Born Player." At about midpoint in the *Never Die Alone*, this first-person story appears—and is contained—within the larger third-person narration of Pawlowski's story. This form of representational containment is a reflection of the larger modes of spatial and racial containment that occur in the novels themselves, and Goines's self-conscious use of it works to expose the streamlined production process that was required of him at Holloway House. King David's diary looks a lot like the standard autobiographical crime novel of the Holloway House variety. It is an account of how he has ripped off New York's biggest heroin dealer and then traveled to Los Angeles to swindle high-class Hollywood starlets. Written as a criminal confession in the tradition of Iceberg Slim, David's story admits to his many crimes, including his exploitation of a variety of women. There is a passage early in the novel that illustrates King David's swindling women in order to facilitate his escape from his former life of poverty: "The stupid bitch was waiting for me with the check. After taking her to get it cashed, I left her sitting in a restaurant with the promise that I would be back at her apartment in about an hour. As I write this shit, I wonder if anyone would ever read it and believe that people could be so dumb. Since this morning I've collected three pieces of heroin and a check for two hundred and twenty dollars."[37] On the surface, King David's story fulfills the ideological expectations of the black experience narrative by presenting the story of the black criminal's exploitation of women as a pathway to freedom.

As the story continues, however, King David's abuse of women transforms from economically opportunistic to purely sadistic. At the autobiography's conclusion, he professes to raping and killing his girlfriend with a "hotshot," a mixture of heroin and battery acid, because she threatens to turn him over to the police. The description of her death is as explicitly brutal as anything that Goines ever put in print: "I walked over and looked down at her. Snot poured from her nose and a long stream of it fell down on her chin. Her legs were wet from where her bowels had busted on her. As I stared down at her, a lump of shit came running down her leg. I looked at it and the thought flashed through my mind that she wasn't so fuckin' fine after all."[38] Much like Raymond Chandler's detective novels, black crime fiction depends on violated and objectified bodies. But whereas white-authored detective fiction utilizes black male bodies, black-authored crime novels use female ones to construct narratives of heroic masculinity. However, even for a Goines novel, the violence visited on the female body here is excessive, even hyperbolic. King David's diminishment of the female body to snot and shit goes beyond the calculated control of women for economic gain. It is an act of violence motivated by a pornographic desire to reduce women to bodily excrement. While violence against women is a commonplace trope in Holloway House's black crime novel, this sadistic display calls attention to itself as exaggerated overstatement. What this suggests is that in the realm of the popular literary market, even as such pornographic representations are expected to sell books, Goines voices a complex form of protest against these representations through hyperbole. While for many readers, this moment of violence against the female body might seem like an uncritical reproduction of ideologies of misogyny, for the careful reader, it explodes such ideologies through the only strategy available to the popular writer working within the strict confines of the pulp market. That is, in a marketplace where sex and violence are required representations for selling books, Goines pushes such expectations to absurd limits.

Goines employs the framing device of Pawlowski to call attention further to the constructed quality of the black criminal autobiography. When Pawlowski starts reading "The Life Story of a Born Player," he initially thinks David's diary is just an authentic, off-the-cuff confessional of ghetto life. However, after just a few pages, as King David starts adding dialogue between himself and other characters, the narrative suddenly seems less a straightforward confessional and more like a novel. When Pawlowski reads the first exchanges between David and a Hollywood starlet he is fleecing, Pawlowski realizes that David is actively constructing a narrative: "The poor sonofabitch was really trying to write a book! Now I wonder just how much shit in here is real and how much is just an overworked imagination. Paul studied the handwriting before him. Maybe this guy was really planning on trying to sell this shit to some publisher."[39] Through the device of Pawlowski, Goines illustrates that the black crime novel is never an unmediated confession but is an actively constructed literary expression, a stylized narration and reinterpretation of real events. Over and over again throughout Pawlowski's reading of

King David's story, he finds himself wondering if he is reading autobiography or a work of fiction. In this way, Goines uses Pawlowski to call attention to the fact the black criminal autobiography is the result of a process of literary production and not simply a reflection of reality. It is also significant to notice here that even as Pawlowksi's perspective frames King David's, it is a frame that is entirely unstable. In this moment of free direct discourse, there are no quotation marks to separate the thoughts of Pawlowski and the perspective of the omniscient narrator. Thus, even as Pawlowski's story is used as the structure to contain King David's story, Goines collapses the neat differences between Pawlowski and the narrator, thereby calling attention to the instability of forms of representational containment. The novel challenges Holloway House's reduction of the black experience novel into some kind of criminal confessional. Goines highlights the complex forms of literary production at work in the black experience novel by presenting it here as a series of frames within frames.

Ultimately, *Never Die Alone* is a novel that attempts to expose the process of publishing autobiographical black crime stories as a racially exploitative one. Although Pawlowski begins reading because he is curious to find out why King David is killed, as he gets deeper into the diary, he sees an opportunity shape the diary into a novel of his own: "If it remained interesting, he might just make a complete book out of it. Of course it would take some work, but a man didn't stumble over a good story every day, and from what he had read so far, it might just appeal to some sections of the public."[40] Pawlowski sees that King David's story has potential commercial appeal for black consumers not yet hailed by the publishing industry, which is itself reflective of Holloway House's attitude toward publishing black-themed materials following the riots of the 1960s. As with Holloway House's Jewish owners, Bentley Morriss and his partner, Ralph Weinstock, Pawlowski's upward mobility is based on the commercialization of black autobiography. Goines further dramatizes this essentially exploitative relationship by transforming King David's story into a literal treasure map to fifty thousand dollars in drug money. When Pawlowski realizes that the diary holds the secret to the location of King David's hidden fortune through his heroin trade, his reading the novel and his search for ghetto treasure become one and the same search: "If there was any truth in what he read, the diary should give him the key to where the money was. He went back to the bed and reopened the diary. This time his interest was more than curiosity. Greed was mixed with it."[41] Pawlowski starts off in the story as a figure who is going to be potentially exploited by the publishers at the *Evening Star*. By the conclusion of the novel, and with King David's criminal autobiography in hand, he emerges as a potential exploiter of black materials himself.

The final image of the novel provides the most dramatic illustration of this point. Although Pawlowski is initially seduced by the idea of keeping King David's money, he decides to give it away to a drug rehabilitation clinic after reading the concluding chapter of the diary in which David brutally murders his girlfriend. Even though Pawlowski donates the fifty thousand dollars to a drug clinic in an attempt to compensate for King David's horrific deeds, he keeps his white Cadillac. As he drives off through Harlem on the last page of the novel, he says aloud to himself, "I guess I'll keep the car. That much I do owe myself."[42] As we have seen in the pimp autobiography of Iceberg Slim, the white car, especially the Cadillac, is a central symbol of black mobility in the face of conditions of white containment. By taking possession of the car, Pawlowski appears to have achieved at least some momentary freedom as well. But having given away all of King David's drug money, the novel implies that Pawlowski will have to go back to writing in order to earn the income to maintain the mobility that the car allows. The narrator never explicitly states whether Pawlowski will transform King David's story into a novel of his own or not. However, the shape of the literary marketplace that the world of the novel outlines suggests that he will have to exploit King David's diary if he wants to survive and keep his newfound mobility. The Cadillac provides a physical symbol of the potential economic mobility that King David's diary has provided Pawlowski. However, still covered in David's blood, the car signals that this mobility is enabled by violence against black men. The haunting concluding image of Pawlowski cruising through Harlem in David's bloody Cadillac reflects the fact that racial bloodshed underwrites this industry of literary production. It also uncannily reflects Goines's and other black writers' complex position at Holloway House, in which white Jewish copyeditors were able to build a publishing empire on the backs of former pimps and hustlers who sold their stories for pennies on the dollar. With Pawlowski and King David each at various moments standing in for Goines himself (as victimizer of women and victim of the publishing industry), *Never Die Alone* is ultimately Goines's most outspoken and complex representation of the various and uneven forms of racial, gendered, and economic containment facing both the black criminal and the black writer in the American landscape.

Conclusion

After Goines's death, his publishers capitalized on his image as a criminal outlaw. At about the same time Holloway House published his biography, it sent out the following announcement to book distributors: "Donald Goines is dead. Executed. The most talented writer of the black experience novel died in a real life scene from one of his own books. Stock up on all of Goines's books now. Use our special new display. They will be in great demand."[43] Along with creating these new displays, emphasizing the thin line between Goines's life and works, Holloway House also began printing the following on the back cover of each of Goines's books: "Donald Goines, savagely gunned down at the age of 39, was the undisputed master of the Black Experience novel. He lived by the code of the streets and exposed in each of his 16 books the rage, frustration and torment spinning through the inner city maze. Each of his stories, classics in the Black Experience genre, were drawn from reality as Donald Goines poured out the anger, guilt, and pain of a black man in America!" Here we can see how sinister this use of the "real" can become as it is employed as a marketing strategy to sell books in the Holloway House system. Rather than a descriptive or critical category, the discursive use of authenticity becomes a convenient tool for the culture industry of black street literature to rationalize its own existence. While Goines himself interrogates this characterization of black crime fiction in works such as *Never Die Alone*, Holloway House was nevertheless able to subsume such challenges through its advertising fictions.

Although writing within a prejudicial system of mass-market publishing, Donald Goines expanded on the narratives and tropes invented by Chester Himes and Robert Beck in order to push the black crime novel in new directions. Even as he became indentured over the course of his short writing career to the commercially driven Holloway House system, Goines nevertheless transformed the pimp narrative into a story of black radicalism, thereby making the antiwhite, antiauthoritarian politics of the pimp autobiography an explicit part of this literary scene. Unlike any of the black authors before him, Goines also used the black crime novel to comment on the problematic racial politics of the black pulp publishing industry. By connecting the figure of the writer in the marketplace to the figure of the criminal in the street, Goines made overt a relationship between commercial and urban spaces of white containment. In the next chapter, we turn to an examination of the variety of utopian novels created at Holloway House in the post-Beck, post-Goines era. Providing a wide range of imaginary solutions to the problems of ghettoization, incarceration, and economic containment, the Holloway House novels of the mid-to-late 1970s reflected both a worsening outlook for many black urban communities and a consolidating literary market of black pulp publishing.

4 /   Black in a White Paradise: Utopias and Imagined Solutions in Black Crime Literature

In 1976, Roland Jefferson published *The School on 103rd Street*, a novel that extended the black crime fiction genre established by Chester Himes, Robert Beck, and Donald Goines in important ways. As we have seen in the previous three chapters, Himes, Beck, and Goines each illustrated in their novels implicit connections between the carceral space of the prison and the confined space of the black neighborhood. Jefferson, however, makes this relationship explicit by representing the black city as a dystopian space of captivity. After the main protagonist, a black forensic psychiatrist named Elwin Carter, accidently stumbles across an underground prison built beneath an elementary school in the black neighborhood of Watts, he assembles his own militant organization to search for any other prisons hidden in other American cities. They discover that, following the urban insurrections that swept across the country during the 1960s, the government has built underground concentration camps in nearly every American city that has a sizable black population:

> We have uncovered the presence of underground prison compounds in the following cities: Detroit, underneath a health clinic on the edge of the ghetto; in Chicago on the West Side beneath a Baptist church. . . . Oh yes, in Bedford-Sty underneath a tenement house; in Harlem, dig this! Underneath the new wing of Harlem Hospital, which by the way, is the biggest we found, and it's natural, you know why? Wheel niggers into the hospital, they just don't come out! Folks just figured they died. . . . Newark, New Jersey,

under a school; Washington, D.C., below a junior high school; Philadelphia, under a church on Girard Street, south side of the city; Baltimore, under a library adjacent to a police precinct; New Orleans, under a medical clinic; and in Atlanta, under a recently constructed day care center for children of working mothers, not far from Morehouse College.[1]

By suggesting that health clinics, hospitals, tenement buildings, churches, libraries, schools, and day care centers are literal covers for the prison facilities built beneath them, *The School on 103rd Street* illustrates Michel Foucault's point that modern institutions are at their cores also mechanisms of surveillance and discipline. Furthermore, Jefferson's novel suggests that the establishments that house the black middle class are not supportive of the black masses but are themselves bankrupt and corrupted institutions. By placing prisons underneath cities with large black populations—Detroit, Chicago, Brooklyn, Harlem, Newark, Washington, D.C., Philadelphia, Baltimore, New Orleans, and Atlanta—Jefferson's novel makes the statement that black American neighborhoods have become spaces of incarceration for many of their black citizens, and it illustrates black crime literature's continued suspicion of the social and political impact of the black bourgeoisie.

The School on 103rd Street dramatizes the effects of spatial and racial containment created by decades of urban segregation in the mid-to-late twentieth century. The mechanisms that had been developed by whites in the decades following World War II to constrain black populations had by the 1970s produced a racially divided America. The suburbanization of white communities and the segregation of black citizens in inner cities had calcified by the early 1970s, and in all of America's largest cities, African Americans were isolated in centralized urban ghettos. Some black suburbanization mitigated these divisions during this decade; however, the completion of public housing high-rises in the inner city and the construction of vast highway systems facilitating white flight, coupled with deindustrialization and continued racial discrimination in housing and the job market, meant that the black ghetto had become a permanent fixture of the American landscape by the early 1970s.[2]

As the black ghetto solidified as a reality of American life during this decade, Holloway House also emerged as a center of black literary production. The company had established itself as the niche publisher of black crime novels with the publication of Robert Beck and Donald Goines. But it became a cultural institution of black pulp publishing with the addition of writers such as Joseph Nazel, Odie Hawkins, Charlie Avery Harris, Omar Fletcher, James Howard-Readus, Randolph Harris, Andrew Stonewall Jackson, Amos Brooke, Roosevelt Malloy, and others in the mid-1970s. Holloway House's catalogue of novels that developed throughout the decade consists of hundreds of books by dozens of authors, including such titles as *Gentleman Pimp, Trickshot, Macking Gangster, Whoredaughter, Black Renegades, Stack A. Dollar,* and *Black in a White Paradise.* Many of these novels draw on the narratives of criminals, pimps, and revolutionaries first popularized by Goines and Beck. However, the novels of the 1970s push the genre of black crime literature in new directions by providing utopian resolutions to spaces of white containment. Whereas the books of Goines and Beck almost always end in death, incarceration, or tragedy, these newer novels feature narratives of successful escape from spaces of containment or victory over figures of white power. For example, the pimps and hustlers in the novels of Amos Brooke and Charlie Avery Harris successfully con white women into giving them piles of cash, and—whereas the heroes in Goines's and Beck's works are thrown back into spaces of containment—these new characters are able to move out of the ghetto into white suburbs and other free spaces. In another twist on this new utopian trend, the ghetto revolutionaries of Omar Fletcher's books effectively dismantle white authority by killing off figures of white power. The heroes of these novels successfully escape the spaces of white confinement by abandoning the city altogether and taking up residence on a deserted island.

The most fantastical of these utopian black crime novels are by far Joseph Nazel's popular Iceman series. In them, the main protagonist, Henry Highland "the Iceman" West, makes enough money from pimping in Harlem to build "the Oasis," a black-owned Las Vegas–style pleasure palace in the Nevada desert. It is guarded by the Iceman's stable of karate-trained prostitutes and his surveillance supercomputer named Matilda, and it therefore operates as a symbolic inversion of the black ghetto. As a fantastical space that provides black heroes with freedom from sites of white containment, the Oasis is a spatial representation of the new direction the black crime novel took in the Holloway House system during the 1970s. The various representations of the ghetto utopia, or "ghettopia" as I call it, is the main subject of this chapter.

On the surface of things, these more utopian representations of pimps, hustlers, and freedom fighters might seem like a degradation of the black crime fiction genre. For although the novels of Beck and Goines entertain pimping and other illegal activities as potential pathways out of

FIGURE 4.1. *Stack A. Dollar* (1979) by Elroy Waters was one of the many African American crime novels published by Holloway House in the 1970s.

spaces of white containment, they end with the black protagonist unable to maneuver successfully institutional white power. By contrast, many of the Holloway House novels published in the post-Goines era feature black criminals who successfully negotiate spaces of white containment through rather improbable narrative resolutions. While it may be tempting to dismiss utopia as a form of deception and distraction, cultural theorists of mass culture such as Janice Radway, Michael Denning, and Fredric Jameson remind us that the utopian impulse in popular forms is also a political gesture of a shared oppositional stance to the dominant culture. As Jameson states, even the most degraded form of mass culture "remains implicitly, and no matter however faintly, negative and critical of the social order from which, as a product and a commodity, it springs."[3] Even mass culture that reproduces the status quo of the existing social order must do so by first giving expression to the collective anxieties that produce imagined solutions in the first place. In this way, the utopian resolution can be understood as a fantasy of systematic change of a society, one that draws on the material social and political crises of that society in order to shape specific fantasies of transcendence and escape. In the case of the black crime fiction of the mid-to-late 1970s, these novels remain deeply critical of white racism, urban containment, the mass incarceration of black populations, and the economic exploitation of African Americans. That they provide utopian visions of other worlds where black people are empowered illustrates the degree to which such racial divides had become deeply entrenched in American life.

Throughout the twentieth century, utopian fiction has played a significant role in African American political and cultural life. Although utopian elements in black cultural traditions can be traced back to the spirituals and plantation stories of slaves as well as to Martin Delany's unfinished novel *Blake* (1859), the dawn of the twentieth century witnessed the publication of a number of black utopia novels, including Sutton Grigg's *Imperium in Imperio* (1899), Pauline Hopkins's *Of One Blood* (1902), W. E. B. Du Bois's *The Quest of the Silver Fleece* (1911) and *Dark Princess* (1928), and George Schuyler's *Black Empire* (1936–1938). As Dohra Ahmad has recently argued in her excellent study *Landscapes of Hope: Anti-Colonial Utopianism in America*, writers such as Du Bois and Hopkins adopted the romantic mode of utopian fiction to counter the accommodationist strategies of Booker T Washington. These early representations of black utopian thought, Ahmad illustrates, reject both Washington's political pragmatism as well as the larger forces of global imperialism by constructing imminent utopias where black national and international identities can be forged.[4] An examination of utopia in black crime fiction expands on this African American literary and cultural history by viewing these paperback romances as imaginary refusals of the multiple oppressions facing black populations in the post–Civil Rights moment.

To be clear, we can best read the utopian solutions provided by these novels not as anesthetized reflections of black urban struggles but as otherworldly resolutions for black readers who no longer had viable political or social avenues available to them. The 1970s witnessed the end of the Civil Rights and Black Power Movements, the calcification of the division between the black inner city and the white suburbs, and accelerated economic downturns driven by postindustrial decline. In the face of such conditions, the utopian novels in the Holloway House line fulfilled the needs of a black readership by providing both complex wish fulfillments and other imagined geographical and literary spaces to inhabit besides that of the American ghetto. By creating such spaces, the authors of this genre provided entertainment for an incarcerated population, a form of entertainment that offers an implicit critique of the material conditions of ghettoization and white hegemony that produced them.

We also have to consider that the expansion of this genre reflects a mechanization of the marketing strategies on the part of Holloway House. For the most part, the Holloway House novels of the post-Goines era have been considered to be an undifferentiated mass. According to Jerry H. Bryant, whose *Born in a Mighty Bad Land* offers one of the only sustained academic treatments of these later Holloway House authors, the black experience novels of the mid-1970s lack the individual aesthetic or literary value of Beck or Goines. To quote him directly, "The emotion comes from the collective impact of these novels rather than their individual literary merit. They command our attention by their cumulative power, not by their individual esthetic success."[5] While it is no doubt true that many of the novels published in the post-Goines era are of inferior quality in terms of plotting, editing, and overall readability, neither Bryant nor any other critic has attempted to explain why this is so. I believe that we can read these apparent flaws as reflections of a larger shift in the literary marketplace, in which the owners at Holloway House encouraged high output and low quality. By featuring stories with happy endings, the company shifted its focus from individual stories of the black experience to serialized novels that could be sold one right after another. For instance, six of the seven novels in Nazel's Iceman series were published within months of another, while authors such as Charlie

Avery Harris, Omar Fletcher, and Roosevelt Mallory each wrote serialized stories of pimps, hit men, and black gangsters, all published roughly between 1975 and 1979.

We can interpret this mode of entertainment in installments as another form of containment of the black author in the literary marketplace of Holloway House books. For while the autobiography of Beck experimented with a kind of recognizable "literariness" in terms of innovative language and sophisticated character and plot development, by the mid-1970s these qualities were viewed by the publishers as expendable luxuries. As Holloway House was a closed literary system of production, its writers were forced to meet the expectations of an industry that increasingly valued output over innovation. Therefore, the commodification of the black crime novel in the mid-to-late 1970s was also a reflection of the calcification of the black urban ghetto of the same period. As African Americans found themselves isolated in inner-city neighborhoods that were suffering from economic decline and white disinvestment, the serialized black crime novel provided utopian fantasies of entertainment and escape from these conditions. At once fulfilling the expectations of a readership in need of popular fantasies of escape and at the same time further constraining black authors within the confines of a limiting marketplace, the black experience novel of the 1970s constituted a significant new moment in the genre and industry of black crime publishing.

Bryant's assumption that the novels of the post-Goines era lack individual literary merit is not quite true, as there are specific authors who do expand the genre of black crime literature in new ways from the earlier books of Beck and Goines. While Bryant's book should be commended for bringing long-overdue attention to authors in the Holloway House line, further work can be done to categorize and evaluate them. The first section of this chapter looks at the expansion of the pimp and revolutionary novels in the Holloway House line written throughout the 1970s. It examines the ways in which key authors such as Charlie Avery Harris, Amos Brooke, and Omar Fletcher extend the tropes and narratives of the books of Beck and Goines. In particular, this section looks at how the pimp and revolutionary novels emerge as two significant strains of the black crime novel, each providing imaginary solutions to the real-world problems of ghettoization, incarceration, and other forms of white containment. The second section investigates the novels of America's most prolific black author in history, Joseph Nazel. The author of the widest variety of pimp fantasies, black detective novels, and other fictions in

Holloway House's history, Nazel is the writer who created the most significant and expansive representation of the ghettopia. The conclusion of this chapter investigates the hazardous position of the black writer in this new literary marketplace of pulp publishing through a brief examination of the writing careers of Odie Hawkins and Roland Jefferson, two authors who attempted to work against the constraints of this more rationalized system. Writing within the confined commercial space of Holloway House, a core group of authors expanded the representation of the black urban criminal in new directions by infusing the black experience novel with incredible conclusions of victory, escape, and a transformation of American society.

Imaginary Resolutions in the Black Experience Novel

Throughout the 1970s, Holloway House greatly expanded its list of titles by publishing the works of dozens of aspiring black writers. These novels took a variety of forms, including prison novels, pimp stories, and narratives of black revolution. Some were straightforward imitations of the pimp autobiography invented by Robert Beck. Replicating the conventions of the genre as outlined in *Pimp: The Story of My Life*, a few authors published their own pimp narratives, which detail their criminal exploits as street hustlers, their confrontations with spaces of white containment, and their eventual incarceration.[6] Some examples of these kinds of imitative autobiographical novels include first-person confessionals, such as Andrew Stonewall Jackson's *Gentleman Pimp: An Autobiography* (1973), Randolph Harris's *Trickshot: The Story of a Black Pimp* (1974), Bruce Conn's *The Horror of Cabrini Green* (1975), and Odie Hawkins's *Sweet Peter Deeder* (1979), as well as third-person stories of pimp exploits, such as Amos Brooke's *Last Toke* (1977), Elroy Waters's *Stack A. Dollar* (1979), William Cook-Bey's *The Way It Came* (1983), and John Springs's *Kansas* (1984).

Marketed by Holloway House as books written "in the searing tradition of Iceberg Slim and Donald Goines," many of these autobiographical novels often do little more than replicate Beck's pimp autobiographical form. For example, Andrew Stonewall Jackson's *Gentleman Pimp* opens with the narrator sitting in Wayne Country Prison awaiting a transfer to Jackson State Penitentiary in 1967 on the eve of the Detroit riots. Having just finished reading Beck's *Pimp: The Story of My Life* and *Trick Baby: The Biography of a Con Man*, the narrator realizes that "brother Beck" and he "had a good deal in common," and these books inspire him to tell his own story. As he puts it, "Since brother Bob's books proved to me that my life story could be told, and since it should be told honestly, in the raw nitty gritty fashion, I'm going to tell it like it was. So sit back and be prepared to read a confession that only a fool would write."[7] Following the stylistic model invented by Beck—to confess to his crimes in the "raw nitty gritty" vernacular of a street pimp—Jackson replicates the first-person confessional strategy of *Pimp*. What follows is a story that in many ways impersonates Iceberg Slim's narrative. The narrator provides a series of vignettes about his various street capers, including boosting, conning, and, of course, pimping prostitutes, and at the conclusion of the story, he ends up in prison. A pioneering work of literature, Beck's *Pimp: The Story of My Life* proved to be an imitable form for aspiring black writers looking to enter the literary marketplace of black pulp publishing at Holloway House.

Although these pimp narratives are not particularly innovative in their use of the form, what makes them interesting both individually and collectively is their articulation of updated black street vocabulary and style. In other words, in the hands of the Holloway House authors of the 1970s, the pimp autobiography became a vehicle to showcase a living, breathing black urban style and linguistic innovation. For example, Elroy Waters's *Stack A. Dollar*, a third-person pimp narrative, follows the basic genre conventions of *Pimp*, including the protagonist's street education in pimping, confrontations with figures of white authority, and incarceration at the conclusion of the book. At one point in the novel, the protagonist and title character, named Stack A. Dollar, gives one of his many pimp philosophy sermons: "'That's why jails are overcrowded now!' Stack blew. 'A mothafucka' be sleepin', when they should be thinkin'.' He took the last sip of his drink and let out a long ah. 'Anyhow,' he said, 'don't nothin' come to a sleeper, but a dream, and when he wakes up . . . that's gone!'"[8] This moment when Stack shows off his verbal skills is reminiscent of the tirades of Iceberg Slim's mentor Sweet Jones in *Pimp*. Stack's speech also serves as a platform to demonstrate the innovativeness of pimp poetics. Although essentially repeating the central principle of survival from *Pimp*—that pimping is a thinking man's prerogative, a "skull game"—Stack's speech nonetheless says it in a new way and for another generation. He emphasizes that in order to stay out of prison, hustlers and pimps need to wake up from a state of unconscious and approach the profession with thoughtfulness and linguistic innovation.

These pimp autobiographies and hustler stories therefore provide readers with the pleasure that comes with a repeated reading experience, but in new linguistic modes of expression. In other words, much like the hip hop music that later modeled itself on narratives such as *Pimp*, the form of the black crime novel was used as a vehicle to showcase updated street talk and tactics for survival. Waters's novel, like many in the Holloway House line throughout the 1970s, uses the form of *Pimp* in order to parade new expressions of urban poetics. The popular pimp novels published by Holloway House therefore offer black readers something of similar value to what romances offer female readers. Janice Radway writes, "Romance reading, it would seem, can be valued as much for the sameness of the response it evokes as for the variety of adventures it promises."[9] As Radway explains, the pleasure offered to readers by popular literature comes from the combination of varying escapades *and* a repeated experience. In the case of the black experience novel, the pleasure of the pimp story is derived from meeting certain generic expectations and varying the style in which those expectations are met. In the pimp autobiography of this type, the variety of adventure is less important than the changing stylistic choices that constitute the story. Pimp literature thus emphasizes the importance of individual voices who make up the genre, each offering a singular expression of black urban language through the form of the popular novel. Taken together, these pimp autobiographies represent a repository of black culture and storytelling that documents the hidden struggles and verbal innovativeness of black urban America in the 1970s.

While the straightforward imitation of pimp autobiography represents one strain of the black crime novel during the 1970s, another interesting development of the genre is pimp and hustler stories that feature the total subversion of white power. Especially following Goines's death in 1974, a number of talented black authors emerged at Holloway House to fill the gap left by his absence. Writers such as Charlie Avery Harris, Omar Fletcher, Roosevelt Mallory, James-Howard Readus, and Amos Brooke each wrote multiple novels featuring fast-paced narratives of pimps, hustlers, con men, hit men, prisoners, prostitutes, and revolutionaries. Though these books feature the usual cast of urban characters from Goines's and Beck's books, the majority of them depart significantly from these earlier novels by featuring black heroes who are able to overcome forces of white power and spaces of urban containment.

The writer who provided the most sustained articulation of this type of crime-does-pay pimp fantasy is Charlie Avery Harris. The author of six novels, *Whoredaughter* (1976), *Macking Gangster* (1976), *Black and Deadly* (1977), *Broad Players* (1977), *Fast Track* (1978), and *Con Man*

(1978), Harris is one of the many Holloway House authors whose books were popular upon their first publication in the late 1970s but disappeared after only a few reprints. Very little is known about Harris's personal life, except for the brief life history printed on the last page of his final novel, *Con Man*. It describes him as follows: "Born during the forties in Baltimore, Maryland, growing up within the walls of Baltimore's dense jungle of Sandtown on the northwest side which is an area sometimes peopled by pool sharks, pimps, militants, cunning con men and women of all breeds whose first thought is of money."[10] Like Goines and Beck before him, Harris is marketed by Holloway House as a product of the "jungle" of the ghetto streets and an author who became "a writer of intensely realistic black fiction" while serving time in prison. Harris himself acknowledges a literary debt to Goines in particular at the opening of nearly every single one of his novels. For example, Harris opens the novel *Whoredaughter*, a book whose title is a clear play on Goines's first novel, *Whoreson*, as follows: "Dedicated to the everlasting memory of my friend and tutor, the late, great Donald Goines, whose patience and guidance still preside over my words. Thus, it's mandatory that I preserve this beautiful brother's image."[11] On the surface, it would seem, Harris simply repeats the plot points, gritty street vernacular, and tropes of black crime fiction transplanted onto the grounds of the Baltimore ghetto.

Although Harris's six books do feature hit men, prostitutes, pull artists, revolutionaries, and other ghetto characters made famous in the novels of Beck and Goines, his novels depart from the work of his forebearers by featuring the story of the most successful pimp who ever lived, Junius. With the exception of *Black and Deadly*, all of Harris's novels chart the rise of the pimp Junius, whose verbal prowess and magnetism make him an untouchable figure of black masculinity. A much more romanticized figurate of ghetto manliness than those represented in the novels of Beck and Goines, Junius never faces the consequences of a life of crime that befall his literary ancestors. His gift of gab protects him from pimp rivals, disgruntled prostitutes, and even imprisonment. This marks a distinctive shift in the genre from the cautionary tale to the fantasy of mobility. As the central figuration of linguistic power in Harris's books, Junius is able to negotiate spaces of white containment in ways that border on the absurd. For instance, the main plot of *Broad Players* features a bet among Junius and his pimp competitors over who is the greatest pimp in New York City. Each of the pimps has one year to collect, in the words of Junius, "the most cash, the fliest ride, the hippest wardrobe, the better history during this period, jewelry, and above all, the baddest broad or broads."[12] After spending six months in Chicago, refining his skills with the game's master pimp, named Craig, Junius then uses his linguistic expertise to enlist a white mother-and-daughter pair named Freda and Myra from the suburbs of Connecticut to be part of his prostitution ring. After spending three months in the women's mansion horseback riding, playing croquet, and golfing, Junius returns to New York with his new stable of white women in order to win the bet. Junius arrives at the players' ball in a black Rolls Royce with eight armed white guards, two million dollars in cash, and Freda and Myra, whom he introduces as Countess Nicole de Beaumarchais and Princess Cassandra von Hardenberg. Convincing the other pimps that he has courted European royalty to be part of his stable of prostitutes, Junius emerges at the end of *Broad Players* as the embodiment of the fantastical resolution to the problem of white containment. With his move to the suburbs underwritten by two rich white women, Junius is able to bypass altogether the various social, political, and racial constraints facing the characters of Beck's and Goines's novels.

Just like the pimps in the novels of Beck and Goines, Junius emphasizes that mastery over language is the primary strategy that allows him to combat spaces of white containment. However, in Harris's novels, linguistic expertise takes on a magical quality to overcome all obstacles. As Junius states in Harris's final novel, *Con Man*, "Nothing in the world has the power of words, not even money! This is because words earn money, from the President's speech down to the street pimp's rap. A blind man can beg for anything, but a mute can't request nothing. This is how precious words are, and anyone who doesn't believe that they are should try to count the millions of dollars that authors have earned with the tools of words."[13] Drawing an explicit connection between language, capital, and power here, Junius makes explicit how "rap" is critical to obtaining influence at every level of society, from president to pimp. Harris's novels also make the point that such a mastery of the linguistic is also crucial to black authorship in the literary marketplace of black crime fiction. As Junius boasts to one of his prostitutes when he is educating her in the history of pimping,

> These were the town players who wore plenty of silk, attended fabulous sets, rapped real slick, and spent U.S. currency like they owned the mint. I set my goal, patterned after them. But, baby, today, this same group of guys envy me, because I passed these niggers on the

way. They're has-beens. But I'll never let this generation coming up under me have this to say about me. Before I be looked upon as yesterday, I'll . . . I'll write a goddamn book like Iceberg Slim did and immortalize my name with fame.[14]

Junius exhibits the ways in which the language of street life has become by this moment an apparently marketable skill, and he illustrates the degree to which pimp linguistics is central to success in both black criminal life and black pulp publishing. By the late 1970s, pimp poetics had come to have overt literary value, as Holloway House had emerged as a commercial space where former criminals could publish their own versions of the stories created by Beck and Goines. While providing the pimp protagonist with a utopian solution to the problem of white containment, vernacular fluency also supposedly provides the pimp author access to the world of black publishing. However, this access is of dubious merit; for as we have seen in the cases of both Beck and Goines, publishing books at Holloway House did not provide its authors with the kind of hoped-for escape from life on the margins of American society. Therefore, Junius's desire to solidify his fame with a published account of his life is also a kind of utopian wish that cannot actually be fulfilled in the market of black pulp publishing.

Amos Brooke's *Black in a White Paradise* (1978) offers the most dramatic illustration of this new manifestation of the utopian Holloway House novel. Brooke had begun his writing career with Holloway House first by publishing a Manhattan pimp novel titled *Last Toke* (1977), followed by an exposé of prison life at New York's Green Haven Correctional Facility, titled *Doing Time* (1977). Although these first novels feature some elements of fantasy as imagined solutions to spaces of white containment and incarceration, it is Brooke's final novel, *Black in a White Paradise*, that provides the clearest expression of the black crime novel's turn toward the unreal. The story features two small-time drug operators named Lenny Thompson and Jason Cribs, who at the opening of the novel move from Harlem to a Southern California luxury condominium complex known as Palmwood Gardens. A part of Los Angeles's suburban expansion project, Palmwood Gardens is an exclusively white community, which, according to the colorful ad copy on the book's back cover, is populated by "racist honkie broads hungry for hard loving and by drug starved surfer dudes."[15] It is microcosm of the forbidden white world outside the boundaries of the black ghetto, and Brooke represents Palmwood Gardens as a fantastical inversion of the streets. As Lenny, one of the main protagonists, explains it, "Most white people go crazy when they hit the streets. The world's too real out there. White folks live like they're on television or something. Like this apartment house, one big television show."[16] Composed of narratives of Lenny's and Jason's erotic triumphs over the various white women who populate the complex, *Black in a White Paradise* offers black male readers fantasies of sexual domination in this white fantasy world as the pathway to freedom from spaces of white containment.

At the center of the novel is the story of Lenny's sexual and economic conquest of Wanda, the white manager of Palmwood Gardens. After Lenny awakens her long-repressed sexuality, he takes compromising pictures of her, which he then uses to blackmail her out of twenty thousand dollars in cash. This repeats the trope of conning rich white women as a form of escaping the ghetto that is central in both Robert Beck's *Pimp: The Story of My Life* and Donald Goines's *Whoreson: The Story of a Ghetto Pimp*. The main difference, however, is that in *Black in a White Paradise*, this con is the fulcrum of the novel's happy ending. Lenny and Jason, using Wanda's money to finance their own large-scale heroin operation, kill off Los Angeles's main drug financier in the final pages of the story. At the conclusion of the novel, they chase off Wanda's white boyfriend from his home in the affluent white neighborhood of Bel Air, where they plan to set up their drug-running operation. On the last page of the novel, Wanda joins Lenny at his newly acquired home, and they begin making plans together to take over Los Angeles's drug trade. The final lines read. "'Now,' he began softly, 'you a white woman in a black man's paradise.' He moved quickly across to her and began undressing her. Wanda closed her eyes, a soft smile working its way across her full lips."[17] This final resolution showcases the way in which Brooke's novel provides readers with a fantasy of escape from forms of white containment not available to the protagonists in either Beck's or Goines's books. Having bilked the white Wanda out of her twenty thousand dollars, set up a drug business, and moved to one of the most affluent neighborhoods in America, the novel's hero effectively creates what he calls a "black man's paradise." Unlike earlier Holloway House novels of the Beck and Goines variety, mobility here is actually achieved. The novel elides the gender violence in the novels of Beck and Goines altogether; rather than offering any justification for it, the novel simply encodes a pornographic male fantasy that Wanda submits to and even likes the exploitation that victimizes her. The fantasy of mobility and the fantasy of female submission are actually connected, as they are both imaginary solutions in the black crime novel. Reflecting the degree to which potential real-world solutions to problems of ghettoization had been all but foreclosed for the majority of black urban citizens by the mid-1970s, the movement toward fantasy in black crime novels such as Brooke's text provides hope within spaces of popular literature. These fantasies create imaginative outlets for a male community increasingly beset by the material constraints of white containment.

While these types of pimp and hustler romances represent some of the significant expansions of the black crime novel in the 1970s at Holloway House, one other important direction is the developed representation of the black revolutionary. As we have seen in the novels of Beck and Goines, the pimp and the revolutionary are parallel figures in the black crime literature genre, as they each attempt to overcome spaces of white containment. While the approaches to combating these forms of containment may be different (individual versus collective action, for instance), each of these figures in the novels of Beck and Goines attempt to negotiate the structures and spaces of white power, only to fail. A number of black writers at Holloway House following Goines developed this revolutionary character as an imaginary combatant to the violence of white containment. Black militants who are successful at dismantling forms of white power feature centrally in a variety of Holloway House novels, including James-Howard Readus's *The Black Assassin* (1975), Randolph Harris's *The Black Connection* (1974) and *The Terrorists* (1980), Roosevelt Mallory's four-book Radcliff series (1973–1976), and five out of the six of Omar Fletcher's novels: *Hurricane Man* (1977), *Walking Black and Tall* (1977), *Black against the Mob* (1977), *Black Godfather* (1977), and *Escape from Death Row* (1979).

The author who created the most sustained use of the successful black radical in his novels is Omar Fletcher. Advertised by Holloway House as "a great new discovery in the tradition of Donald Goines," Fletcher consistently used his novels to express that violent black militancy against white society is sometimes the only viable way of encouraging that society to recognize the humanity of black people. For example, Fletcher wrote a two-part series about two militant crime partners named Tyrone Abraham Jones and Omar Nusheba, *Walking Black and Tall* and *Black against the Mob*. These two books restage much of the black-on-white violence of Goines's Kenyatta series. At the opening of *Walking Black and Tall*, the novel introduces us to Tyrone Abraham Jones, whose family has been murdered by white policemen during the Newark riots of 1967:

Nothing would ever make him forget the burned bodies of his wife and two children, trapped in the nightmare of a police sniper squad: cops popping off shots each time a black face appeared at a window or door, and insisting, after the deed was done, that they had cornered two rioting looters in the house, and it was them, not Marcy and the kids, that the bullets were meant for. That no other bodies were found in the house seemed not to matter at all to the press and the police review board. So many niggers had died in the riots that two or three more didn't matter.[18]

Grounded in the urban insurrections of the 1960s, in which African Americans burned and looted the ghetto neighborhoods to which they had been confined, Fletcher's novel uses the riots as the crucial staging area for the creation of its politicized black hero. This is significant, as it suggests that the unorganized violence of the riots might be usefully organized into more productive black radical channels. Jones becomes radicalized after he loses his family to the riots, and he changes his name to Malcolm Lumumba, a composite name derived from the black nationalist leader Malcolm X and Patrice Lumumba, the first elected prime minister of the Republic of Congo following its independence from Belgium. This signals the novel's indebtedness both to the colonial struggles of Africa and to Goines's use of Kenyatta's name in his final books. Following Lumumba's radical transformation, he becomes a stick-up artist and hit man, because, as the narrator puts it, "his Luger pointed at a white face was the only thing he had found that could make the hurt go away for a little while."[19]

The bulk of both *Walking Black and Tall* and *Black against the Mob* consist of Malcolm and Omar robbing members of the white syndicate. At the conclusion of *Black against the Mob*, Malcolm and Omar, after robbing and killing dozens of members of the mafia, escape to a deserted island off the coast of Hawaii. Even as institutional racism remains intact at the conclusion of the Lumumba/Nusheba series, the two protagonists are able to escape from these conditions. The final fantastical image of *Black against the Mob* is of Malcolm and Omar paddling an outrigger to the remote island, free of urban spaces and violent white constraint: "Malcolm kicked off his shoes. Omar did likewise. Together they stepped into the surf—two city boys on their way to a place that harbored no cities, no threats."[20] Here it is the city, rather than the white police or racism, that bears the burden of oppression. This is a dramatic shift in the novel, as it both explicitly spatializes and deflects the symbols of domination from white racist cops onto the city itself. Providing moments of cathartic violence against white oppressors and then a utopia in the form of a deserted island, black experience novels such as these engage the social crises of ghettoization and white racism while also providing fantastical resolutions to these divides.

Even though the white police are responsible for the death of Lumumba's wife and children, it is the white Italian syndicate that becomes the object of his violence. As targets of black vengeance, these figures provide convenient marks for black violence that cannot be enacted on the overall system. By displacing justifiable black rage onto scapegoats who are, as Omar puts it, "jive mothers somewhere 'tween white folks and gorillas,"[21] Fletcher's novels provide black audiences with fantasies of striking out against figures of white power without directly threatening the larger institution from which that power emanates. In other words, in the utopian world of post-Goines crime literature, the white mafia provides a convenient substitution for those forms of systemic white power that oppress black populations. For as we have seen in Goines's Kenyatta series, even black militants are unequal to the combined economic and military forces of white power. By contrast, Malcolm and Tyrone consistently defeat these stock characters of white control through liberating violence. At the end of *Walking Black and Tall*, for instance, Lumumba hires a band of black Muslims to go to war with the syndicate. Repeating the final image from *Kenyatta's Last Hit*, Lumumba and his gang of black militants ride the elevator to the top floor of an exclusive white apartment complex. However, in this version of the story, they successfully kill off all the members of the syndicate who live there. For Lumumba, this victory has important therapeutic value: "It was the reality of black men striking back against the white hoodlums and thugs the police could not control. It was, to the old-timers and those too honest or weak to pick up a gun, pride in the knowledge that black men, their motives be damned, were standing tall in the face of an oppressor more vicious than the slave master of old. More deadly in that he attacked free of the law."[22] In an interesting sleight of hand here, the deadly white cops that threaten the black community at the opening of *Walking Black and Tall* have been replaced by white thugs and criminals. Black violence becomes a force of social good, and, in this post-Goines novel, such violence finds expression in the murder of targetable white oppressors rather than the racist cops or businessmen who are responsible for black exploitation. This imaginary provides a palatable form of black-on-white violence, one that does not directly challenge the status quo, even as it provides readers with the pleasures of dismantling white criminal authority.

The pimp novels and black radical fiction written at Holloway House during the mid-to-late 1970s expanded on the narrative forms and literary tropes created by Robert Beck and Donald Goines in a range of ways. Although these books create utopian solutions to black struggles, they nonetheless take a critical stance toward systematic forms of white power and containment. In the novels of Harris, Brooke, and Fletcher, the protagonists sidestep the problems of violence, poverty, police harassment, and riots by literally moving outside such spatial containments. Islands, suburbs, and even rich white communities themselves become utopias for the black heroes of this genre. This reflects a social and political moment in which many avenues toward black liberation had been foreclosed through institutional racism and acts of white violence. The emergence of this new, more fantastical black crime novel represents a significant development of the genre. On the one hand, these novels promise an experience of cathartic victory over individuated white figures of power. At the same time, however, they contain such representations by making the violence "safe" by directing it toward figures that are less politically problematic to scapegoat. In this way, black crime literature of this moment carefully negotiates the tension between a radical dismemberment of white power structures and consumable expressions of problack, antiauthoritarian violence.

"A Fantasyland of Pleasure and Recreation": Joseph Nazel and the Ghettopia in Black Crime Literature

Joseph Nazel was the most prolific and multifaceted representative of black crime literature's utopian turn in the post-Goines era. Nazel is author of countless articles and short stories under a variety of pseudonyms, including Dom Gober, Brother Skip, and Joyce Lezan. He was the former editor of *Players* magazine, the *L.A. Watts Times*, and the *Sentinel*, and he authored over sixty books with Holloway House. As such, Nazel is one of the most productive black American authors in history. At Holloway House, Nazel expanded and diversified the publisher's black experience imprint, publishing a wide variety of narratives, including black detective fiction, pimp action-adventure tales, horror stories, a series about a black investigative reporter, biographies on black historical figures such as Ida B. Wells and Richard Pryor, romance novels, and even a "high-brow" novel titled *Every Goodbye Ain't Gone*, which is a kind of popular version of Ralph Ellison's *Invisible Man*. Following on the heels of Robert Beck and Donald Goines, Nazel transformed black crime fiction by infusing the gritty street sensibility and edgy cultural politics of the genre with utopian solutions and spectacular fantasies of escape from spaces of white containment. Nazel's unique contributions to the black experience genre and to Holloway House's men's magazine, *Players* (the subject of the next chapter), also signaled a new moment in the production of the black crime novel. Unlike Himes, Beck, and Goines before him, Nazel did not have a criminal background; he was a college-educated journalist. Nazel was a part of an emerging contingent of Holloway House writers—Roland Jefferson, Wanda Coleman, Odie Hawkins, and Emory Holmes—who viewed Holloway House as an opportunity to promote black cultural politics through mass-market literature. Although the black experience novel was initially created by affiliates of the criminal underworld as a creative response to white racism and an ineffectual black bourgeoisie, it was appropriated by Nazel and other members of an oppositional coalition of black literary talent. With less direct ties to the criminal underworld, Nazel and others capitalized on the popularity of black crime literature in order to stage a creative critique of white racism and ineffectual black politics. Nazel's two longest-running series, one about a pimp action hero and one about a black detective, dramatize Nazel's ambivalence toward adopting the black crime novel. On the one hand, Nazel's pimp hero novels, known as the Iceman series, reveal his affinity for the pimp as subversive to forms of white economic and social power. On the other hand, Nazel's creation of a black detective hero shows his deep suspicion of illegal methods of resistant to bring large-scale freedom for black people. This ambivalence toward postures of black criminality is an organizing feature of the works of Himes, Beck, and Goines, albeit expressed on lower frequencies. Through Nazel's pimp and detective novels, he created utopias and imagined solutions to manage the contradictions posed by black criminal self-representation.

Nazel's most interesting contribution to the pimp fiction tradition is his seven-novel Iceman series. These books feature the ongoing story of a Manhattan pimp named Henry Highland "the Iceman" West, who hustles his way out of "the darkest jungle in New York, Harlem," in order to become America's most powerful black man.[23] Named after nineteenth-century abolitionist Henry Highland Garnett, the Iceman pimps up enough money by the time he is thirty to create the Oasis, a black-owned version of Las Vegas. As the omniscient narrator states it in the first installment of the series, the Oasis is a distinctly utopian space: "The Oasis, a fantasyland of pleasure and recreation, situated in the burning desert sands fifty miles outside of Las Vegas, Nevada, was a rich man's dream and the Iceman's reality. It was a self-contained city. A city where the international jet set, politicians, stage and screen stars, gangsters who had advanced from striped suits to business suits and industrial tycoons congregated to indulge in whatever pleasures met their fancy."[24] As a fantastical revision of the ghetto space represented in the earlier novels of Beck and Goines, the Oasis is a reflection of the black crime genre's move toward the utopian. The Oasis inverts the containment of the ghetto by granting the powers of surveillance and security to the Iceman himself. With his band of black-belt prostitutes and his supercomputer named Matilda, the Iceman builds a fiefdom geographically and socially separate from the rest of America. As one of Iceman's friends puts it, the Oasis is an alternative space to the ghetto and the consciousness that it produces: "It's a dream that all black men have at one time or the other. It's something beyond what we have known and what we have been conditioned to believe was all that was open to us."[25] Providing a form of wish fulfillment for black populations entrenched in urban ghettos, Nazel's Iceman novels construct an otherworldly escape, the realization of a collective dream to move outside the boundaries of spaces of white containment. In other words, it is the very definition of a ghettopia.

While utopian in nature, Nazel's Iceman novels, like earlier novels of the black crime fiction genre, are grounded in a form of critique of the economic, racial, and cultural exploitation facing African America. The plots of nearly all these novels are virtually the same: the Oasis is threatened by figures of white power—represented variously by the Italian mafia, oil company executives, crooked American politicians, slave-labor lords, and white capitalists—and the Iceman and his stable of sex workers save the Oasis through ritualized violence against these white figures of authority. Importantly, the pleasure of these confrontations comes not only from the physical defeat of white authority but also through the Iceman's verbal besting of his foes. For example, in the second installment in the series, titled *The Golden Shaft*, the Iceman tangles with a white South African slave-labor lord named Robert Martin who tries to muscle the Iceman out of a hidden gold mine on the edge of the his property. The novel's central figuration of white power and economic exploitation of black labor, Martin believes that he will easily be able to bilk the Iceman out of his property: "Blacks are notorious for wanting gaudy things. All we have to do is wave some money in front of his face and tell him how he will be the big man with the ladies and how he can buy a big red car and that will be that. He probably needs the money. They are terrible businesspeople, you know."[26] Echoing the stereotypes that surround black men, particularly black pimps—that they like gaudy things, money, and big cars and that they lack basic business sense—Martin here embodies the white racist attitudes toward black urban subcultures of this period. As a manager of the South African Mining Company, he exploits black laborers at his mine, withholding their pay and physically abusing them in methods entirely sanctioned by South Africa's notorious apartheid, a fully realized version of white containment. Martin is the quintessential white bad guy of black crime literature.

Martin's status as oppressor makes the Iceman's verbal and physical victories over him all the more cathartic and entertaining for black readers. When the Iceman meets Martin for the first time, he thinks,

> He would enjoy putting the bigoted honkie through a few changes before he told him to go to hell. It wasn't often that he had the opportunity to deal with a contemporary slave driver. He had heard about the conditions in South Africa. The horrid conditions that Black Africans, who were the majority, had to live under. It was inconceivable that these Africans who made up two-thirds the population, were forced to live in utter poverty on less than one-tenth of the land. And the reservations that were set aside for Blacks were on very unproductive lands. Yes, he would enjoy toying with the honkie bastard.[27]

Reminiscent of Goines's Kenyatta series—in which an analogy is created between black American populations and African colonies—Nazel's novel highlights that white-controlled spaces are the main issue facing blacks both globally and nationally. The novel literally brings African colonization into the United States, underscoring America's own internal colonization. In this version of the story, however, the black hero triumphs over the embodiment of white power, first through verbal sparring and then through violent action, thereby providing readers with a magical solution to the problems of colonization and ghettoization. When Martin approaches the Iceman at poolside of the Oasis in an attempt to trick him out of his mine, the Iceman exaggerates the stereotypical black identity that Martin expects. Picking up a newspaper and feigning a southern drawl, the Iceman says, "Got's to finish lookin' at these here pictures in this comic section. Sho' wish I could read, so I'd know what they was saying. Know what I mean, boss? Us poor iggnrent

niggers jus' sho' ain't worth a darn sometimes."[28] Parroting the stereotype that black people cannot read, the Iceman uses his linguistic skills
to insult Martin by performing a version of the blackface minstrel. As in
many other black experience novels, linguistic aptitude and theatrical
expressions of black identity are critical to overcoming white foes. Following this moment, and other confrontations like it, and after Martin
murders Iceman's most loyal prostitute, Brenda, the Iceman tracks Martin back to his South African labor camp. Here the Iceman foments a
black uprising among Martin's slaves and buries Martin alive in his own
mineshaft. Unlike Goines's Kenyatta series, which dramatizes a frustrated black revolution at home and abroad, Nazel's novels provide black
readers with pleasurable confrontations with and subversions of white
authority as the Iceman traverses international boundaries to overthrow
white power. In Nazel's imaginary, the pimp is emblem of heroic black
masculinity, capable of dismantling the economic and political structures of racism itself.

Joseph Nazel's much more ambiguous literary project that registers
his ambivalence toward black criminality is his serial about a black
detective named James Rhodes. Written under the pseudonym Dom
Gober, the four novels in the series, *Black Cop* (1974), *Doomsday Squad*
(1975), *Killer Cop* (1975), and *Killing Ground* (1976), follow the cases of
Los Angeles narcotics detective James Rhodes as he does battle with
racist cops and small-town sheriffs, but also black freedom fighters and
political assassins. At one level, Rhodes is a heroic figure capable of dismantling figures of white authority. For example, *Black Cop* opens on
Los Angeles's Central Avenue, with Rhodes and his white racist partner
debating the causes of the ghetto. Looking out at the city before them,
Rhodes sees that Central Avenue is the product of strategies of white
society. The first lines of the novel read, "His eyes were focused on the
derelicts that comprised the foot traffic on Central Avenue on the south-
east end of Los Angeles. He had seen the motley army of cast-offs all
his damn life but somehow he was always bothered by what the white
world had done to so many of his people. He was pissed! His gut churned
as a drunk stumbled and crashed to the filthy, glass-sprinkled sidewalk
under his feet."[29] Reminiscent of the opening of Raymond Chandler's
novel *Farewell, My Lovely*, in which the white detective surveys the very
same streets of Central Avenue, *Black Cop* returns to Los Angeles's Watts
neighborhood to introduce the black detective hero to the audience.
Written over thirty years following Chandler's novel—after Central Avenue had undergone a total racial transformation—the representation of

the street here is distinctly different from Chandler's book. Rather than an encroaching threat, the black neighborhood along Central Avenue for the black detective Rhodes is the unfortunate product of white racism and urban containment. As the image of the drunk crashing to the sidewalk suggests, the white-controlled city itself is a menace to black people who reside there.

While Rhodes is critical of the structural racism that constrains black people in the ghetto, his partner, Turner, is the embodiment of those white racist attitudes that underwrite such structures. When Rhodes voices his compassion for the people of Central Avenue, Turner replies, "They're getting just what they deserve. . . . When are you going to get off that bleeding heart bullshit? Shit, if it was up to me, I'd bust them all down and throw the damn jail away. They're not worth a damn."[30] Here, Turner exemplifies the institutional and ideological modes of white racist power that produce spaces of containment. In Turner's mind, the black ghetto and the prison system are both justifiable forms of control, as black people are criminals to be locked up in prison cells or behind ghetto walls. Just as this argument begins to escalate between Rhodes and Turner, the detectives find themselves in a shootout with some black drug dealers. Even though one of the suspects surrenders, Turner murders the unarmed black man in cold blood. Over the course of the novel, Rhodes learns that Turner's murder of the young man is not just an isolated incident of racism but is emblematic of his larger corruption as an informer for the mob. At the conclusion of the novel, Rhodes and Turner shoot it out on the deck of a freighter carrying illegal shipments of heroin, and Rhodes in the end kills the racist cop: "'You can't kill a nigger unless he's unarmed, can you?' Rhodes moved in on Turner, laying down a steady barrage with the rifle. The night that Turner had killed the unarmed man came back to him. How many more had Turner ripped off and gotten away with? Rhodes was settling the score for them all. 'Can you honkie? Can you honkie?' The hot lead belched from the barrel of the gun and thumped into Turner's already dead body."[31] This moment is distinctly different from the final showdown between the white detective Walker and the black protagonist Jimmy in Chester Himes's *Run Man Run*. Whereas in Himes's narrative the white detective shoots and nearly kills Jimmy before he even has a chance to see his attacker, in Nazel's story, the black detective Rhodes provides black audiences with cathartic entertainment of killing racist figures of authority. In this hyperviolent moment, not only is the white detective killed, but his body is riddled with bullets even after he is dead. Dismantling and desecrating the novel's figure of racist white authority, Rhodes is in the utopian space of this novel "settling the score" for all black people who have themselves been the victims of white racist violence. As in the Iceman novels, the imaginary overthrow of white hegemonic power is represented through a defilement of the white body. In this story, the city itself remains intact, and the imaginary solution is provided through the literal annihilation of a corrupt white authority.

But while Nazel's first Rhodes novel deploys the black detective as an imaginary figure capable of taking down representatives of white power, he also represents Rhodes as a figure who contains black militants. Both *Doomsday Squad* and *Killer Cop* feature narratives about black radical organizations that Rhodes must neutralize in order to restore the social order. Rhodes is initially sympathetic to these organizations, likening their forms of organized violence to the riots of the 1960s. As he says to his new partner at one point in *Doomsday Squad*, "It's only a matter of time before people get pissed enough to do something about the foot that's crunching down on their heads. You remember the riots, Danny. The ones in East L.A. and in Watts. People get mad and then they explode."[32] Like many other novels in the Holloway House line, the riots of 1965 are a significant starting point for the narration of black power, as these are expressions of unorganized violence that might be harnessed for useful political effects. Even as Rhodes displays an understanding of why people join these militant organizations in the face of white containment and violence, and even as he actually considers at various points joining up with these organizations, he ultimately defuses them.

Nazel's novel provides tricky narrative justifications for this seemingly conservative turn. First of all, it turns out in both *Doomsday Squad* and *Killer Cop* that black militants in Nazel's novels are not the product of spontaneous grass-roots militancy but the calculated efforts of white power brokers. The militants who follow the rhetoric of black uprising are not freedom fighters in the tradition of the Panthers; they are represented as pawns of institutional racism. For example, in *Killer Cop*, Nazel lampoons the black militants by showing them to be mindless celebrators of violence without a real political program. At the end of the novel, one representative militant named Burley agitates for the black cause of freedom by misquoting Claude McKay's famous militant poem "If We Must Die." He speaks to his crowd of followers: "'We ain't cowards,' Burley bellowed, mad because he couldn't remember the rest of the poem he had stolen the die boldly line from. 'We're through with rhetoric. We will die boldly in the streets. We will die boldly out there,' he jabbed his finger toward the front of the building, conscious of the dramatic effect. 'Die boldly in the streets killing cops. Breaking honkie heads.'"[33] Of course, McKay's sonnet was written in response to the wave of 1919 race riots in order to protest the ways in which whites attacked blacks who had just begun moving to urban centers en masse. The poem begins,

> If we must die, let it not be like hogs
> Hunted and penned in an inglorious spot,
> While round us bark the mad and hungry dogs,
> Making their mock at our accursed lot.

Characterizing the newly forming black ghetto as an "inglorious spot" where blacks are "penned," the poem then goes on to call for militant and heroic resistant to these forms of white violence. In Nazel's novel, by contrast, armed resistance to white forms of containment and violence is represented as hopelessly misguided, as the novel's radical character encourages rioting in order to boost his own ego. Unlike the Iceman novels, Nazel's detective novels reveal the limits of violent confrontation and criminal posturing as a sustainable approach for combating white racism. Extending a theme initially represented in Goines's Kenyatta novels, the Rhodes detective novels explore the pitfalls of armed resistance and misguided black radicalism.

While black radicalism is represented as naïve and poorly conceived in Nazel's Rhodes novels, the black detective himself is characterized as the heroic, and perhaps even revolutionary, character. As the omniscient narrator states it at the opening of *Killer Cop*, "Drugs sapped the life of black people. A drugged people can in no way be a productive people. A revolutionary people. Maybe, in his own way, he [Rhodes] was one of the leaders of the revolution. Maybe."[34] Resistance to forms of white power and even the possibility black revolution are central concerns of the Nazel novels; however, as this quote indicates, the black detective is characterized as the legitimized figure of defiance to forms of racism and injustice. This is a striking shift in the world of black crime literature, as it displaces the power to subvert white authority onto the character of the black lawman. In doing so, Nazel's black detective novels bring us full circle back to the literature of Himes, who invented the black detective team of Coffin Ed Johnson and Grave Digger Jones. In this version of the story, however, the black narcotics detective is represented as an emblem of social good, as he works to rid the ghetto of the neutralizing effects of the ghetto's drug epidemic. This represents a new direction in the genre, as the black detective is upheld as a legitimate character of potential social change in this utopian world. In refashioning the black experience novel to include the story of a black detective, Nazel registers the limitations of black outlaws to act as agents of true change, and he expresses hope that these oppositional stances of heroic black masculinity might be redeployed as lawful responses to a corrupt social order.

Conclusion

We can therefore understand the expansion of the black crime novel at Holloway House in the 1970s as a complicated development. On the one hand, the utopian novels of Charlie Avery Harris, Amos Brooke, Omar Fletcher, Joseph Nazel, and many others provided black readers with utopian escape and entertainment from the real-world problems of ghettoization, incarceration, and economic exploitation in the postindustrial age. Providing a range of imaginary solutions to systematic modes of white containment that calcified during the 1970s, the black crime novel operated as a flexible form to handle these conditions. On the other hand, black crime novels with happy endings lent themselves to serialization and simplification, and this streamlining of the form played directly into the marketing strategies devised by Holloway House to sell books. Of course, any publisher's goal is to sell as many books as possible, but Holloway House increasingly sacrificed all other literary and political imperatives in order to rationalize the market of black pulp publishing.

In order to appreciate the full extent of this transformation, consider, for example, the case of one of the most prolific and talented members of the original Holloway House set, Odie Hawkins. A former member of the Watts Writers Workshop who grew up in the same neighborhood as Robert Beck, Hawkins published more books with Holloway House than any other author with the exception of Joseph Nazel. Self-described on his website as "the underground master," Hawkins is the author of twenty-four novels, numerous articles, short stories, screenplays, radio programs, and television scripts, and he is the last of the original Holloway House writers still actively publishing today. Like Donald Goines, Robert Beck, and Joseph Nazel, Hawkins employed the Holloway House format to create a distinct fictionalized world, populated with the customary cast of characters found in the black crime novel, including pimps, sex workers, dopefiends, and black revolutionaries, as well as working people and aspiring authors.

Although Hawkins is the author of a broad range of fiction and nonfiction materials, his greatest literary accomplishment is his first novel,

FIGURE 4.2. *Ghetto Sketches* (1972) by Odie Hawkins.

Ghetto Sketches, published in 1972 by Holloway House. Defying many of the literary conventions that had established Holloway House as a publisher of "authentic" black street stories from former pimps and hustlers, *Ghetto Sketches* is an experimental novel written in the present tense. It portrays the overlapping and often competing perspectives of pimps and revolutionaries, as well as a variety of women who sit on the neighborhood stoops and comment on the actions of these characters. Anticipating postmodern literature's lack of a central perspective, *Ghetto Sketches* pushes against the expectations of black mass-market fiction by creating an imaginary universe that continually calls attention to its formal innovations and stylistic trademarks. The opening line of the novel provides an illustration of the novel's stream-of-consciousness aesthetic: "A ramshackle, three-story, rim-shot building, stuffed full of people . . . a ramshackled rim-shot neighborhood, stuffed . . . overlapped with people, uncollected garbage, reeking with swift running Black Earth, Saturday night smells . . . on any Saturday afternoon, in any city in this country, in any of its black ghettos" (ellipses in original).[35] Although starting with the image of the contained black ghetto that is familiar in black crime literature—a derelict building, garbage in the streets, an overcrowded neighborhood—Hawkins's innovative use of language signals that this is anything but a standard representation in the Holloway House line. Deploying a combination of present tense, ellipses, and various images of the street piled on top of one another, Hawkins creates an evocative literary voice that resists the customary depiction of the black neighborhood. Refusing both the autobiographical impulse and the standard depiction of the ghetto, Hawkins's book is avant-garde compared to many of the other works published by Holloway House at the time, as it refuses to be reduced to another pimp and hustler narrative. While books such as Robert Beck's *Pimp* and Donald Goines's *Kenyatta's Last Hit* became the models for other black writers to follow at Holloway House, a text such as Hawkins's *Ghetto Sketches* illustrates the wide range of literary talent of authors who did not neatly fit into the commercial niche created by Holloway House.

As Hawkins continued his writing career at Holloway House throughout the 1970s, the company began placing a higher premium on quick production. As he explained in an interview, "None of my books were ever edited. I wish they had been. *Black Casanova* was an outline. I wrote what I wrote and gave it to Ray Locke [an editor at Holloway House]. I said, 'What do you think of this?' I was willing and ready to flesh it out and make a book out of it. Next thing I know it was in print. Very often I did not receive galleys to correct. At the time, what did it matter? Because

I could correct the galleys, and they could still print the damn thing in a horrible way."[36] As this quote attests, by the time that Holloway House had established itself as the exclusive publisher of this niche of black fiction in the mid-1970s, all pretensions at creating quality literary product were gone. As black crime novels gained popularity throughout the decade, Holloway House found that it could forgo the standard publishing practices of showing authors galleys for approval or even publishing completed works of fiction and still turn a profit. In other words, just as ghettos became calcified spaces of containment throughout the decade, so too did Holloway House emerge as a space of commercial incarceration. The creation of the black novels of this period can be understood as a creative response to both the historical realities of ghettoization and the commercial restrictions of the pulp fiction marketplace.

By way of conclusion, a brief return to Roland Jefferson's *The School on 103rd Street* can help us understand the degree to which such a parallel holds true. Jefferson had originally self-published the novel with the small Vantage Press in 1976 and then republished the novel a few years later as a sensationalized paperback with Holloway House under the title *The Secret below 103rd Street*. Although self-published black crime books have become a driving force of the African American literary market in the past decade—a subject that is discussed in greater detail in chapter 6—in the 1970s, such books were considered insignificant to the larger literary scene. As Jefferson himself explained it in an interview, "When *103rd Street* came out, I couldn't get a major bookstore in Los Angeles to carry it. Their response was, 'We don't carry self-published books.' Then you would send it to major newspapers, and their response was, 'We don't review self-published books.'"[37] Here Jefferson illustrates the dubious position of the popular black writer working with political themes in this literary marketplace. Although similar to political novels such as Sam Greenlee's *The Spook Who Sat by the Door* and John A. Williams's *The Man Who Cried I Am*, Jefferson's novel found a difficult time securing an audience because it was not published by a major imprint.

After a few years, the book was picked up by Holloway House, and its advertisement of the novel reveals its singular approach to pimping black fictions. According to Jefferson, although Morriss was excited about publishing it, he wanted to reshape it in order to downplay its political implications:

> I told them that the book really is political. It is clearly a political book. He [Morriss] said, "We know. It's got that strange title. We

are going to change it so that it will have a more popular appeal." We were talking about where it was going to be advertised. I gave him a list of all of the publications that I knew that were primarily African American political instruments, like *The Black Scholar* and *Freedomways*. There were two or three others. I said, "This is really where you should take the ads out because this is the readership for this book." Well, they really didn't want to do that. I think they took out an ad in *Players*, the black version of *Playboy*. I said, "You really need to send it to a political magazine." So they submitted an ad to *Freedomways*. The ad, instead of addressing the political ramifications, said this was a sexy, sensuous book. They sent that back so fast and said, "Not in this magazine."[38]

As this quote describes it, Holloway House actively resisted advertising Jefferson's book on the basis of its obvious political merit, even going so far as to change the title. Secure in its understanding of what constituted commercial success among black readers, Holloway House attempted to promote Jefferson's novel instead as a "sexy, sensuous book." The spaces of secret confinement that Jefferson represents in his novel—the prison and the ghetto—are themselves reflections of this marketplace of black pulp publishing. Caught between a self-publishing market that remained unrecognized by the majority of the literary world and a publishing house that advertised all its novels as sensationalized black fiction, Jefferson is emblematic of the incarcerated black popular writer of the 1970s who nevertheless attempted to employ the black crime novel to protest these methods of containment.

5 / "For He Who Is": *Players* Magazine and the Reimagining of the American Pimp

In one of the early issues of Holloway House Publishing Company's *Players* magazine—the first commercially successful men's magazine targeted specifically toward African Americans—a reader provides an insightful analysis of the significance of the publication's title: "Players is not a 'demeaning' name for the magazine for it is not really saying that all Black men are pimps and hustlers. To me, it is saying that we all, Black Men and Black Women, are players in our own right. For it is true that we all have roles to play in life. We are all actors. Not just the Black race, but all people on this earth are players."[1] In part, the reader's defense of *Players'* title recalls William Shakespeare's famous lines from *As You Like It*, in which the melancholy Jaques states, "All the world's a stage, / And all the men and women merely players: / They have their exits and their entrances; / And one man in his time plays many parts." While consciously or unconsciously channeling Shakespeare, the reader here also emphasizes the theatrical quality of the black urban identity. Extending the definition of *player* to mean more than simply a pimp or hustler—though still overshadowed by the pimp's preence—the reader emphasizes the idea that the player is essentially an actor who survives the perils of white society by self-consciously playing black urban identity as a role. This expansion of the idea of the player to mean something more universal than "pimp" or "hustler" is emblematic of *Players'* larger contribution to African American cultural production. Although drawing on the representations of the pimp and hustler figures invented in the pages of Robert Beck and Donald Goines, *Players* rearticulated these figures of black cool as legitimate icons of upward mobility in American society. This chapter investigates how the über-utopian space of the men's magazine was utilized to promote the figure of the player as a logical expansion of the protagonists in black crime literature. It examines the diverse ways in which black writers and editors at *Players* transformed the pimp, hustler, and revolutionary into politically charged figures of cosmopolitan black identity.

As we have seen in previous chapters, with the publication of dozens of black novelists by the early-to-mid 1970s, Holloway House gained a significant foothold in the marketplace of black book publishing. Its stories of pimps, hustlers, prisoners, and revolutionaries launched an underground literary renaissance of black literature that was culturally and geographically distinct from mainstream America. Confined to inner-city neighborhoods and prisons across the country, many black readers turned to these black crime narratives of Robert Beck, Donald Goines, Joseph Nazel, Odie Hawkins, and others as a form of entertainment and imaginary escape, thereby constituting a new black urban literary scene. Holloway House and black crime writers formed a troubled coalition to create a new popular genre of black literature, offering a wide range of literary expressions of the black criminal experience from the grittily realistic to the fantastically utopian.

It was at this very same moment in the early 1970s when Holloway House was cornering the market of black mass-market fiction that it also launched *Players*, a men's magazine targeted specifically at African Americans. Originally subtitled "For He Who Is," *Players* was imagined as a cross between *Playboy* and *Ebony*. At first, it contained a hundred pages of fiction and nonfiction, black political and social news, interviews with black celebrities, film and music reviews, advice on grooming and fashion, and nude images of black women. The publication initially sold for one dollar per copy, and it was published at first bimonthly and then monthly between November 1973 and 2000. During its heyday in the mid-1970s, *Players* was printing just under half a million copies of each issue, and it featured one of the most wide-ranging collections of criticism, art, and entertainment found in any American publication. It included the editorial work of poet Wanda Coleman and novelist Joseph Nazel, monthly columns by Stanley Crouch and Julian Bond, nude pictorials of black movie stars Pam Grier and Roz Miles, fiction by Ishmael Reed and Robert Beck, and celebrity interviews with countless black personalities, including Gil Scott Heron, George Foreman, Maya Angelou, Sam Greenlee, Don King, James Baldwin, O. J. Simpson, and Dizzy Gillespie.

Much like the black experience novels that had established Holloway House's niche position in the industry of paperback literature, *Players* provided black readers with recognizable and consumable images of heroic black urban identity. *Players* did this by expanding the existing prototypes of the pimp, hustler, and revolutionary characters invented in the novels of Beck and Goines into the figure of the black player in its pages. While owing something to the street figures created by Beck and Goines, the player of the magazine is imbued with an air of legitimacy and intellectual high-mindedness. This is a figure that achieves mastery over urban spaces not through pimping, drug deals, or violence but rather by employing wit, guile, and style to survive in a racist America. This player is well versed in jazz and literature, is knowledgeable of hip urban styles, and is equally comfortable discussing both popular culture and black radical politics. The magazine helped expand the parameters of African American urban identity in the sphere of the mass-market magazine by promoting the character of the player as an idealized figure of black masculinity in a post–Civil Rights America. However, the development of this figure by writers such as Coleman, Nazel, Crouch, and Holmes was distinctly different from the novelistic representations of this figure by Beck and Goines. These writers did not create out of their prison and street experiences but rather co-opted the representation of the player for their intellectual and political ends. As members of a radicalized black middle class, these authors sought to capitalize on the popular fascination of street characters in order to promote cultural education for the black mass readership through *Players*.

Players was also a new site of struggle between the writer and the machinations of the literary marketplace, as owners, editors, writers, and fans fought over how this emerging figure should be characterized in the pages of the magazine. Like the black experience novels published at Holloway House, *Players* was created in an uneasy alliance between white capital and black talent. It was initially imagined by its first editor, Wanda Coleman, as a politicized popular magazine, but then it was eventually co-opted by the white owners, who wanted to make it into a more baldly commercial instrument. Coleman and other black writers at *Players* paradoxically used the forum of the "girlie" magazine to rewrite the violence against women inherent in the pimp narratives of earlier writers such as Beck. They did so by infusing the images of nude women with black militancy and intellectual high-mindedness that was circulating in popular discourse at the time. However, Morriss and Weinstock eventually put a stop to this by narrowly circumscribing the style and content of the magazine to be tawdry and sensationalist. Ironically, this did not increase the popularity of the magazine among black readers but actually diminished it. By the early 1980s, the magazine had lost the support of national advertisers, half its sales in circulation numbers, and about 20 percent of its original one hundred pages. Although Morriss and Weinstock wrested creative control away from *Players'* black editors in an ostensible attempt to sell more magazines, in effect, they produced another form of symbolic containment of the figure of the player.

As a textual analysis and cultural history of *Players* magazine, this chapter builds on histories of the black press, as well as recent scholarship that has examined the relationship between mass-market magazines and the making of modern masculine identity. As a number of scholars of African American literary history have shown, the African American print media has from its beginning struggled with the dual goals of political relevance and commercial viability. Black magazines, newspapers, and periodicals prior to magazines such as *Jet* and *Ebony* operated largely independently from the forces of consumer capitalism that shaped the white literary marketplace, because they lacked advertising support from national brands as well as access to large distribution networks. For instance, while the dozens of black newspapers invented in the antebellum period provided an important outlet for black political expression, including the first black newspaper, *Freedom's Journal* (started in 1827), these early publications all folded after a few years because of a lack of circulation and sales.[2] Even the most famous abolitionist newspaper of the nineteenth century, Frederick Douglass's *North Star*, found itself fighting a dual battle of trying to abolish slavery and competing with William Garrison's *Liberator* for readership in the emerging marketplace of print culture.[3]

Finding the balance between commercial viability and political efficacy remained a problem for the black press throughout the twentieth century as well. Influential journals of the early twentieth century, such as the National Urban League's *Opportunity*, the Brotherhood of the Sleeping Car Porters' *Messenger*, and the NAACP's *Crisis*, were kept afloat by subsidies from those political organizations. Although the first black magazines such as *Colored American Magazine* and *Crisis* successfully attracted some advertisers, the advertisers were predominantly local and African American. This affirmed W. E. B. Du Bois's observation that the white commercial power structure would not underwrite black dissent, a primary function of the early black press.[4] The most commercially successful black publications of the twentieth century were those that made concessions to mass-market expectations at the expense of a directly political agenda. Black newspapers such as the *Defender* created unprecedented circulation numbers by adopting the "yellow press" model of reporting sensationalized stories of violence, scandal, and sex, a model that had been created by figures such as William Randolph Hearst.[5] In 1945, John Johnson's *Ebony* created a commercial formula that became the model for future black publications, including *Players*. A publication dedicated to "mirror the happier side of Negro life," *Ebony* departed from the rights-based agenda of earlier black publications and emphasized a consumerist ethos, thereby linking black identity to ideologies of purchasing power. By adopting this strategy, *Ebony* attracted the first national advertisers in a black publication on a large scale, thereby demonstrating the viability and sustainability of a black consumer market for the first time in history.[6]

Following this model, *Players* attempted to strike a balance between commercial and political concerns, and it did so by capitalizing on the growing interest in and debate over the figures of the pimp, the hustler, and the revolutionary in black popular culture. *Players* essentially caught the black public's imagination by addressing audiences overlooked by *Playboy*, as well as by the middle-class-oriented *Jet* and *Ebony*. Following *Ebony*, *Players* linked black success to consumerism, but with an important difference. As the first major black serial publication to emerge following the Civil Rights Movement and the collapse of viable black radicalism such as the Black Panthers, *Players* presented the consumption of black urban styles as an imagined solution to the social crises of segregation, postindustrial decline, and ideologies of racial hatred. *Players* incorporated political radicalism and the cult of cool as mutually inclusive markers of black urban identity, emphasizing the personality, style, leisure, and work ethic embodied in the figure of the player.

As the first commercial black magazine to court working-class black urban readers, especially prisoners and military personnel, *Players* represents an unacknowledged link that connects early black publications, such as *Colored American Magazine*, *Crisis*, and especially *Negro Digest* and *Ebony*, to later arbiters of black popular taste, such as *Vibe*, *The Source*, and *F.E.D.S.* As such scholars as Tom Pendergast, Noliwe Rooks, and Elizabeth Fratterigo have recently argued, mass-market magazines such as *Ringwood's Afro-American Journal of Fashion*, *Esquire*, *Ebony*, and *Playboy* are important cultural artifacts because they helped broker the anxious relationship between gender and racial identities and consumer society in the twentieth century.[7] As an extension of the literary genre of black crime literature and a theater where various expressions of black masculine and feminine identity were staged in the post–Civil Rights moment, *Players* represents a significant missing chapter in the history of black cultural production and identity politics in late-twentieth-century America. The player was invented as a strategic expansion of the urban criminal prototypes from the Holloway House corpus. He is politically informed and culturally self-aware but maintains an edge of urban cool outlined in the black experience novel. A history of this magazine helps us expand our understanding of the black crime literature genre by revealing how the player was developed as a character who could successfully negotiate spaces of white containment through a crossover into mainstream society. At least in the utopian fantasy space of the mass-market men's magazine, the player could employ his style, cunning, and knowledge of black culture to overcome the class and racial oppressions he faced.

Players and the Expansion of Black Urban Identity

In the premier issue of *Players*, one of the pictorials presents a spread on "Hustlers' Cars." It features photos of black film star James Cousar posing with two topless women next to a variety of slick cars—including a Mercedes Benz, a Bentley, and a Cadillac—and it emphasizes how a stylish ride is a central part of the ideal hustler's identity. However, as the narrative that attends the photos states, this new kind of "hustler" has not achieved mobility through pimping, drug deals, or other illegal activities. He has become successful by first working late nights at a barbeque joint and then investing in a black advertising and public-relations firm. Advising the reader that the Mercedes is the right type of car for this kind of figure, the attending copy reads, "It's the car for the man who likes to hustle from behind a desk, keeps his shoes tied, and don't want his 'business' in the streets."[8] As in the novels of Robert Beck and Donald Goines, the flashy car is represented here as a central symbol of freedom from containment for the black "hustler." However, the significant difference is that the model hustler is portrayed here as a legitimate businessman, whose work ethic and entrepreneurial savvy has granted him the freedom associated with the car. Moving the hustler from the streets to the boardroom, *Players* in the premier issue expands on the image of the hustler created in the pages of Beck and Goines to be more of a mainstream embodiment of American values. Even while this figure retains the flair and coolness for which the black hustler is known—he wears a red velvet smoking jacket and sips champagne in the photos—his

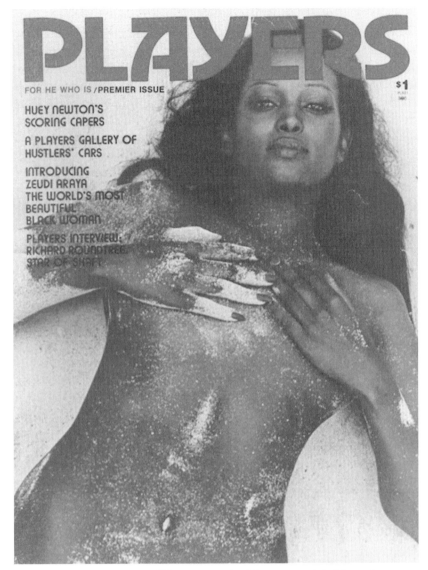

FIGURE 5.1. Premier issue of *Players* magazine hit newsstands in November 1973.

hipness is sanctioned as a logical outgrowth of capitalist production and consumption. This pictorial is emblematic of the range of strategies that *Players* created in its inaugural issues in an attempt to redeploy the figures of the pimp, the hustler, and the black radical as mainstream figures of black cultural identity, all under the larger banner of the black player.

Players essentially broadened the meaning of the terms *pimp, hustler,* and *player* to denote any black person who is able to use guile in order to outwit an exploitative system. Especially in the interviews with black celebrities that grace the pages of each issue, the subject of the interview points out how hustlers, pimps, and players are not just criminals in the street but figures who have been able to survive in white-controlled institutions. Although featuring a wide range of personalities—including black film stars Richard Roundtree, Cambridge Godfrey, and Raymond St. Jacques; authors Sam Greenlee, Gil Scott Heron, and Robert Beck; and musicians Bill Withers, Dizzy Gillespie, and Bobby Womack—many of these interviews illustrate that being a hustler or a player means negotiating the constraints of white society through an ethos of cool. For instance, in Michele Kidd's interview with actor Raymond St. Jacques, there is an exchange that dramatizes this point. Kidd states, "People who survive in the streets—you may call them hustlers or players or whatever, but they've learned to do cool business." In response, St. Jacques replies, "We all have to learn it. Everybody sitting up here in high places—they're all hustlers. The higher you go, the more difficult the hustle. They're all hustlers up here."[9] Expanding the definition of the hustler to mean black actors who have found success in white-operated Hollywood, St. Jacques suggests that hustling is crucial to black achievement and upward mobility. Much like the black figure of the "Hustlers' Cars" pictorial, the hustler is not so much a criminal as he is a savvy survivalist in white America.

Players also expanded the definition of the hustler and player to mean someone well versed in black arts, literature, politics, and music. The magazine constructed an ideal reader who is invested in a range of "high" and "low" black cultural products. For example, in each issue, *Players* features reviews of popular black-themed films such as *Shaft in Africa, Superfly TNT,* and *Blackenstein,* as well as art films such as *Ganja and Hess* and Ralph Bakshi's *Coonskin.* Even more significantly, in its book-review section, *Players* promotes Holloway House authors alongside more overtly political black nonfiction. In *Players'* inaugural issue, for instance, Roosevelt Mallory's Holloway House novel about a black hit man, titled *Harlem Hit,* is reviewed next to James Forman's autobiography about his involvement with the Student Nonviolent Coordinating Committee, titled *The Making of Black Revolutionaries.* In the second issue, Donald Goines's *White Man's Justice, Black Man's Grief* is reviewed right next to Richard Gibson's *African Liberation Movements: Contemporary Struggles against White Minority Rule.* In the space of *Players* magazine, Franz Fanon, Angela Davis, and James Baldwin get the same attention

as Robert Beck, Donald Goines, or any of the other dozen writers working for Holloway House during this moment. Such a strategy illustrates
Players' attempt to constitute its audience as a known quantity. But it is
also an acknowledgment of the flexibility and expansiveness of *Players'*
community of readers. By reviewing the popular fiction of the Holloway
House variety next to the political literature of Fanon and others, *Players*
indicates that the apparent distinctions between "high" and "low" literature and black culture are in fact arbitrary. By placing these authors on the
same page together, *Players* encourages its readers to draw connections
between the pulp representation of the American prison system and the
historical documentation of the colonies of Africa, or the action heroes
of the black hit-man novel and the protagonists of the Civil Right Movement. In other words, these strategic pairings are more than just baldly
commercial strategies to legitimize Holloway House fiction; they also
create explicit symbolic relationships between and among black crime
literature, African and African American history, and the black political
struggles at home and abroad. *Players* extended the strategy of marrying
the popular and the political that is evident in works of Goines, Nazel,
and others, and it thereby solidified Holloway House's unique position in
the marketplace as a promoter of a black cultural aesthetic that tried to
negotiate the tensions between the radical and the trendy.

The editors and writers at *Players* attempted to constitute a politically
minded and socially aware reading audience by utilizing the popular figures of the pimp and the hustler as the critical starting point for creating
an informed black cultural consciousness. This can be seen not only in
the choice of books that the magazine reviews but also in the literature
that the magazine excerpts. *Players* features the original fiction of Robert
Beck, Joseph Nazel, and Odie Hawkins side by side with the reprinted
works of established black authors such as James Baldwin, Chester
Himes, and Ishmael Reed. When reprinting the work of better-known
black figures, the magazine features those selections that are a recognizable reflection of the Holloway House crime literature ethos. Consider,
for instance, that in 1973, both *Players* and its main rival, *Ebony*, each
reprinted selections from Huey Newton's recent autobiography, *Revolutionary Suicide*. Their respective selections highlight the contrasting
strategies each magazine used for reaching an audience. In the May 1973
issue, *Ebony* features the chapter titled "Freedom," in which Newton
tells of his incarceration in Alameda County Jail and the radicalization of his consciousness in solitary confinement. By contrast, *Players*
in its premier issue published Newton's chapter titled "Scoring," which

Players advertises as "Huey Newton's Scoring Capers." In it, he details how he studied the law in order to become a better criminal. Describing his various illegal exploits, including burglary, short change cons, and credit card fraud, Newton's "Scoring" chapter looks a lot like the autobiography of Iceberg Slim and other authors in the Holloway House line. By emphasizing the subversive aspects of criminality embedded in Newton's work, *Players* attempted to distinguish itself from its main competition by focusing on the illicit behaviors that are the starting point leading to a revolutionary consciousness.

Thus, although at first glance *Players* might appear to be simply a "nudie" magazine, the editors and writers at *Players* sought to create a radical and enlightening publication under the guise of a black *Playboy*. A survey of the articles written in the first decade of the magazine's lifetime illustrates a broad range of interests in black arts, culture, social news, and political movements. Some of the important articles on American politics include, but are not limited to, an investigation of the Watergate scandal by humorist Dick Gregory (January 1975), an analysis of black people's freedom at the moment of the bicentennial by *Players* editor Art Aveilhe (July 1976), a retrospective on the Scottsboro Boys trial by Senator Julian Bond (July 1977), and a remembrance of Martin Luther King Jr.'s political legacy by Joseph Nazel (June 1978). *Players* in these early years also promoted knowledge of a variety of black arts and artists, including the black portraiture of Los Angeles artist Walk Walker (February 1975), the modern dance choreography of Eleo Pomare (June 1975), African American graffiti (November 1975), the photography of Harlem Renaissance documenter James Van Der Zee (February 1976), and South African theater (July 1977). Finally, *Players* tried to expand the consciousness of its audience by exploring African America's relationship to larger global issues. The magazine features a number of articles by expatriate Ollie Smith on his experiences in Europe (November 1973, November 1974, December 1975, and April 1977), as well as travel sections on African-diaspora geographies such as the West Indies (January 1974), Haiti (March 1974), and Barbados (July 1974). Taken together, these varied representations of black art, politics, and culture signal an attempt on the part of the black editors and writers of the magazine to utilize the "nudie" magazine to advance an informed black national and international consciousness.

In these first years, through the editorial work of Wanda Coleman, Joseph Nazel, Art Aveilhe, and Yazid Asim-Ali, *Players* tried to strike a balance between the genre expectations of the erotic men's magazine and the imperatives of promoting a black political culture. While as a novelist, Joseph Nazel used the form of black experience fiction to create utopian fantasies of pimp entrepreneurs and invincible black detectives, he used the men's magazine as a forum to air more radical political views. In his introductions to the thematic focus of many issues, Nazel weighs in on politics, black arts, and social movements. He discusses the history of boxing as a source of black pride (September 1975), the legacy of the riots of the 1960s and Civil Rights Movement (November 1975), the scapegoating of the urban poor (February 1976), Martin Luther King Jr.'s murder (April 1976), and even the possibilities of black revolution (June 1976). In Art Aveilhe's premier issue as editor in July 1976, he criticizes America's celebration of its bicentennial by describing how black Americans live as "prisoners of war." He writes, "At present, many of us are actually behind bars, prisoners of war. In fact, some of our finest writers and most gifted artists are in jails. As an editor who receives submissions from prisoners, I can testify to that grim fact. Our prisoners of war are increasing in number. And that is one reason for our belief that Black people have no valid reasons for celebrating this ugly nation's 200th birthday."[10] Echoing Frederick Douglass's famous "What to the Slave Is the Fourth of July" speech, Aveilhe suggests that the American prison system is a modern form of slavery for black Americans. Such a radical focus might seem surprising for a mass-market men's magazine. However, as a brief survey of the letters to the editor reveals, many readers were black prisoners and servicemen, two all-male communities living in strictly regulated institutional spaces. The letters from the prisoners especially express a radical political critical stance toward the justice system. These letters display an informed social consciousness, discussing topics such as the racial oppression of prisoners (December 1976), South African apartheid (May 1977), and the systematic injustice that many prisoners face in the American prison system (May 1978). As many of the readers of *Players* were themselves prisoners, military servicemen, and citizens of America's ghetto spaces, such a political message certainly must have had wide appeal.

Perhaps *Players'* most significant effort to use the magazine as a forum to constitute a culturally aware mass black audience was Stanley Crouch's monthly jazz reviews. Beginning in the fifth issue of the magazine in July 1974 and running regularly for the next two years as the lead feature, "Crouch on Jazz" represents *Players'* most daring strategy at creating an avant-garde black publication. In the first issue that features Crouch's review, he explains exactly why it is so important for him to reclaim jazz music in the pages of *Players*:

As a result of the various sell-outs to fashion, radio play, platform shoes, European rock specialists or to what a blind man named Tom Wolfe calls "funky chic," very few people in the streets have any idea at all what jazz is, almost all thinking now that it is some foul pastiche of spastic rock rhythms, electric gurglings and wah-wah pedals. No good. However, there are certain musicians who will always be about jazz, which is the most advanced art form to ever develop in the western so-called civilization, a form far beyond the most serious probings of the brain being that it deals with recognition, reaction and creation.[11]

Responding to the co-optation of jazz by white audiences in the 1950s and 1960s—consider the white hipster's fascination with bebop or *Playboy*'s incorporation of jazz into its white masculinity ethos—Crouch here sets out to recoup jazz for black audiences. Crouch's reviews, which are actually more like miniessays, cover every important name in the jazz scene, including John Coltrane, Miles Davis, Thelonious Monk, Duke Ellington, and Dizzy Gillespie.

In style and content, Crouch's essays exemplify *Players*' attempt to utilize the mass-market magazine to constitute a readership educated in the history of black musical production. These reviews try to reclaim jazz for black audiences by specifically linking the improvisational genius of the jazzman to the stylistic inventiveness of the "player." Consider, for example, one of Crouch's early essays on jazz improvisation. He writes,

The great jazzman is something else altogether, and what he is exactly has not really been figured out because western academic traditions have no means of truly assessing improvisation, for it has to do with the *mind in action*, decisions being made at velocities that are absolutely terrifying when the clarity of the creations is considered: for the improvising jazzman is maintaining or playing with a tempo, maintaining or playing with key centers and meters, maintaining or playing with harmonic laws all the while expressing himself and listening to (as well as reacting to) the total emotion, thought and musicality of the whole ensemble. But we must realize western white thought is not prepared for these kinds of realizations about the cohesive possibilities of the mind in motion—particularly when the greatest exponents of this mental magic are black people.[12]

Drawing attention to the ways in which the jazz improviser both maintains and plays with tempo, meter, and harmonic laws, Crouch creates here an implicit link between the jazz "player" and the street "player." Both of these figures perform what Crouch calls mental magic by becoming virtuosos of extemporization; while the street player performs this with black urban vernacular, the jazz player performs it with the language of music. Further, Crouch's own prose reflects the improvisational dynamic he describes, repeating "maintaining or playing with" three times, while changing the object to which this repeated refrain refers. Mirroring jazz music's central principle, which is to improvise themes over a repeated chord progression, Crouch's essay celebrates and performs playing as a uniquely black American approach to self-expression.

Players' representation of the player as successful businessman, the player as literary and cultural critic, the player as political radical, and the player as jazz maestro are just a few of the ways in which the magazine attempted to expand the meaning of this figure into a more legitimate character on the American stage. However, even as *Players* constituted a new representation of black masculinity in its pages, it did so through the containment of women as objects of the male gaze in the nude pictorials—a strategy that would, as I have described in the preceding chapters, already have been familiar to readers of black crime fiction. To take but one illustrative example, returning to the "Hustlers' Cars" pictorial that opened this discussion, the two topless women featured in the photographs are pictured as supporting characters subordinate to the successful player. Underneath a photograph of one of the bare-breasted women serving the player champagne and chauffeuring him in his Bentley, the description reads, "He's hired *two* natural beauties to sign his checks, remind him of his important appointments, chauffeur him around and in general, see to it he doesn't die of heart failure before the age of thirty."[13] Mimicking the gender dynamic of Iceberg Slim's *Pimp: The Story of My Life* and other books in the Holloway House line, black women are represented as sexual objects and supporting characters, who are nonetheless critical to the player's status and economic success. At the most basic level, *Players* seems to reproduce uncritically these gender roles through narratives of masculine triumph and objectifications of female sexuality.

However, a careful discussion of the trends of the selection of nude photographs at *Players* is necessary for understanding the complex gender politics at work at the magazine, as the representation of women is not as straightforward as it might seem. The original concept for *Players* was created by poet Wanda Coleman. She had formerly worked as a copyeditor for her father, who had tried to create his own black *Playboy* magazine out of his garage in the late 1950s.[14] Although Coleman was editor of *Players* for only its first six issues, she created the template for presenting black female nudes that was followed by subsequent editors of the magazine. In part, Coleman set out to capture the market of black men who purchased *Playboy*.[15] Although *Playboy* began including the occasional black model in 1963, around the same time it published interviews with Miles Davis, Malcolm X, and Martin Luther King Jr., these representations tended toward the "construction of the exotic as erotic," in the words of *Playboy* scholar Elizabeth Fraterrigo.[16] Coleman's nudes, by contrast, attempt to rewrite these representations of gender and race in a variety of significant ways. For instance, many of the early issues of *Players* feature nude pictorials of black couples posing together, emphasizing the beauty of the black body without completely isolating and objectifying women (July 1974, January 1975). Additionally, many of the first nude sets feature women both topless and sporting the latest urban fashions. The pictorial set of film star Pam Grier in the third issue, for example, features Grier both nude and wearing a variety of outfits created by Hollywood costume designer Ruthie West. This mix of nudity and high fashion is the hallmark of the early *Players* issues, and it is an effort to revise exoticized representations of the black female body by recasting them as emblems of sophisticated urban chic.

Many of the early pictorials also feature components of militancy in the presentation of the black female nude, mirroring the magazine's incorporation of elements of black radicalism and intellectual high-mindedness in its construction of the ideal player. As opposed to *Playboy*'s "girl next door" image, *Players* presents a female counterpart to the male player, well versed in international politics, black nationalism, and high culture. For example, the copy that attends the photos of Pam Grier provides an illustration of the incorporation of these aspects. It reads, "Pam considers herself one of the militants of the black motion pix scene and her current Molotov cocktail is aimed at *Playboy* Magazine who, according to Pam used photos of her in one of their last year's issues without so much as a phone call to the black 'godmother of them all.'"[17] This combination of nudity, fashion, and politics is one of the trademarks of the early pictorials. Here *Players* attempts to capture the *Playboy* market by offering images of black female sexuality together with the language of militancy that would have been familiar to a black audience of this moment. By presenting the consumption of black female nudes as a radical political act, *Players* attempted to use the form of the nudie magazine to capitalize on the rallying cry of the late 1960s, "Black Is Beautiful."

Although there are a number of examples of this strategic combination of radical black style and intellectualism in the nude photos throughout the first few years of the magazine, none is more dramatic than the pictorial for "Gaye" in the May 1975 issue. In the composition and content of the photos, the pictorial tells a story of an emerging black consciousness that echoes the magazine's characterization of the player. The opening photos of Gaye feature her bare breasted, bound in chains, and framed by a Confederate flag. On the next pages, Gaye has broken free from her chains. She is dressed up to look like Angela Davis, and she is reading a copy of the Bill of Rights. The text that attends these photographs reads, "Instead of thumbing through tired catalogues brushing up on the price of platform shoes, and 'living' bras, hip city ladies of the Sassy Seventies, sit back with Rimbaud, Franz Fanon, quotations from Chairman Marcus, and Ralph Ellison, and drop a cool thumbsdown to the jive historic okey-doke their mammas and pappas lived and struggled through."[18] Here the presentation of Gaye as a politicized intellectual reflects the magazine's larger project of using the form of the "girlie" magazine to bring the figure of the player into the mainstream. However, displaying the contradictory impulses that define mass culture, the commercial magazine itself is paradoxically a space where vacuous consumerism in the form of "tired magazines" is rejected in favor of radical black consciousness. Significantly, this is the very issue that a few pages earlier reviews Franz Fanon's manifesto of decolonization, *The Wretched of the Earth*. This pictorial of Gaye draws an explicit connection between erotics and politics by featuring Fanon as one of the authors that Gaye reads. Although this trend of incorporating elements of black radicalism into the pictorials disappeared from the pages of *Players* over the years—a subject to which we will turn in the second section of this chapter—at its beginning, *Players* sought to construct politicized consumer male *and* female players through its interconnected pictorials, books reviews, and articles. Although commodified as a consumable fashion, radical black thought was a key component of *Players'* style and ethos.

Before we turn to a discussion of *Players'* position in the literary marketplace, it is worth noting that, even as *Players* adopted some complex and even subversive strategies of representation, it was, at the end of the day, still a magazine for men. Following the conventions of such a mass-market product, the magazine also promoted an objectification of the female body. We can think about the tension between the representations of race and gender in the magazine as mirroring those in the black experience novels of Robert Beck and others. In the pages of the magazine, black freedom from white constraint depends on the further containment of black women. One representative reader of the magazine writes, "After seeing thousands of *Playboys*, *Quis*, *Penthouse* and others, I take a personal pride and pleasure in exhibiting the pictures of Beautiful Black Women upon the walls and doors of my locker."[19] As this quote suggests, while *Players* provides readers with representations of black identity that defy ideologies of a universal white beauty, it does so by specifically objectifying black women. The women of these photographs are literally put away in the space of the locker, a clear sign of their vulnerability to modes of containment.

However, this is not to say that women are entirely voiceless in this mode of representation. In fact, a survey of the letters from fans in these early years indicates that the audience of *Players* was wide ranging, including many women. The letters from these female readers express a range of opinions on the female nudes, from the complimentary to the critical. While some praise the photography of black women as a historical first (March 1976, September 1976), others complain about the thinness or light-skinned color of the models (January 1976). Some female readers unsurprisingly object to the photographs altogether. As one reader writes, "The nude photos are disgusting, and although I do not deny the audience they must bring you, I feel that they are further oppressive to the black woman. It is just an imitation of one of the many low-life traditions of our oppressors."[20] However, the majority of these women who write in advise that *Players* needs to have an equivalent balance of male nudity. As one representative reader writes, "Now we have *Players* for the brothers but what do you have for us? . . . Besides giving out some wonderful articles let's have some beautiful black men to pin up on Our! wall-lockers, dormrooms and to just look at when We! Pick up your magazine."[21] This quote reflects the sentiments of many of the female readers who write letters to the editor. No doubt responding to the reader quoted earlier, who thanks *Players* for producing pictures for him to put on his locker door, this reader points out that some female readers would like pictures that they can lock away as well. The reader essentially expresses a desire to reverse the gender dynamic that the magazine has set up in its pages. This quote not only reveals a female readership at a magazine targeted to black men but also showcases the way that *Players* had become a significant forum for conversations about the representation of the black body among a variety of black readers. Of course, the representativeness of these letters can be called into question by the fact that they were handpicked by the editorial staff and are not in any way meant as a poll of reader opinion. However, that the editors chose these letters illustrates precisely their desire to show the diversity of voices of people who read the magazine. In this way, these letters operate as textual traces of the discussions concerning radical black politics, gender dynamics, and racial oppression that *Players* attempted to generate.

"The Business of Building Stereotypes": *Players* Magazine and the Literary Marketplace

In the introduction to the June 1975 issue of *Players*, editor Joseph Nazel, discussing the historical legacy of the American minstrel tradition, provides a statement which also encapsulates the racial dynamics at the magazine: "Whites who control images are still about the business of building stereotypes. But there is a viable group of blacks who are about the business of challenging those images."[22] Although Nazel is specifically describing here the relationship between contemporary black comedians and white-controlled culture industries, his remark may also be understood as a larger meditation on the conflict between white and black image makers at *Players*. By this moment, Nazel had already written a number of novels for Holloway House, and he took over the job of lead editor after Wanda Coleman's departure in September 1974. Thus, Nazel was uniquely positioned to comment on the growing conflict between white owners Bentley Morriss and Ralph Weinstock and black writers over the shape and direction of *Players*. For although black creators, such as Wanda Coleman, Stanley Crouch, Emory Holmes, and many others, attempted to use the magazine as a vehicle to expand the black player into a more mainstream figure, the white owners adopted a variety of strategies in order to contain this figure further.

The conflict over the magazine's advertisements is the first significant site for tracking the racial struggles at *Players*. Although adult magazines for black men had been attempted before, such as the short-lived *Duke* (1957), these publications had gone out of business because of a lack of access to national distribution and institutionalized corporate support. *Players* succeeded where others had failed partly because it was able to entice national advertisers with its edgy style that was nevertheless fitted to the mainstream of American society. Initially constituting ten of the original one hundred pages of the magazine, the full-page glossy ads include Benson and Hedges, Kool, and Salem cigarettes; liquor from Old Taylor Whiskey and Jose Cuervo; men's fashions from Eleganza and Flagg Brothers; and black hair-care products Head Start and Afro Sheen.

In both style and content, the advertisements in the first few issues of the magazine are strikingly similar to those found in its main competitors, *Ebony* and *Playboy*. In fact, the advertisements for Flagg Brothers and Eleganza black fashions, Head Start Hair Vitamins, Kool, and Benson and Hedges, are virtually identical in both *Ebony* and *Players*, while those advertising Jose Cuervo, Brass Monkey, and Bell and Howell televisions are exactly the same in both *Playboy* and *Players*. The inclusion of these national advertisements suggests that *Players* initially fashioned itself as a mainstream mass-market product; such a strategy was symptomatic of the magazine's attempt to recast the player as a figuration of legitimized black urban culture and style.

However, as the magazine began to gain popularity in its first year, the owners decided to replace much of *Players'* content with more advertisements. By the magazine's sixth issue, the ads constituted an astonishing thirty pages of the total magazine. As former editor Wanda Coleman remembers the experience, "There were so many ads coming in, it became competitive with the content. So I would make commitments to people. I'd say, 'Your story is going to be in the next issue,' and then it would be cut for ad space. Instead of making the magazine larger, they would cut my content. My content was being pared away."[23] Although Coleman was originally given total creative control over *Players*, as it became a more popular publication, the owners began to execute more power. Cutting content in order to make more room for advertisements, Morriss and Weinstock compromised the artistic integrity of *Players* in order to increase revenue. In the face of these strictures, Coleman left the magazine to pursue her career as a poet, and as a result, the magazine began to change direction. Although Nazel retained many of the stylistic touches and contents that Coleman created, there were a few noticeable transformations. The magazine's "Drum" feature, which reported black political and social news in New York, Washington, D.C., Philadelphia, Miami, and Los Angeles, disappeared following Coleman's departure. The travel sections on postcolonial geographies such as Haiti and Barbados were replaced with features called "Girls of Fiji" and "Jamaica Girls." Although these were small shifts in focus, they are emblematic of *Players'* trajectory of downplaying the political and social aspects of the magazine in order to emphasize a focus on nude pictures. Ironically, however, these changes did not increase interest by advertisers but decreased it. In the face of the widening gap between editorial goals and advertising revenues, the national advertisers started to abandon the publication. By the middle of 1976, *Players* only featured four full-page advertisements.

This is a trend that continued throughout the 1970s and into the 1980s, as *Players* displayed between four and eight full-page national advertisements. Although the "radicalish" quality of *Players* may have initially attracted mainstream advertising, as soon as that focus began to disappear, so too did national support.

Another way that the white owners attempted to control the shape and style of the magazine was to institute a list of rules of what could and could not be published. According to Emory Holmes, who was the assistant editor for *Players* in the mid-1970s and then its primary editor in the early 1980s, Morriss and Weinstock created a very strict set of policies in order to evacuate the more radical aspects of *Players*. As he recounted it in an interview,

> We could never publish any story about blacks in history. In other words, no stories about Dr. W. E. B. Du Bois. No stories about the slave trade. No stories about emancipation. No stories about blacks in history at all.
>
> No stories about blacks in any other country, unless they are American blacks on vacation. In other words, no stories about Jamaica's Trenchtown, or South Africa, or apartheid. No stories about blacks in any kind of trouble in any kind of foreign land, unless it's the girls of South Africa or the titties of South Africa. Then you could write the story, because there's lot of pictures.
>
> No stories relating to black painting and black plastic arts. You can do stories about music, but not about these arts which no one is interested in. Painting, sculpture, and classical jazz. You can do stories about the Boogaloo and the Frug and all that as connected to the pop world. But you could not do any stories that dealt with any kind of high-minded pursuits.
>
> No stories about politics.[24]

As this quote attests, despite the black writers' and editors' attempts to expand the representation of the player into a more legitimate American icon—interested in a variety of black political issues, arts, international affairs, and culture—the owners had very different ideas for the magazine. The cutting-edge content and wide-ranging representations of black culture had vaulted *Players* into a national spotlight; however, it was these very things that became the target of censorship by the owners. This method of representational containment in many ways reflects Holloway House's approach to publishing its black experience novels. By publishing the works of Robert Beck, Donald Goines, and others as "authentic" reflections of the ghetto "jungle," Holloway House could maintain some symbolic control over the representations it was producing. Similarly, by severely curtailing the scope of what could be published in *Players*, the owners could reduce the publication to a black "titty" magazine, thereby containing the figure of the player as a subcultural curiosity of the American scene. The strictness of these rules, in other words, can be understood as an economic and affective response to the black writers' attempts to extend the figure of the player into mainstream society. No longer simply a criminal to be dismissed or imprisoned, the player represented a threat by potentially crossing over into the public sphere, a threat that the white publishers felt the need to contain through elaborate strategies of representational control.

However, the most significant site of struggle at *Players* was the contentious battle between the white owners and the black editors over the selection of the nudes. Following Coleman's departure from the magazine, Weinstock took control of the selection process. Again, according to Holmes, the conflict between him and Weinstock over the choice of photographs became increasingly volatile during Holmes's tenure there. At the core of this conflict was Weinstock's narrow conception of what qualified as beautiful. According to Holmes, he decided to quit the magazine in the mid-1970s after Weinstock called him into his office and told him, "You don't know what a beautiful black woman is. A beautiful black woman has three qualities: she looks like she is eighteen years old, she has European features, and she has big tits."[25] Holmes attempted to extend Coleman's initial vision for the magazine by choosing the most artfully composed black nude sets, including photos that focus on women's faces. By contrast, Weinstock selected the most exoticized and explicitly sexual portraits of black femininity. The vast number of the nude sets chosen by Weinstock feature full-body shots of black women masturbating as well as explicit pictures of what is known in the industry as "pink" (close-ups of the vagina). This trend toward more sexually explicit nudes is one of the defining features of *Players* as it devolved as a quality publication throughout the 1970s. In this way, *Players'* change in composition mirrored national trends in the men's magazine business toward the sexually explicit, as more graphic publications such as *Penthouse* and *Hustler* entered the market during this period.

Unsurprisingly, in the face of such constraints, many of the black writers and editors abandoned *Players* throughout the 1970s, until there was not a single black staff member at the magazine by 1980. Joseph Nazel, Emory Holmes, Julian Bond, Stanley Crouch, and many others all left *Players* between 1975 and 1979. As *Players* hemorrhaged black talent, its style and content also deteriorated. The "Who It Is" section, which provided a forum for the editor to introduce the thematic focus of a particular issue, disappeared by 1978. Articles on black politics, international issues, and the arts, which had been part of the original vision of the magazine, were replaced by football-season previews, personal ads, and increasingly racist and misogynist articles, such as the unfortunately titled "The Black Woman: Why Black Men Hate Her!" (January 1982). By the mid-1980s, the book and jazz reviews had been replaced by reviews and ads for the "nastiest and hottest interracial videos around." Meanwhile, advertisements for nationally recognized brands were traded for advertisements featuring sex toys and such items as the Hot Stud, reputed to be "the world's most exciting vibrator." The materiality of the magazine itself also changed over this period as well. Whereas the magazine had started out with a hundred pages, by the late 1970s, there were only eighty pages. A decade later, *Players* comprised only sixty-eight pages. The slick paper on which the magazine had been printed was replaced by pulp paper in 1981, so that about one-third of the pages were composed of the cheaper material. Paradoxically, even as the owners of the company instituted these changes in an ostensible attempt to increase sales, the very opposite occurred. While at the end of the first year, *Players* published an average of 450,000 copies of each issue, by the end of 1981, the number of copies sold per month had dropped to about 200,000.[26] Some readers began to notice the changes and to criticize *Players*. In one of the representative letters disparaging the new *Players*, one reader writes, "You've taken a damn good idea and managed to mess it up. . . . First off, the gaudy new contents page is garish and unattractive. The older contents page looked better by far. Too, the presence of blemishes on your models marks inferior photography. Your articles are sometimes good, but as suggested by another reader, often blatantly racist. The fiction is shitty—there is no other word for it."[27]

Even as *Players* began its steady decline starting in the early 1980s, there were a few moments when black editors briefly returned the magazine to its former status as a significant publication. When Emory Holmes returned to *Players* in 1982, he did so with the goal of making an appealing magazine for two confined populations: the black American prisoner and the American GI. As the editor of *Players* from 1982 to the middle of 1984, Holmes fought his own form of guerrilla warfare at the magazine, returning to *Players* a focus on black politics, culture, and the arts. Morriss and Weinstock still instituted restrictive rules for what could and could not be published in the magazine. In the face of this, Holmes found creative ways of circumventing these strictures. Taking a cue from Invisible Man's grandfather in Ralph Ellison's novel, Holmes presented an image of compliance in order to transform the magazine from the inside. Little by little, over the course of his two-and-a-half-year tenure as lead editor, he began including more political articles in the magazine, including a piece on prison riots (July 1982), a discussion of the Tuskegee syphilis experiments (August 1983), and a story on black teenage unemployment (October 1983). By small degrees, Holmes over-hauled the style, advertisements, and even content of *Players*, thereby repairing some of the integrity the magazine had in its heyday.

Holmes's most significant achievement in transforming *Players* into a subversive publication was his black history issue, published in February 1984. Although he had begun sneaking articles on black politics and history into earlier issues—such as the Africa issue published in August 1983—the infamous history issue published in February 1984 represents the most politically radical of what *Players* could be within the strictures created by Morriss and Weinstock. With "Collectors Issue" embossed on the cover, this issue features articles on Paul Robeson, slave poet George Mason Horton, black astronaut Guion Bluford, Martin Luther King Jr.'s March on Washington, the return of "Crouch on Jazz," and the legacy of Marxism in Africa. The issue's central pictorial set features actress Lynn Whitfield dressed up as Marie Laveau, Josephine Baker, and Doro-thy Dandridge. It was the most expensive photo shoot commissioned by the magazine, and remarkably, it features no nudity. Attempting to bring the magazine back to its roots of balancing coverage of black politi-cal and cultural issues with images of beautiful black women, Holmes manipulated the institution of the mass-market men's magazine to cre-ate an underground forum for populist expressions of black art. Read-ers seemed to appreciate this change in strategy. In 1984, the year that Holmes published both the history and the political issue, the circula-tion increased to nearly 300,000 copies per month.[28] This suggests that creating a healthy mix of the popular and the political met the needs of a black reading audience more than the owners' strategy of showcasing nude photos at the expense of the content did.

Although Holmes was able to restore a certain amount of artistic and political respectability to *Players* in the early 1980s, following the history issue, the magazine began its slide toward oblivion. Following Holmes's departure in 1984, Nazel returned to the magazine to edit it on and off for the next ten years. Although Nazel introduced new features to the

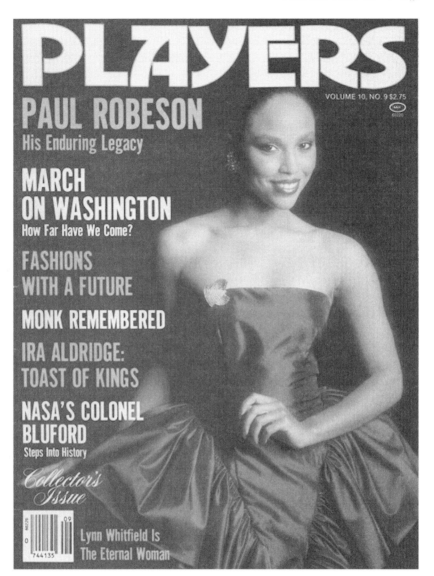

FIGURE 5.2. The infamous "history" issue of *Players* magazine was published in February 1984.

magazine, such as the "Book Bonus" section, *Players* was a shadow of its former self by the time he took over the helm for the last run. By the late 1980s, it had dropped from its original one hundred pages to two-thirds that length, there was not a single national advertisement in the magazine, and *Players* had been overrun by previews and reviews for pornographic videos. Although *Players* had started off using the form of the men's magazine as a forum to promote black arts, culture, and politics, about fifteen years after its inception, it had been reduced to an instrument of white-controlled consumerism.

Conclusion: The Legacy of *Players* and the Contemporary Magazine Market

Players ceased publication in 2000, though Holloway House began publishing a number of more sexually explicit magazines to replace it. In 1997, Holloway House began publishing *Players Nasty* as a substitution for *Players*. In the opening issue of the magazine, editor John Slade announces how this publication will differ from its predecessor:

> Here it is. A stroke book that breaks all the rules. No more photo sets of girls slowly getting undressed in bedrooms only to give you a peek at their pussy and maybe a taste of pink. Nasty is dedicated to all those horny guys who want to see wide open pussy and ass. Dripping wet pussay, greasy buttholes, sweaty faces, and women who like getting down. We promise to publish the best looking flesh, spread wide and blown up to extreme proportions so you can put this mag on the floor and get down to business.[29]

As this editorial suggests, *Players Nasty* is a very different kind of publication from its predecessor. Dropping all pretensions of balancing pictorials of nude women with stories about black arts, politics, and culture, *Players Nasty* represents the ultimate degeneration of the black men's magazine from its original intent. With a focus on the graphic objectification of the female body, specifically a focus on close-up shots of female body parts and orifices, *Players Nasty* is designed to be what Slade calls "a stroke book," or masturbation aid. Although the editorial presents this as a publication that readers have demanded, as the publication history of *Players* suggests, *Players Nasty* represents the logical end point for Holloway House's vision for a black men's magazine. Reduced to their body parts, women are simply objectified for the sake of filling the company's coffers. In this way, the politics and radical representations of the earlier magazine are contained through the exclusive focus on hypersexualized and contained female bodies.

But while Holloway House's *Players Nasty* represents one development of the men's magazine in the modern era, more representative of *Players'* legacy are other publications born out of the hip hop movement.

With the emergence of hip hop as a cultural and economic influence on mainstream America, magazines such as *As Is*, *Don Diva: The Original Street Bible*, *Straight Stuntin Magazine*, *XXL*, and dozens of others have emerged in the past ten years. Featuring a mix of articles, fiction, reviews for urban literature and hip hop music, interviews, and pictorials of black women, these magazines are the more direct descendants of *Players* for the way that they balance the political and erotic elements of the men's magazine. What is most suggestive about these new magazines is that although they feature pictorials of women, none of the women are photographed nude. This is because one of the primary audiences for these magazines is incarcerated black men. What is and is not allowed into prisons has precipitated a transformation in the style and content of popular black men's magazines. As these magazines must make it through the increasingly restricted prison censors, publishers have begun making the photographs of women less graphic. With the American prison population now soaring well over two million people—nearly 40 percent of whom are African American—the American prison system constitutes a coherent literary marketplace. Although black prisoners have always constituted some portion of the audience for the African American men's magazine, these recent shifts in the publication approach toward the less sexually explicit reveal that the prison is now a major marketplace driving the production of such magazines. This acknowledgment of the growing significance of the black prison community among magazine sellers represents just one development of the black literary marketplace. The other, which is the development of the street literature genre, is the subject to which we now turn in the final chapter of this study.

6 / The Women of Street Literature: Contemporary Black Crime Fiction and the Rise of the Self-Publishing Marketplace

In Vickie Stringer's third novel, *Dirty Red* (2006), eighteen-year-old Raven "Red" Gomez uses her charm and sexual magnetism to con various men into giving her gifts of clothes, cars, and cash. Reversing the usual gender dynamics of pimp literature invented by Iceberg Slim, Red uses cunning and deceit to exploit male rivals in an attempt to escape the confines of the Detroit ghetto.

> Even Oprah said it so it had to be true: Detroit was the poorest big city in the country. Littered with abandoned buildings, trashy casinos and with a sky-high unemployment rate, you'd never believe it was once called the "Paris of the Midwest." After the closing of many of the automobile factories that gave Detroit its livelihood and the subsequent rise of drug and gang activity, the gap between the "haves" of the suburbs and the "have nots" of the city was gaping.
> Red despised Detroit and everything in it. In Red's crazy-ass mind, she planned to make the city her bitch and strike it rich by exploiting as many residents as she could reach.[1]

Reflecting the ongoing problem of racial and spatial divides between the suburbs and the inner city in Detroit in twenty-first-century America, *Dirty Red* updates the story of the black criminal in spaces of urban containment for a female audience. As the antihero of the novel, Red adapts the cool poses and manipulative ethos of the pimp to con and steal from men and to achieve financial independence. Once the object of sexual exploitation in the narratives of Iceberg Slim and Donald Goines, the urban female is now the organizing figure of contemporary street literature who uses her sexuality as a form of mobility. Red, like other female protagonists of the genre, gains power by adopting a number of tactics to subvert the aims of would-be pimps, hustlers, and gangsters and reverse the power dynamics in those misogynist relationships. As Red writes in a letter to one of the victims of her deceit, "The pimp game got flipped on your ass."[2]

Like the earlier black experience novels of Donald Goines, *Dirty Red* also self-consciously draws a symbolic parallel between these dramas of the black criminal and the dilemmas of the writer in the black literary marketplace. At one point midway through the novel, Red publishes her ex-boyfriend Bacon's novel titled *Bitch Nigga, Snitch Nigga* while he is still in prison and pockets the twenty-five-thousand-dollar advance and royalties for it best-selling sales. After Bacon is released from prison and learns of Red's betrayal and that the publisher has no record of him as the legitimate author of the manuscript, he goes to the Triple Crown Publications office and burns the company to the ground. As the building is reduced to ashes, a reporter arrives on the scene to interview the owner of the company: "Tears streaming down her face, the owner, Jennifer Nicholas, stood in front of the camera near the rubble. The reporter wondered who would do such a horrible thing to such a fantastic urban publishing house, and why. Ms. Nicholas shook her head. 'I have no idea. If anyone has any information, please call the police department.' Bacon stared at the TV screen, thinking, *They know why*."[3] As in Goines's *Never Die Alone*, Stringer's *Dirty Red* uses the black crime novel as theater to reflect on the racial and gender politics of black popular publishing. In this version of the story, the criminal/author Bacon, perceiving that he has been exploited by the publishing industry, takes his revenge by actually destroying the organization itself. In line with the utopian impulses of the genre, *Dirty Red* on the surface stages a revenge fantasy in which the criminal/writer dismantles the symbols of ideological and economic containment.

But the racial politics of publishing are not so straightforward in this novel. Triple Crown Publications is actually the most successful black-owned independent imprint of street literature today. Furthermore, the publishing company is the creation of *Dirty Red*'s author, Vickie Stringer. Stringer is just one of many entrepreneurial African American writers who has in the past ten years built independent publishing companies supported by the growing popularity of black crime literature.

Thus, we might read here a more complex allegory about the gender and race politics of black publishing than just a revenge fantasy. For in *Dirty Red*, Triple Crown is represented as a "fantastic urban publishing house," as the reporter calls it. Red finds the rules for submitting Bacon's manuscript straightforward, and she is paid promptly upon the book's publication. As a savvy author/publisher, Stringer uses the street literature novel as a platform to promote her company. Bacon is Red's nemesis and the book's central male antagonist, and therefore his destruction of Triple Crown indexes his excessive and illegitimate criminal status. Representing new gender configurations and representations of the publishing world, the rise of contemporary street literature is the most significant transformation of the genre of black crime fiction since Holloway House published *Pimp: The Story of My Life* in 1967. In the literary landscape of black-owned publishing houses and female power brokers, black crime literature and the business of pulp publishing reflect new social, economic, and political realities of the twenty-first century. Further, with the entrance of women into this literary marketplace, the representations of pimps, players, revolutionaries, and writers have been rewritten in order to give voice and agency to female characters.

Over the past dozen years or so, street literature (or hip hop literature, ghetto fiction, or urban literature, as it is also known) has exploded on the American scene as one of the driving forces of the African American literary market. With the publication of such titles as Teri Woods's *True to the Game* (1999), Sister Souljah's *The Coldest Winter Ever* (1999), Vickie Stringer's *Let That Be the Reason* (2001), Shannon Holmes's *B-More Careful* (2001), K'wan Foye's *Gangsta* (2002), Wahida Clark's *Thugs and the Women Who Love Them* (2002), and Nikki Turner's *A Hustler's Wife* (2003), street literature has emerged as the most recent expression of the black crime fiction tradition created by Chester Himes, Robert Beck, and Donald Goines. Broadly defined, street literature can be understood as black-authored crime narratives of pimps, hustlers, drug cartels, and con artists and their struggles with inner-city life and crime. Much like the Holloway House novels that predate these books by a few decades, street literature highlights the stories of black criminals who attempt to escape the ubiquitous spaces of white containment—the ghettos, prisons, and projects that have becoming a defining feature of black urban America.

However, these material forms of white containment have developed somewhat since the years of Himes, Beck, and Goines, and street literature is a cultural form that is alive to the changing character of history. While the ghetto spaces that were created in the postwar decades have remained a defining feature of black American life—and in many ways have experienced greater hardships since the time of Beck and Goines—the systematic imprisonment of black populations has grown astronomically since the 1970s. Over the past three decades, prison populations in the United State have reached epic proportions with the criminalization of drug-related offenses. In 1975, just as the black experience novel was reaching the height of its popularity, there were 360,000 people serving time in American prisons. Currently, there are about 2.3 million people in local, state, and federal prisons.[4] This prison population has been constituted by a disproportionate number of African Americans. Nearly 40 percent of inmates are African American, and African American women represent the fastest-growing incarcerated population in America.

With close to one million black people behind bars, America's correctional facilities have unexpectedly become cultural centers for the creation, distribution, and consumption of street literature. As one of primary producers and consumers of this genre, America's black prison population has become a "captive" audience for the expansion of the street literature market. Many black bookstores that carry large amounts of street literature, such as Black and Nobel books in Philadelphia and Black Star in Harlem, ship to correctional facilities, and on any given day, family members, friends, and partners crowd these stores with lists of books and magazines to purchase and ship to incarcerated loved ones. Understanding street literature's growing popularity as a reflection of the larger influence of prison culture in African American and American life is one of the keys to comprehending the significance of this body of work and this community of readers.

Although both black experience fiction and street literature can be understood as part of the black crime literature genre, there are a number of important qualities that distinguish contemporary street literature from its black experience predecessor. Of greatest significance for the purpose of this study is the fact that many of the most successful street literature authors and publishers are women—including Sister Souljah, Vickie Stringer, Nikki Turner, Teri Woods, Wahida Clark, and Tracy Brown. There are no doubt a number of popular and influential male authors of street literature, including K'wan Foye, Shannon Holmes, and Carl Weber, among others. Steeped in the literary traditions of Robert Beck and Donald Goines but updating black crime literature for a contemporary audience, these male authors deserve more critical attention than space allows for here. In the remainder of this chapter, I hope to outline the revisionist narratives offered by female writers in response to the masculine stories that have traditionally constituted black crime fictions. This female perspective is a significant development, not only for the way that it challenges misogynist gender dynamics of the black crime novel but also for the way that these transformed dynamics have produced a massive female readership and a new literary market. While the Holloway House novels primarily feature the narratives of male pimps, hustlers, and other criminal figures attempting to overcome spaces of white containment—often at the expense of the women who populate the novels—much of the new street literature focuses on stories of madams, female hustlers, and "wifeys." By featuring female criminals as the protagonists, street literature retains the hustler ethos that has defined the black crime literature of Beck and Goines, but female protagonists hijack this masculine power for themselves. In much of female-authored street fiction of the past decade, the women protagonists con, exploit, and outfox their male and female rivals. This new kind of black crime narrative not only rewrites the gender politics of earlier pimp-inspired literature by providing narratives of female struggle and triumph, but it signals the emergence of a new mass-market literary culture in black America.

The creation of this new cultural movement has been underwritten by a number of material changes to the mass-market paperback industry—these factors include the emergence of the self-publishing industry, the rise of the independent book imprint, and the mainstream crossover success of many street literature titles. Holloway House may have invented the niche market of black crime fiction; however, significant changes to the ways that books get published and consumed has democratized the marketplace, allowing new voices into the space of the book industry. For example, a number of successful authors have established their own independent black publishing companies. Vickie Stringer established Triple Crown Publications following the success of her first novel, *Let That Be the Reason*; Carl Weber created Urban Books; and both Teri Woods and Wahida Clark have each created their own successful imprints. These companies publish between one dozen and two dozen titles a year, many of them from first-time authors, and they tend to have loyal fan bases. In addition to these more well-known independent publishers, there are dozens of smaller imprints arriving on the scene every year, each with its own coterie of aspiring black authors. A short list of some of these independent publishers includes Street Knowledge Publishing, Amiaya Entertainment, Flowers in Bloom Publishing, Hard Hustle Publications, Life Changing Books, and Melodrama Publishing.

This new, decentralized African American book-publishing industry has produced about a thousand titles by nearly a hundred authors in just a single decade, creating an unprecedented popular literary culture among black readers.

Street literature has even begun to influence the mainstream publishing industry, as trade presses such as St. Martin's, One World Ballantine, Grand Central Publishing, and Atria have signed the biggest names in street literature to six-figure, multiple-book deals.[5] This is no doubt because these publishers see the high sales of these books at a moment when the book market is shrinking practically everywhere else. In black bookstores in cities all over America—Black Images Book Bazaar in Dallas, Alexander Books in San Francisco, Hue-Man Books in Harlem, Black and Nobel Bookstore in Philadelphia, and Endeavors Bookstore in Baltimore—the owners report that street fiction constitutes a massive portion of their total yearly sales, accounting for upward of 50–70 percent of titles sold.[6] African American street literature now represents a major portion of the black literary marketplace, and it is sold in a wide range of venues, including street-corner tables, in Barnes & Noble, on Amazon.com, and in prison communities across the country. What began as urban subculture at the margins of American society has emerged as one of the driving forces of the book-publishing industry and critical to contemporary debates over the shifting definitions of authorship, literature, and even the book itself. A marketplace where the street-corner book table and the prison have become sites of sustained literary production and consumption, and that involves potentially millions of readers, thousands of books, and hundreds of authors, contemporary black crime literature is a cultural phenomenon that demands our attention if we wish to understand more fully the dynamics between race and popular culture in twenty-first-century America.

While street literature has garnered a loyal constituency of readers, there has been a growing controversy concerning the genre's popularity, its quality, and its social message. Mirroring many of the recent debates in the mainstream literary world that have been precipitated by the economic crisis in the book-publishing industry, critics complain that the popularity of cheaply published street literature has helped contributed to the death of the "literary" author. The most vocal and well-known criticisms of street literature were published by Nick Chiles in his 2006 *New York Times* op-ed piece titled "Their Eyes Were Reading Smut." In it, he argues that the popularity of street literature represents the "sexualization and degradation of black fiction" and that these prurient titles,

FIGURE 6.1. One of the many book tables in New York City that sells the latest street literature titles.

with their "lurid book jackets," have come to take up too much shelf space, effectively eclipsing the higher-quality African American literature of Toni Morrison, Terry McMillan, Edward P. Jones, and Chiles himself.[7]

There are a number of issues that Chiles articulates here worth considering. Chiles's objections to the sexual explicitness of street literature echo much of the "moral outrage" discourse that has surrounded controversial black literature of the past. Although considered literary classics in many circles now, Richard Wright's *Native Son*, Alice Walker's *The Color Purple*, and even Toni Morrison's Pulitzer Prize–winning *Beloved*—a novel that is, we recall, about a mother's murder of her infant child—have all been criticized and even banned for their explicit depictions of violence and sex. The more productive question that we might ask of street literature is, what are the politics and messages of these explicit representations of black sexuality? In the case of female-authored street literature, the protagonist's expression of sexuality illustrates her agency within the very limiting confines of society defined by patriarchal capitalism. Additionally, these representations of women who use their female power to defeat male rivals challenges the representations of hegemonic male authority created in the works of Beck and Goines.

Chiles's objection to the mass-market quality of street literature, the "lurid book jackets" that grace the covers of these books, repeats earlier objections to the literature of Beck and Goines. Moving past these books' covers, we might understand street literature as a complex and multifaceted response to the persistent conditions of racial and gender oppression. Its growing popularity suggests that the carceral conditions that produced it have not subsided since the Civil Rights Movement, the continued gentrification of the American city, or the election of a black president. Additionally, street fiction, like any other genre of popular fiction, is not monolithic but has its pioneering works, its imitators, and its fan favorites. In the world of street literature, dozens of fan websites have been created to rank and debate street literature titles. Internet sites such as The Urban Book Source, Rawsistaz Literary Group, Urban Reviews, and many others have become significant sites where readers of this genre of fiction as a community actively judge these texts and arbitrate their success in the marketplace.[8]

Finally, perhaps the hard and fast division between street literature and canonical African American fiction is not as clear as Chiles makes it. Consider, for example, a moment in the middle of Shannon Holmes's third novel, *Never Go Home Again*. As the novel's protagonist, Corey Dixon, serves his time in prison, he finds that urban literature provides an important starting point for the radicalization of his consciousness:

> He started out reading urban literature: Donald Goines, Iceberg Slim, and Terry McMillan. Soon he advanced beyond reading stories he could relate to; he also enjoyed reading about things and people he was curious about.
>
> He read biographies of civil rights leaders, including Martin Luther King, Jesse Jackson, the reverend Al Sharpton, and Dick Gregory, and about the Black Panther Party. He learned about all the lives that were lost and the sacrifices that were made for his sake. He learned about black culture. The more he read, the more he seemed to hunger for more knowledge.[9]

Echoing many other works of black literature in which literacy is equated with freedom, this moment provides a critical illustration of the value of street fiction and its relationship to black struggles for freedom. Starting with the "classics" of urban literature, Donald Goines and Iceberg Slim,

Dixon then moves on to the literature of McMillan, one of the authors whom Chiles characterizes as a canonical figure of African American literature but who here is characterized as in the same league as Goines and Beck. In Holmes's novel, these mass-market fiction books serve as a gateway for Dixon to historical works on Dick Gregory, Martin Luther King Jr., and the Black Panthers. Such descriptions of the protagonist's pathway from popular black fiction to black political and cultural history are everywhere in the works of street literature. These moments suggests that the boundary separating canonical and noncanonical black literature is not a rigid one and that a wide range of African American literary traditions inform the works of street literature. It also suggests that street literature is a vital tool in the ongoing cultural and political education of black people because it speaks directly to the experiences of its audience, and it inspires a passion for knowledge across a broad spectrum of forms and subjects. This balance of the popular and the political, the radical and the mass market, is one of the features that characterizes street literature and that links it to earlier black publications such as *Players* magazine and black experience fiction.

This final chapter expands on our understanding of street literature by contextualizing its emergence as the extension of a black crime fiction literary tradition created by Robert Beck and Donald Goines, as well as a reflection of a changing literary marketplace. Paying close attention to the literary innovations of key female street fiction writers, particularly Vickie Stringer, Sister Souljah, and Nikki Turner, the first section outlines the genealogy of street literature over the past decade, providing a clearer sense of its social and literary value to audiences unfamiliar with the genre. Much like the novels of Beck, Goines, and others in the Holloway House line, these books engage the persistence of racial and economic injustice in America and promise readers fantasies of temporary escape from these real-world problems through the stories of female criminals. The first section examines the first novels of Stringer, Souljah, and Turner as prime examples of female narratives of the pimp, the revolutionary, and the utopian romance, respectively. The second section focuses on the publishing industry of street fiction, with specific attention paid to the relationship between self-publishing, imprisoned populations, and female authorship. The book concludes with a short discussion of how we might ultimately understand the value of popular black crime fiction given the trajectory of this study.

Pimpadams, Female Hustlers, and Wifeys: Street Literature and the Feminist Rewriting of Black Crime Fiction

Street literature can be understood to have a number of different points of origin. As noted earlier, Sister Souljah's *The Coldest Winter Ever* (1999), Teri Woods's *True to the Game* (1999), and Nikki Turner's *A Hustler's Wife* (2003) are important novels that heralded the arrival of a new brand of female-authored urban literature. And these are just a few of the hundreds of novels published by young black authors in the first few years of street literature's emergence. However, it is Vickie Stringer's 2001 novel *Let That Be the Reason* that is perhaps best representative of a female-authored revision of the pimp tradition of Beck and Goines that I outline in this book. In the acknowledgments section of the original publication of *Let That Be the Reason*, Stringer directly recognizes the influence of Goines on her work, writing, "you set the path for those with a street story to tell."[10] Written in the final months of her incarceration for drug trafficking, Stringer's semiautobiographical first-person novel helped redefine the black crime novel by focusing on the struggles and victories of the female hustler.

Let That Be the Reason follows the story of Pamela Xavier, who graduates from a call girl to a madam (or "pimpadam," as she calls it) to a high-level drug dealer over the course of the novel. Although this story of the journey of the black criminal is similar to the novels of Beck and Goines, Stringer's book transforms the genre by focusing on the female experience in the sex and illegal-drug industries. At the novel's opening, Pamela becomes an escort in order to pay her bills and support her young son. Her first customer is a white man who hires her for a hand job for one hundred and fifty dollars. As she states, "Three minutes of work. I was so ashamed. I felt dirty and so low. I've never had any desire to be touched by a white man, but there I was, touching him, giving him pleasure."[11] Books such as Robert Beck's *Pimp* represent the black woman as a figure all too willing to have sex with white men; such a representation serves as the pimp's justification of his exploitation of her. By contrast, Stringer's book reveals that performing sexual services for a white john is done purely out of economic desperation as a single mother. Especially at the opening of the novel, Pamela documents her shame and anger toward these figures who sexually exploit her. In need of money to care for her son, Pamela submits to the sexual desires of white and black men and women. As she states,

It had my head all messed up. But for my son, I'd do anything—
even turn tricks. I blocked out my feelings and focused on a come-
up to help my son and me. I went on seven more outcalls that day:
a well-to-do businessman, a sixtyish black man in a wheelchair,
another who was blind and only wanted to eat me out, a couple
who wanted me to watch as they had sex, a diabetic with both legs
amputated who asked me to climb into his bed and ride 'im like a
cowgirl and an elderly white man who wanted to be called "massah." I opted to call him "mister," and he just flipped up my skirt
and got on top of me, fucking me, calling me "Kizzy."[12]

Although Pamela is subjected to the sexual desires of a number of people, it is this last customer who provides the most vivid illustration of
the racial violence of the sex industry. By insisting on being addressed as
"massah" (a term which Pamela tactically refuses to employ), the elderly
man is the novel's figuration of abusive white power. "Kizzy," of course,
is the name of the female slave who is raped in Alex Haley's *Roots*, and
the elderly white man's use of this name recalls the history of the sexual
abuses of slavery, in which black women were subject to the rape of their
white masters. Rewriting the black crime novel from the perspective of
women, Stringer's *Let That Be the Reason* shows the persistence of this
racial and sexual oppression. This moment illustrates the importance of
female authorship of African American crime literature for exposing the
violence of the contemporary sex industry and linking this violence to a
long lineage of ideologies that subjugate black women.

However, while using the black crime novel to showcase the female
perspective in the sex industry, Stringer also shows how street success
still depends on a reproduction of the power dynamics at the center of
books such as *Pimp*. In the face of the demands of the escort industry,
Pamela decides to start up her own escort service in order to circumvent
her sexual exploitation. Following the strategy that Iceberg Slim devises
in *Pimp*, Pamela creates an alter ego that she calls Carmen: "From that
day on, I became Carmen, my alter ego, a totally different person from
Pamela. Carmen was strong, emotionless, and untrusting. Pammy, well,
she was the opposite: weak, emotional, and trusting."[13] Adopting a posture of streetwise indifference, Pamela essentially constructs a masculine
pose to perform while transacting her business. Throughout the novel,
Pamela equates her new identity to actually acting like a man. Early in
the novel, when she first picks out her girls for the escort service, she
states, "I scanned the room with the mind and eye of a man."[14] Later in

the novel, when Pamela becomes a large-scale drug dealer, she further enacts this masculine persona: "In the streets, you try to keep everything a secret, but I wanted this man to see that not only was I a woman in a man's role, but I was a human being in this life and just trying to make it. Not really as a baller or a gangsta, but more or less as a businesswoman with big ideas who could be trusted."[15] Much like Beck's *Pimp*, Stringer's novel features a protagonist who adopts an icy masculine persona as a way of surviving the criminal life. A key difference, however, is that Pamela takes on the identity of Carmen, not to be seen as a pimp, baller, or gangster but in order to be viewed simply as *human*. In a world where femininity is contained and exploited by sexual predators, adopting a posture of cool masculinity is one of the few ways to have agency. This illustrates the degree to which participation in the life of street crime is a masculine domain and that these women need to take on a masculine role in order to be part of it.

Also like Iceberg Slim in *Pimp*, Pamela obtains her freedom in these illegal economies through the exploitation of others, particularly women. Thus, while showing the specific struggles of female hustlers in a male-dominated industry, *Let That Be the Reason* also illustrates that female triumph still depends on the further containment of other women in the industry. For example, early in the novel, when one of Pamela's workers, Spice, demands more money for her work, she thinks through the problem much like Iceberg Slim does in *Pimp*. She reasons, "Let's see, she feelin' herself 'cause she's made about two thousand today, and off that two grand, I'm getting eight hundred, and she has a problem. . . . So what are my choices? I can tell her to fuck off, or I can try to silk it, 'cause she makes money for me. Do I want to miss out on my cut of what she makes? No. At this point she's valuable. But this disrespect shit gots to go. So I gotta flip on her."[16] Pamela essentially mimics the strategy invented by Iceberg Slim by verbally muscling Spice into submission. Using *Let That Be the Reason* as a primary example, we can see female-authored street literature of the new millennium as an ambiguous development of the genre. The female hustlers of this new era, without other avenues of freedom available to them and tired of the male oppression that they face on a number of fronts, take on the personae and strategies of entrepreneurial exploitation created by figures such as Slim and Goines. In this new literary landscape, the female hustler is able to escape from the spaces of containment and the forces of gender and racial oppression by adopting and revising the very approaches that have been historically used to subjugate her.

Also like the novels of Beck and Goines, Stringer's book concludes with the protagonist in prison. Pamela starts out the novel with the plan of retiring from the game after earning fifty thousand dollars. However, over the course of the book, she is lured deeper into a life of crime by the promise of Armani suits, flashy cars, and most importantly, a suburban home for her and her son. As she starts stacking large amounts of cash midway through the novel, she thinks, "Nothing on my mind but my son and our new life. Safe in a suburban home, streets lined with mature trees and me getting his school bus at the corner. Dreams can come true."[17] This follows the form of other black crime novels, as *Let That Be the Reason* represents pimping and hustling as potential methods of escape for the female protagonist from economic and spatial forms of containment. Furthermore, it registers the novel's ambivalence toward criminality as a path to freedom, as there is this insistent pull toward middle-class life in the suburbs. Pamela's dreams of a life in the suburbs update the representation of success modeled in the novels of Beck and Goines, though Pamela's dream of escape into the suburbs is explicitly connected to her role as a mother. Like the earlier novels on which *Let That Be the Reason* is based, this dream turns out to be short-lived, as Pamela is eventually arrested and incarcerated for her participation in the drug game. At the conclusion of the novel, as Pamela sits in prison, she witnesses firsthand the consequences of her involvement in the drug business: "I saw the effects of drugs more vividly than I ever had in the streets. I watched women violently sick from heroin withdrawal and go into crack comas and come in with tracks all over their bodies. This was up close and personal. I couldn't believe I had a hand in contributing to this, putting poison in people, my people. I was being educated on a whole new level, a spiritually conscious level."[18] Following the pimp autobiography of such figures as Iceberg Slim and Whoreson Jones, Stringer's novel concludes with the protagonist in prison, coming face-to-face with the inevitable consequences of a life of crime. She progresses from escort worker to pimpadam to a major player in the drug trade. But then Pamela must finally confront the victims of her hustle, the women who suffer from heroin and cocaine withdrawal. Pamela ultimately arrives at the decision to give up pimping and hustling (and then to write her autobiography), and she does so because in prison, she must encounter directly the various women she has exploited. Thus, the popular genre of street fiction, like its predecessor black experience fiction, bears a complex and contentious relationship to issues of freedom and containment, race and gender dynamics, and black radical politics. Freedom for the pimp and hustler can be won, but such freedom is always fleeting, and participation in the life of crime finally leads to a transformed social consciousness. Further, in novels such as *Let That Be the Reason* this transformed social consciousness is shown to be the product of a confrontation with the damage that drugs do to the society of women. Unlike the novels of Beck and Goines, then, which focus on the male individual's struggle and eventual transformation, Stringer's novel emphasizes the female criminal's larger connection to the community of which she is a part.

While the pimpadam story represents one significant strain of the street literature novel, the female-authored radical political novel represents another important development that continues yet another register of the black experience novel. The black political novels of the street literature genre are quite different from, say, Goines's Kenyatta series of the early 1970s. While these earlier novels of Goines feature the black revolutionary as a central hero of the book, street fiction introduces elements of black radical thought through more indirect literary strategies. Such strategies reflect the degree to which overt radical black politics has been neutralized through methods of white containment—including the persistence of large-scale ghettoization and the mass incarceration of black populations. Thus, the strategy of utilizing the street literature novel to convey surreptitiously a subversive political agenda represents a new moment in the development of the genre. Consider, for example, what is perhaps the best known and most influential work of modern street literature, Sister Souljah's 1999 novel *The Coldest Winter Ever*. A self-described "raptivist," Souljah had tried to employ the popular form of hip hop music as an explicit political forum with her 1992 album *360 Degrees of Power*. Unfortunately, the album was a financial and critical failure. Although Souljah achieved some recognition for her 1996 memoir *No Disrespect*, it was not until she published *The Coldest Winter Ever* that she found a literary voice capable of expressing a radical political agenda under the guise of popular fiction. The book was published by the trade press Atria Books, the imprint of Simon and Schuster which eventually also published the later works of Vickie Stringer and Shannon Holmes, and it was reviewed widely in publications such as *Essence*, *Publisher's Weekly*, the *New Yorker*, and the *Source*. *The Coldest Winter Ever* eventually sold over a million copies following its publication, and it inspired countless female authors to publish their own books, including Nikki Turner, one of the most important authors of the genre.[19] A different literary project than Vickie Stringer's *Let That Be the Reason*, *The Coldest Winter Ever* is not an autobiographical recounting of a life of crime. Instead, Souljah invents the first-person story of a female hustler in order to stage a radical black political agenda in a consumable popular form.

The Coldest Winter Ever follows the hustles and eventual incarceration of the self-proclaimed "queen of this ghetto," Winter Santiaga, the privileged daughter of a New York drug lord. In what is perhaps one of the most ingenious literary innovations in the genre of street literature, Souljah writes herself into the novel as Santiaga's nemesis. As Santiaga states it in the first line of the novel, "I never liked Sister Souljah, straight up. She the type of female I'd like to cut in the face with my razor."[20] With this dramatic opening line, we are introduced to Souljah's unexpected strategy for showcasing her political agenda. Souljah the author airs her ideas about black community building, the need for class consciousness, and the dangers of the illegal drug industry, while still containing these messages within Santiaga's story, which serves as the narrative vehicle. Souljah sidesteps the ambiguities associated with being the implied author by writing herself directly and explicitly into the text. For example, early in the novel, Sister Souljah comes on the radio, discussing how drug dealers are destroying the black community. Listening to this message, Santiaga reacts with typical disdain: "I sucked my teeth, rolled my eyes, and sat stiff while Souljah went on to talk about some black struggle. *Humph*, I thought, *if there is some kind of struggle going on, she must be the only one in it. Everybody I know is chilling, just tryna enjoy life.* She, on the other hand, with these Friday and Saturday night comments, busting up the radio hip-hop flavor mix, is the only one who is always uptight."[21] Moments like these, in which Souljah articulates a significant political message, and Santiaga actively rejects it, constitute much of the novel. At various moments, Souljah appears in order to speak about African heritage, the problem of AIDS among African American women, and even black cooperatives, and at every turn, Santiaga dismisses Souljah's messages.

As the novel progresses, Sister Souljah emerges as a more significant figure in the novel. Santiaga even begins living at Souljah's house, and at this point the book becomes an ideological debate between their two ideas about black femininity in a world of injustice and crime. Santiaga hopes to use her wiles, beauty, and charm to ensnare a rap star or drug dealer. When she sees a rap star by the name of GS—who is friends with Souljah—at a party, she thinks, "Some trick in that party was gonna bankroll all of my fantasies one way or another. Just to keep it real, I had my eyes set on GS. I knew that if I could hook him, my problems would be over. Life would be all Range Rovers, rugs, chips, cheddar, and pleasure. He was wasting his time with Souljah. She was no trophy."[22] Santiaga's attitude reflects the attitudes of many of the female hustler protagonists in much of street literature. She is invested in using her style and sexuality to "hook" a masculine figure of economic power. Short of adopting the pimp's masculine ethos, as Stringer's Pamela does, Santiaga's strategy of becoming a "trophy" is one of the few opportunities for advancement available to the female protagonists in these novels. Santiaga's sole desire is to become what she calls a "wifey" and to reap the material benefits that come with this position. By contrast, Sister Souljah consistently articulates an ethos of black community building, especially among women. At one of the most significant moments in the novel, Souljah gives a speech to a group of incarcerated women with AIDS. At its conclusion, she states, "Somewhere along the line, many of us as women are led to believe that being pretty is enough. And while we rely on that, we forget to strengthen our minds so that we can learn how to think, how to build. How to survive. We forget how to live our lives to protect our spirit, to be clean and decent. We forget that everything we do matters so much."[23] Preaching a message of self-education and female solidarity over beauty and individual ambition, Souljah's philosophy is the very antithesis of Santiaga's hustler ethos.

Although as narrator Santiaga is the novel's organizing figure, the structure of the book itself privileges Souljah's perspective by revealing that Santiaga's attempts to maneuver her way to fame and fortune are inadequate strategies for achieving freedom. Every effort that Santiaga makes to con and steal backfires, and at the conclusion of the novel, her face is disfigured from a fight with a street rival, and she languishes in prison with a fifteen-year jail sentence for possession of narcotics. In the final pages of the story, Santiaga is allowed to leave her cell briefly to attend her mother's funeral, where she encounters her sister Porsche, now a successful female hustler in her own right. Santiaga has served the first half of her prison sentence, and she wants to warn her younger sister about a life of crime. The final lines of the novel read,

> She was perfect. Her hair was perfect. Her legs were perfect. Her clothes were perfect. But I wanted to warn her about certain things in life. Usually I'm not at a loss for words. But I didn't feel good enough to tell her what I really thought. I knew what she would think: Winter, you're just saying that 'cause you're in jail. Winter, you're just saying that because you're old. Winter, you're just saying

that because you're ugly. Winter, you're just saying that because you're jealous. So instead of saying what I had learned, what was on the tip of my tongue, I said nothing at all. Hell, I'm not into meddling in other people's business. I definitely don't be making no speeches. Fuck it. She'll learn for herself. That's just the way it is.[24]

This last moment serves as a reflection of the novel's strategy as a whole. Rather than Santiaga's attempting to convince her sister that her attempts of cultivating the perfect individual style are inadequate to the larger social problems of racial and gender inequality, she withholds her social message from her sister. However, her story of her failed attempts to hustle her way into wealth serves as an indirect didactic message to the book's audience. This represents the primary rhetorical strategy of this brand of female street fiction. While it ostensibly showcases the glamour of the hustler lifestyle through the "autobiography" of the criminal protagonist, it finally does so in the service of demystifying it as a pathway to individual or collective black freedom. As a pioneering work in the genre, *The Coldest Winter Ever* illustrates how deconstructing the hustler persona is a necessary first step in the creation of a radical black political ethos. In this way, Beck's *Pimp*, Stringer's *Let That Be the Reason*, and Souljah's *The Coldest Winter Ever* all expose the figures of the hustler and the pimp as unable to combat larger systemic forms of oppression, even as they promote these antiheros. Santiaga's imprisonment at the end of the novel leaves only Souljah as the last viable option for readers looking to identify with a female protagonist or to find a social message. Although Souljah the character does not exactly emerge as *The Coldest Winter Ever*'s hero, her radical political ideology is indirectly endorsed through the novel's containment of the novel's female hustler. Souljah, like Wanda Coleman, Roland Jefferson, and Joseph Nazel before her, capitalized on the popular fascination with the black criminal figure in order to promote an agenda of large-scale black freedom from material and ideological forms of containment.

The third significant development of the black female-authored crime novel is something we might call street romance. Although there are a number of examples of this type of story published in recent years, Nikki Turner's influential and popular *A Hustler's Wife* offers a model of the genre. The story focuses on the romantic relationship between Des, Richmond, Virginia's most powerful crime boss, and Yarni, a fifteen-year-old from the upscale community of Richmond Hills. The story opens *in medias res*, with Des being sentenced to sixty years in prison for a murder he did not commit, while Yarni looks on helplessly from the back of the courtroom. The novel then recounts Yarni and Des's early courtship and Yarni's various romantic relationships with other men while Des is in jail, and it concludes with Yarni and Des getting married after he has served ten years in prison. Although the novel is told in the third person, it focuses primarily on Yarni's perspective and her experiences as a hustler's wife. Like Stringer's novel, *A Hustler's Wife* shifts the focus of the story from the pimp/hustler/player figures to the women who love them. In particular, Turner's book recounts the specific difficulties facing women whose husbands and boyfriends face lengthy prison sentences. For example, when Yarni goes to visit Des in prison, she faces a range of humiliations. When she tries to make it past the check-in, she is subjected to the petty whims of the correctional officers, she is forced to change her jeans (because they are supposedly too tight), and she must submit to a thorough pat-down search. As she is searched for contraband by one of the guards, she thinks, "The things a girl's gotta do to be supportive of her man while he's in prison. I realize, though, that this is the way the system is set up, to discourage us from coming in here to see our loved ones. . . . So me giving into these people would be allowing them to win this political war."[25] *A Hustler's Wife* shifts attention from the perspective of the prisoner to that of the prisoner's partner, and it focuses awareness on the interiority of women who confront institutions of surveillance and containment in ways that are distinctly different from the convict himself. Although Yarni is not herself guilty of any crimes, her association with prisoners makes her vulnerable to bodily inspection and other forms of institutional scrutiny (which are themselves forms of containment). Scenes such as this one—in which women are forced to deal with invasive and systematic forms of inspection while visiting imprisoned partners—proliferate in the street literature novels authored by women. This reflects the degree to which the mass incarceration of black men has become a large-scale crisis in African American communities, a repeated motif in black crime fiction. Turner's novel represents the gendered effects of methods of containment by theatricalizing how the incarceration of black men also adversely affects the society of black women on the outside. By representing such a disciplinary system as a "political war" that must be fought tactically, Turner's novel illustrates how even the most fantastical of street literature novels are nevertheless always grounded in the persistence of institutional racism and oppression.

While Turner's cross-class romance is grounded in this and other crises of modern forms of racial containment, the majority of the story offers readers fantasies of female triumph over such struggles. In this way, Turner's novel expands on the earlier utopian novels of authors such as Joseph Nazel by offering fantasies of female-centered success. For example, much of the novel narrates Yarni's romances with and ultimate outwitting of Des's hustler rivals, Rallo, Bengee, and Rich. While Des is still behind bars, Yarni employs her good looks, charm, and education in order to fleece some of Richmond's biggest hustlers. One of the reasons that these moments are so pleasurable is that they offer detailed descriptions of conspicuous consumption about which readers can fantasize. Through her relationship with these hustlers, Yarni gets vacations to New York and the Caribbean islands, diamond jewelry, helicopter rides, property with which she can start a business, and copious amounts of cash. These successful cons are not represented as betrayals of Des but as Yarni's successful negotiation of her role as a female hustler. These moments are represented as fantastical yet suitable compensations for a protagonist whose boyfriend faces long-term imprisonment.

However, the most gratifying moments of the text are actually those in which Yarni outwits these male figures of power. Although Rallo, Rich, and Bengee all lavish expensive gifts on Yarni, each of them is finally revealed as a figure of abusive and manipulative masculine power. Yarni is kidnapped, sent to prison, and subjected to mental and physical violence by these men, and she gets revenge on each of them through street smarts and cunning. There are a number of these scenes of female triumph and revenge, but perhaps the most cathartic is her besting of Rallo, a Richmond gangster who threatens Yarni with physical violence. When Yarni encounters Rallo in a club late in the novel, she concocts a plan to take apart his glorious hustler image. As Rallo first enters the club, he is the embodiment of the well-dressed player: "Rallo walked up to the table bling-blinging with a nice, expensive Cubian Link necklace and an iced out cross on his chain, a big baguette pinky ring, crème linen suit, some colorful shades of brown, gator shoes and, some Cartier glasses."[26] Pretending to be impressed by this display of wealth and style, Yarni feeds him drink after drink laced with Exlax. Soon, Rallo soils his sharp outfit, which the narrator reports with glee: "He shitted so much, that when he got up, his knees were weak. He reached for some tissue to wipe the sweat dripping from his face only to realize that there was no toilet paper on the roll. He realized that he had shit running down the insides of his legs and all over his brand new Gator shoes. When he walked out of the stall, he immediately headed right back in. 'Oh God, God, Lord Have Mercy!!' He shouted out."[27] This moment significantly rewrites the gender dynamic of earlier black crime fiction novels, such as *Never Die Alone*, in which women are reduced to bodily fluids by male pimps and hustlers. Here, Yarni dismantles the image of the hustler by tricking him into soiling his symbols of affluence with his own excrement. By the end of the scene, Rallo has stained his crème-colored suit and the white leather seats of his car with shit. *A Hustler's Wife* stages scenes such as these to undercut the image of the hustler invented in the works of Beck and Goines by reducing the markers of masculine mobility and wealth to refuse.

A Hustler's Wife can be understood as a novel that fuses elements of the black crime novel with the story of the female romance: gangster meets girl, gangster loses girl, gangster regains girl. At the end of book, through an unlikely series of events, Yarni gets ahold of evidence that implicates a number of city and state officials, judges, and parole officers for a range of crimes, including illegal-drug use, sex with minors, and taking bribes. Using this evidence, she secures Des's release from prison after he has served a decade behind bars. The final chapter concludes with Des and Yarni's wedding atop the Eiffel Tower at the Paris Hotel in Las Vegas: "The ceremony was over right when the New Year, the new millennium, came in. The fireworks began right after Des kissed the bride. The timing was perfect."[28] This "perfect" utopian ending is decidedly different from the conclusion of Goines's *Kenyatta's Last Hit*, which also concludes at the top of a Las Vegas hotel. In this version of the story, the male and female protagonists are able to overcome the various forms of incarceration and containment that they face in order to get married at the end of the novel. Providing a happy ending, *A Hustler's Wife* creates for readers of the genre a fantastical solution to the historical realities of mass incarceration of black populations. As a cross-class romance between a working-class hustler and a middle-class woman, the novel also resolves at the narrative level the ambivalences toward the criminal that has characterized black crime literature. As Turner herself remarked about the novel,

> If you are a true Nikki Turner fan, you'd know that the novel's ending was only a fantasy, my fantasy. It breaks my heart to say that Des didn't come home, but at that time of my life that was the ending I wished for. I absolutely loved that ending, and I know that you did, too. I mean, you tell me what girl who has a man behind bars with a sentence equivalent to football numbers wouldn't? But as you know, in life things don't happen when, where, and how you want them to. I may hold the power in the pen but sometimes no authority in my own reality.[29]

This quote from Turner sums up the social message of her utopian first novel. Although grounded in the realities of an incarcerated black American community, the novel provides a fantastical and cathartic escape from such realities. As Turner says, the novel provides a happy resolution in the space of fiction that cannot be found in the actual terrain of carceral America. This illustrates one of the compelling features of street literature: it stages affordable methods of distraction and escape for female readers who have little access to real methods of transforming the social and political landscape.

The Industry of Street Literature

The same year that Vickie Stringer released her book *Dirty Red*, former Triple Crown Publications author Nikki Turner published her fourth novel, *Riding Dirty on I-95*. The story follows the journey of a female hustler named Mercy, who starts off as a drug runner on the infamous "Cocaine Alley" of Interstate 95 that runs from New York to Miami. About midway though the novel, Mercy gets out of the drug game by teaming up with her friend Tallya to produce Mercy's movie script titled *A Girl's Gotta Do What a Girl's Gotta Do*. Tallya forms her own production company, Bermuda Triangle Productions, in order to produce the film. Even though it is a major success as a straight-to-video DVD, Mercy makes no money from her work. When Mercy realizes that Tallya is the one who is exploiting her, she confronts her former friend. Tallya's reply draws an explicit connection between the pimp game and the publishing industry in this contemporary landscape: "I pays a motherfucker when the fuck I—that's right, when I—get ready. And just for the record, and just so that you know—hoes come and go in this pimp game. So you may be the first to leave, but you won't be the last. What you need to understand is I, Tallya, AKA Bermuda Triangle Productions—that's me, me Natallya—that's right. I own yo shit. I can do whatever I want to do, because your DVD is mine."[30] Repeating and revising the scene from *Let That Be the Reason* in which Carmen bullies her escort worker Spice, Turner's novel represents Tallya, the owner of Bermuda Triangle Productions, as a metaphorical pimp. This moment is a thinly veiled reference to the treatment that Turner herself apparently faced when she published her first novel, *A Hustler's Wife*, with Stringer's Triple Crown imprint. According to The Urban Book Source, one of the premier online resources for the review of street literature, Turner reportedly sold over a hundred thousand copies of her first book with Triple Crown, though she made virtually no money from its sale.[31] Much like Goines in *Never Die Alone*, Turner employs the black crime novel here to indict Stringer's Triple Crown for its exploitation of black writers. Further, it challenges the representation of Triple Crown in the pages of Stringer's *Dirty Red*. But in this updated critique of the industry, the conflict has transformed from the *inter*racial to the *intra*racial. As the emblem of the new street literature industry, Tallya is a figuration of a for-profit culture industry that is no longer exclusively under white control. In this post–Holloway House cultural landscape of self-publishing and independent imprints, the racial and gender politics of black pulp publishing have become more complicated. In an interesting twist on the power dynamics encoded in both pimping and black pulp publishing, female authors-turned-publishing-moguls—fed up with the historically unequal gender relationships in both industries—have adapted elements of street hustling and earlier models of pulp publishing in order to position themselves in places of authority usually held by men.

More than other examples of the street literature genre, *Riding Dirty on I-95* calls attention to some of the complex power dynamics at work in the street literature publishing industry. On the one hand, publishers such as Stringer expanded possibilities in the literary marketplace through self-publishing and the creation of independent black imprints. Her story of self-made success is an inspirational tale told and retold in a variety of mainstream magazine publications. In short, Stringer originally submitted her first novel, *Let That Be the Reason*, to twenty-six publishers following her release from federal prison. After she was rejected by all of them, Stringer borrowed one hundred dollars from each of twenty-five family members and friends in order to print fifteen hundred copies of her book. In only a few weeks, Stringer managed to sell all these books, hustling them at beauty salons, at car washes, and out of the trunk of her car. Based on word-of-mouth success and Stringer's own individual efforts, she went on to print and sell thirty thousand copies of her novel in the next few years. With the money she made from the success of this first novel, Stringer then established Triple Crown Publications. Literary voices, especially female ones that would have never found expression through a company such as Holloway House, were able to reach an audience through houses such as Triple Crown. In the first five years of its life, Triple Crown sold a million books, and it introduced to the world some of the best-selling authors of the street fiction genre, including Deja King, Nikki Turner, K'wan Foye, and many others.[32] Publishing around twenty new books each year, Stringer has established one of the most productive and well-recognized independent publishing houses in the industry.

The company's success also challenged the hegemony of Holloway House as well as mainstream trade presses by illustrating the potentialities of the independent black-owned press. As Stringer herself stated in an interview, Triple Crown offers advances and royalties that are pretty much in line with the practices of the publishing industry more broadly: "I'm committed to our model of signing unknown writers at a lower fee and then helping them move on to bigger publishing houses. My advances range from $5000 to $25,000 and the authors get a 10 percent royalty rate, which is about $1.50 per book. It's easier to work with writers when they're excited and don't have the ego."[33] As Stringer states here, her royalty rate of 10 percent is double the rate traditionally offered by Holloway House, and these numbers are pretty reflective of the practices of the contemporary book market more broadly. Furthermore, Stringer expanded the market of black popular books by enlisting the talents of writers generally overlooked by mainstream publishing houses as well as by the waning Holloway House. Her discovery of K'wan Foye offers as illustrative example. After publishing his first novel, *Gangsta*, in 2002 with Triple Crown, Stringer then helped Foye land a multiple-book contract with St. Martin's Press, staging one of street literature's major coups of the mainstream literary world. However, if Nikki Turner's story serves as any indication of some of the publishing practices at Triple Crown, then perhaps the growth of the independent street literature industry is not entirely free of some of the issues of exploitation that plagued its black experience predecessor. To be clear, the racial and gender dynamics are radically different in this publishing landscape compared to those at Holloway House. It nevertheless also seems true that as an artistic *and* commercial endeavor of black self-representation, black crime literature remains a fraught site where writers, entrepreneurs, prisoners, and many others form troubled alliances in order to produce this new body of fiction. Continuing a tradition started by Goines to use the black crime novel as a symbolic theater to contemplate these relationships, works such as *Dirty Red* and *Riding Dirty* can be interpreted as an ongoing debate about the racial, class, and gender politics of contemporary black pulp publishing.

We can ultimately understand the expansion of the street literature marketplace as a dubious social phenomenon, one that builds on but also transforms the model of publishing created by Holloway House decades earlier. Self-publishing and the emergence of the independent black imprint have indeed provided a forum for new voices, particular female ones, and they have provided publishing opportunities that were denied to earlier writers such as Himes, Beck, and Goines. Furthermore, it seems clear that many contemporary independent black-owned presses pay more in royalties than previous black pulp publishers did, and they provide opportunities for authors to cross over into the mainstream literary world. However, as a capitalist venture that draws on the labor of marginalized writers, many of whom are writing from prison, the industry does have the potential to take advantage of those writers. The case of Teri Woods's rise to fame as a premier author and publisher in the industry of street literature provides perhaps the most instructive example of the problematic relationship between street literature's rise to prominence and the potential problems of using literary labor. Much like Stringer, Woods's story of self-made success is an admirable one. In 1993, Woods began writing *True to the Game*. Although this novel is now considered a classic of the street literature genre alongside *Let That Be the Reason* and *The Coldest Winter Ever*, at the time Woods wrote it, there was no publishing market that would support it. Woods was rejected by twenty publishers before deciding to self-publish the book and sell it out of the trunk of her car, a bona fide method for selling hip hop music in black communities for decades. After selling thousands of copies of her novel on the streets of Harlem, Woods started her own self-publishing imprints, Meow Meow Productions and later Teri Woods Publishing. These imprints are responsible for some of the best-selling books in the street literature genre, including Shannon Holmes's *Be More Careful* and Woods's own *Dutch* series. Even without the help of mainstream distributors, Woods's private publishing enterprise has sold well over a million copies of her various books. On the surface of things, Woods is the very definition of the self-starting paperback hustler, who has adapted successfully the strategies of street hustling for the purpose of selling books. Taken together, Stringer and Woods have recognized and capitalized on the untapped potential of the literary marketplace constituted by America's black population. Further, as self-starting literary artists and publishing moguls, Stringer and Woods have adopted the self-making ethos of both the pimp and the pulp publisher in order to create a new female figure of black entrepreneurialism and hipness.

However, much like the pimps and publishers of Robert Beck's moment, Woods has also been at the center of controversy in the past few years. She has been accused of everything from employing ghostwriters without giving due credit to outright stealing material from published

authors. For instance, although Caleb Alexander is not given credit anywhere for his work, he claims to be the well-regarded author behind Teri
Woods's *Deadly Reigns I, II*, and *III*, as well as *True to the Game II* and
III. Although ghostwriters traditionally do not get credit for their works,
Alexander has apparently also not been properly paid for his labors
either. As he stated it in an interview, "It was about the money. I have my
family to feed and bills to pay. So I continued working with Teri Woods
hoping to get my money."[34] According to this and other interviews with
Alexander, Woods has not only withheld payment from her deserving
authors, but she has also taken undo credit for authoring books that she
did not write.

Perhaps the most dramatic example of this complex dynamic between
independent black publishers and authors is the story of Kwame Teague.
Even though Teague is still serving two consecutive life sentences, he
has penned a number of novels for Teri Woods's imprints, including *The
Glory of Demise* and *The Adventures of Ghetto Sam*, under his own name,
as well as the best-selling *Dutch* series under Woods's name. Like Alexander, even though Teague is considered by fans as the true author of
the *Dutch* series, Woods herself is credited as the author of these books.
According to Teague, Woods's decision to publish the *Dutch* series under
her own name was the result of the lack of commercial success of his first
book: "The Dutch thing was more of a marketing decision. . . . Because
Ghetto Sam [his first book] is a hip-hop book, not a street book and
didn't do too well with the street crowd, although it's a hell of a book.
So I felt if Sam didn't do well and cats saw my name again they'd think
it was another Sam, especially with a name like Dutch. So the decision
was made before World War I (laughs) at the time when we were discussing things a lot, so it was mutual. But the other factors for me was
being incarcerated and the content of the book."[35] As Teague articulates
it here, the publication of the *Dutch* series under Teri Woods's name is
partly a reflection of the demands of the street literature marketplace.
Teague's first novels are decidedly experimental in their language, narrative, and form, and as such, they do not fit neatly into the genre of street
literature. Thus, the *Dutch* series represents Teague's attempt to create
a more standard and commercially successful example of the genre.
However, Woods's ability to keep Teague's authorship a secret because
of his incarceration represents a new moment in the production of
black crime literature. Even as Holloway House paid its literary workers
very little money, the company at least brought recognition and exposure to an underrepresented group of authors. In a literary scene that is

increasingly constituted by an ever-expanding incarcerated population, prison writers have little control over the modes of production of their work. They do not have much access to communication with the outside world, and many states have passed laws that prohibit convict authors from receiving royalties. The physical and social isolation of the American prisoner has thus contributed to the success of street literature, as this is an emerging "captive" population that can be tapped for literary production and consumption of literary commodities.

The final point I wish to make here is not that Vickie Stringer or Teri Woods (or even Bentley Morriss, for that matter) are villainous capitalists who have exploited marginalized literary voices in America. Although many people have testified to this over the course of this book, my purpose here is to highlight that black street literature's creation was also the product of contradictory and conflicting aims. Publishers are in the business of devising strategies for producing and selling as many books as possible. Stringer and Turner expanded the industry of black publishing and the genre of crime fiction by reimagining the strategies of the creation, production, and distribution of crime literature to black communities in the twenty-first century. However, as a genre that has always been sensitive to issues of black freedom, economic, racial, and gender inequality, and the commodification of black culture, black crime literature is a site where the artistic and commercial cross-purposes come into high relief. The testimonies of Teague and Alexander and the fictional representation of black cultural production in Nikki Turner's *Riding Dirty on I-95* and Vickie Stringer's *Dirty Red* testify to the fact that black crime literature remains an important site of struggle over the political, economic, and aesthetic concerns of a ever-diversifying black community.

Conclusion

By way of conclusion, I would like to return to Invisible Man's question that he poses when he encounters the zoot-suit hipsters following the death of Tod Clifton: "who knew but that they were the saviors, the true leaders, the bearers of something precious?"[36] We might think about this question through a brief examination of Kwame Teague's 2003 novella *The Glory of My Demise*. Featuring the interlocking stories of urban hipster Kwame Jamal and a nameless white sociologist who follows him around the ghetto, *The Glory of My Demise* switches back and forth between these competing perspectives. The book presents both the "street" perspective of Jamal and the "official" perspective of the sociolo-gist (which is presented in italics). Late in the novel, while explaining the artistic merits of graffiti to the sociologist, Jamal states, "Why'd I say invisible? I didn't, some cat named Ellison said that shit but I knew what he was talkin' 'bout long 'fore I heard him say it. It's like, yo, you ever notice why brothers always wanna wear big hats and funny suits and drive long pink Cadillacs through the city? The same reason they wear big slave-like gold chains and play they radios in the car full blast. To be *heard*."[37] Taking up the intersecting issues of black urban style, mobility, and linguistic mastery that have been central concerns of this study, Teague's novel provides one potential interpretation of the mean-ing of pimp cool. According to Jamal, pimp accoutrements—the chains, the clothing, the cars—are not merely markers of economic mobility. They are also visual cues that signify a need to be heard within the social order. In a society where black people are made invisible through vari-ous strategies of physical and discursive containment—the ghettoiza-tion and imprisonment of black populations—these markers of hip style operate as tactical responses that give some voice to the voiceless. These supervisible symbols of black fashion display charged defiance against white oppression even as they are not organized or recognized political acts. These styles of black cool are at once an extreme form of individual-ized art, forms of social critique of racial containment, and signs of black solidarity.

So how might we ultimately understand the political, social, and symbolic relevance of the American pimp and the literature he helped inspire? As we have seen, the pimp has been employed by a range of writers, publishers, activists, and artists as a flexible literary figure for a variety of aesthetic, commercial, and political purposes. An ambiguous symbol of mobility, literacy, and economic power in America, the pimp has been simultaneously represented as a working-class folk hero and an oppressor of women, a literary artist of street vernacular and a sellout to mass-market consumerism, a political radical and a ruthless capitalist. As a site of these multiple contradictions, the pimp and the literary tradi-tion which this figure helped foster have given expression to the social realities and collective wishes of a large portion of black America that no other mode of representation could. As Jamal sums it up near the end of the novel,

> So just listen. It's an art form to that. If you listen, you might just hear what a motherfucka sayin' without words. It's all about a

command of words. You can command words whether speakin'
or bein' spoken to, or how we say, bein' spit *at* or spittin' on, i-ight?
That's why Shakespeare get the props he do. Command of words.
But if you think *he* had a command of words, you should see the
average pimp, now *that's* a command of words! Could you imagine
Shakespeare a pimp? "Thy yonder damsel, my money, bet' have . . ."
Wouldn't work. Now when a pimp say it—'Bitch, betta have my
money'—you get attention.[38]

Here, Teague's protagonist returns us to the pimp's primary value as an
innovator of the American language, a central trope in African American crime fiction. Although favorably comparing the pimp to the Great
Bard himself in terms of his "command of words," Jamal also points out
the limits of traditional modes of representation by suggesting that the
pimp has a unique form of artistic self-expression that distinguishes him
from Shakespeare. The pimp, though a politically problematic figure,
has through his radical style and linguistic prowess been the inspiration
for the creation of a singular body of American literature over the past
forty years. Black crime literature has given shape to the social critiques,
collective wishes, and political struggles of much of black urban America. Despite ties to mass-market publishing and figures of the criminal
underworld (or maybe even because of these ties), black crime literature
and the pimp at the center of it provide a distinctive perspective on the
development of twentieth-century America. Inviting us to look at the
American city through a mirror darkly, black crime literature exposes
institutional racism, urban segregation, and the economic disparities
that are defining characteristics of postwar society. Writing from the
perspective of the street, the prison, and other spaces of racial confinement, black crime writers give voice to those who have been silenced by
institutional methods of containment.

In the preceding pages, I have sketched out the cultural and literary
history of black crime literature from the mid-twentieth century to the
present. I have drawn connections between the materiality of spatial/
racial confinement in the United States and the emergence of the popular genre of crime fiction written from the perspective of black criminals.
Further, I have outlined the metaliterary qualities of black crime literature, paying particular attention to the ways in which many of the novels
reflect critically on the position of the black crime writer in the literary
marketplace. Although this particular approach to understanding the
black crime novel is useful for bringing attention to this understudied

body of works, it is by no means exhaustive. Future research on black crime literature could focus on a number of texts and issues not taken up in this study. For instance, there are a number of black crime fiction authors who were contemporaries of Chester Himes who have remained off the radar of most literary and cultural scholars. These include but are not limited to Clarence Cooper, Robert Deane Pharr, Herbert Simmons, Charles Perry, and Nathan Heard. Ranging from standard mass-market genre fiction to radically experimental novels, the works by these authors provide new points of entry into the representations of criminals and the spaces they occupy. While this book focuses on the most well-known works by Robert Beck and Donald Goines, each of these authors published many more novels with Holloway House. For instance, Beck's 1969 first-person novel *Mama Black Widow* (about a gay, cross-dressing black man named Otis Tilson) comes to mind as one of the many significant books in the genre that can extend the understanding of race, gender, sexuality, and space that I outline here. Additionally, Holloway House published hundreds of novels by black authors from the 1960s to the 1990s. Although I draw attention to the most pioneering and representative of the genre, I by no means cover them all. For example, although Holloway House did not publish many books by women or for them, it did release a few in the early 1980s at a moment when the company was attempting to expand its hold on the literary marketplace. These include Janice Peters's *The High Price of Gratitude* (1980), Carol Speed's *Inside Black Hollywood* (1980), Sadie Tillman's *Cadillac Square* (1981), and Rae Shawn Stewart's many books about her struggles with homelessness, drug addiction, and AIDS, including *Treat Them like Animals* (1982), *Dying Is So Easy* (1984), *Gotta Pay to Live* (1985), *Letters from a Little Girl Addict* (1990), and *Beyond the Pits* (1991). With hundreds of paperback originals published over a period of a few decades, the Holloway House corpus remains a rich site for exploration of black-themed literary materials. In particular, an investigation of these female-authored works may complicate the representations of gender oppression in black crime literature that I have outlined here.

Finally, future research of this black crime literature needs to remain attentive to new developments of the genre and the literary marketplace. There are new voices entering this growing literary marketplace each month, and new subgenres of black crime literature appear all the time. Especially as America's black prison population continues to grow, and this population constitutes a significant number of the writers and readers of the genre, we must pay attention to both these material realities of incarceration and the cultural response of literary representation. If we are to understand, and perhaps even to alter, the continued racial, gender, class, and sexual divisions in America, we could do worse than to use black crime literature as a new starting point for this conversation. Contemporary black crime literature expresses the plights of American prisoners, working-class mothers, communities afflicted with AIDS, and unemployed youth, and it therefore remains a significant symbolic theater where the political, social, and artistic concerns of parts of the black community are staged and imaginarily resolved. This book is an attempt to start a conversation about the origins and legacies of black crime literature so that we might more fully comprehend the evolution of the genre in the future to come.

NOTES

Introduction

1. Ralph Ellison, *Invisible Man* (1952; reprint, New York: Vintage, 1995), p. 439.

2. Ibid., p. 440.

3. Ibid., pp. 442–443.

4. Ibid., p. 441.

5. For examples of how this mode of analysis has been employed to contemplate other black literary movements, see Harold Cruse, *The Crisis of the Negro Intellectual: A Historical Analysis of the Failure of Black Leadership* (1967; reprint, New York: Quill, 1984); Nathan Huggins, *Harlem Renaissance* (Oxford: Oxford University Press, 1971); and David Levering Lewis, *When Harlem Was in Vogue* (New York: Oxford University Press, 1979). For a recent analysis of the merits and limits of the prostitution metaphor to describe the complex power struggles at the heart of the Harlem Renaissance, see Marlon Ross, *Manning the Race* (New York: NYU Press, 2004), pp. 257–267.

6. Michel Foucault, "Of Other Spaces," trans. Jay Miskowiec, *Diacritics* 16.1 (Spring 1986): 22–27.

7. Jerry H. Bryant, *Born in a Mighty Bad Land: The Violent Man in African American Folklore and Fiction* (Bloomington: Indiana University Press, 2003); Jonathan Munby, *Under a Bad Sign: Criminal Self-Representation in African American Popular Culture* (Chicago: University of Chicago Press, 2011).

8. In the realm of literary analysis, "vernacular criticism" has become one of the dominant modes of reading African American literature. As Kenneth Warren has argued in his book on Ralph Ellison, citing the work of Horace Porter, Paul Gilroy, Hazel Carby, and Houston Baker, some African American literary critics have emphasized black vernacular culture as the source of artistic and political inspiration in the African American canon-building project. Kenneth Warren, *So Black and Blue: Ralph Ellison and the Occasion of Criticism* (Chicago: University of Chicago Press, 2004), pp. 25–26.

9. Madhu Dubey, *Signs and Cities: Black Literary Postmodernism* (Chicago: University of Chicago Press, 2003); Carlo Rotella, *October Cities: The Redevelopment of Urban Literature* (Berkeley: University of California Press, 1998).

10. Eric Lott, *Love and Theft: Blackface Minstrelsy and the American Working Class* (New York: Oxford University Press, 1995).

11. Twenty years ago, H. Bruce Franklin issued a plea, in the introduction to the expanded version of his important study *Prison Literature in America: The Victim as Criminal and Artist* (New York: Oxford University Press, 1989), that literary scholars study Iceberg Slim, Donald Goines, Nathan Heard, and other black writers of the 1960s and 1970s alongside—not instead of—Frederick Douglass, Harriet Jacobs, Malcolm X, Chester Himes, and the criminal artists in the American literary tradition. Stephen Soitos, *The Blues Detective: A Study of African American Detective Fiction* (Amherst: University of Massachusetts Press, 1996); Erin Smith, *Hard-Boiled: Working-Class Readers and Pulp Magazines* (Philadelphia: Temple University Press, 2000); and Sean McCann, *Gumshoe America: Hard-Boiled Crime Fiction and the Rise and Fall of New Deal Liberalism* (Durham, NC: Duke University Press, 2000).

12. Some of the important scholarship in this category includes Robert Steptoe, *From Behind the Veil: A Study of Afro-American Narrative* (Urbana: University of Illinois Press, 1979); Robert Hemenway, *Zora Neale Hurston: A Literary Biography* (Urbana: University of Illinois Press, 1979); Jean Fagan Yellin, introduction to *Incidents in the Life of a Slave Girl*, by Harriet Jacobs (Cambridge, MA: Harvard University Press, 1987), pp. xiii–xxxv; Hazel Carby, *Reconstructing Womanhood: The Emergence of the Afro-American Woman Novelist* (New York: Oxford University Press, 1987); William Andrews, ed., *African American Autobiography: A Collection of Critical Essays* (Englewood Cliffs, NJ: Prentice Hall, 1993); Lewis, *When Harlem Was in Vogue*; Ross, *Manning the Race*; and Jodi Melamed, "The Killing Joke of Sympathy: Chester Himes's *End of a Primitive* Sounds the Limits of Midcentury Racial Liberalism," *American Literature* 80.4 (2008): 769–797.

13. Langston Hughes, "The Negro Artist and the Racial Mountain," *Nation* 23 June 1926: 692.

14. Richard Wright, "Blueprint for Negro Writing," in *The New Negro: Readings on Race, Representation, and African American Culture, 1892–1938*, ed. Henry Louis Gates Jr. and Gene Andrew Jarrett (Princeton, NJ: Princeton University Press, 2007), pp. 268–272.

15. Ralph Ellison, *Negro Quarterly* Winter–Spring 1943: 301.

16. See, for instance, Janice Radway, *Reading the Romance: Women, Patriarchy, and Popular Literature* (Chapel Hill: University of North Carolina Press, 1984); Tania Modleski, *Loving with a Vengeance: Mass-Produced Fantasies for Women* (London: Methuen, 1984); Michael Denning, *Mechanic Accents: Dime Novels and Working-Class Culture in America* (New York: Verso, 1987); Nancy Armstrong, *Desire and Domestic Fiction: A Political History of the Novel* (New York: Oxford University Press, 1990); Soitos, *The Blues Detective*; Smith, *Hard-Boiled*; and McCann, *Gumshoe America*.

17. Theodor Adorno and Max Horkheimer, *The Dialectic of Enlightenment: Philosophical Fragments*, ed. Gunzelin Schmid Noerr (Stanford, CA: Stanford University Press, 2002). Some of the other significant texts in this tradition of cultural studies are Richard Hoggart, *The Uses of Literacy* (Harmondsworth, UK: Penguin, 1958); Raymond Williams, *Culture and Society: 1780–1950* (Harmondsworth, UK: Penguin,

1960); E. P. Thompson, *The Making of the English Working Class* (Harmondsworth, UK: Penguin, 1968); Stuart Hall and Toni Jefferson, *Resistance through Ritual: Youth Subcultures in Post-war Britain* (1976; reprint, London: Routledge, 1993); and Paul Willis, *Learning to Labour: How Working Class Kids Get Working Class Jobs* (New York: Columbia University Press, 1977).

1 / "He Jerked His Pistol Free and Fired It at the Pavement"

1. W. E. B. Du Bois, *The Souls of Black Folk*, in *Writings: The Suppression of the African Slave-Trade / The Souls of Black Folk / Dusk of Dawn / Essays and Articles* (New York: Library of America), p. 359.

2. Robert Beauregard, *Voices of Decline: The Postwar Fate of U.S. Cities* (Cambridge, UK: Blackwell, 1993).

3. My understanding of the early creation of black ghetto neighborhoods comes from a number of sources: St. Clair Drake and Horace Cayton, *Black Metropolis: A Study of Negro Life in a Northern City* (Chicago: University of Chicago Press, 1945); Allan Spear, *Black Chicago: The Making of a Negro Ghetto, 1890–1920* (Chicago: University of Chicago Press, 1969); Gilbert Osofsky, *Harlem: The Making of a Ghetto: Negro New York, 1890–1930* (1966; reprint, Chicago: Elephant, 1996); Kenneth L. Kusmer, *A Ghetto Takes Shape: Black Cleveland, 1870–1930* (Urbana: University of Illinois Press, 1976); Oliver Zunz, *The Changing Face of Inequality: Urbanization, Industrial Development, and Immigrants in Detroit, 1880–1920* (Chicago: University of Chicago Press, 1982); Joe William Trotter Jr., *Black Milwaukee: The Making of an Industrial Proletariat, 1915–1945* (Urbana: University of Illinois Press, 1985); John F. Bauman, *Public Housing, Race, and Renewal: Urban Planning in Philadelphia, 1920–1974* (Philadelphia: Temple University Press, 1987); Mike Davis, *City of Quartz: Excavating the Future in Los Angeles* (1990; reprint, New York: Vintage, 1992).

4. Robert Caro, *The Power Broker: Robert Moses and the Fall of New York* (New York: Vintage, 1975); Kenneth Jackson, *Crabgrass Frontier: The Suburbanization of the United States* (New York: Oxford University Press, 1985); Thomas Sugrue, *The Origins of the Urban Crisis: Race and Inequality in Postwar Detroit* (Princeton, NJ: Princeton University Press, 1996); Arnold Hirsch, *Making the Second Ghetto: Race and Housing in Chicago, 1940–1960* (Chicago: University of Chicago Press, 1998); John F. Bauman, Roger Biles, and Kristin M. Szylvian, eds., *From Tenements to the Taylor Homes: In Search of an Urban Housing Policy in Twentieth-Century America* (University Park: Pennsylvania State University Press, 2000); Robert O. Self, *American Babylon: Race and the Struggle for Postwar Oakland* (Princeton, NJ: Princeton University Press, 2003); Kevin M. Kruse, *White Flight: Atlanta and the Making of Modern Conservatism* (Princeton, NJ: Princeton University Press, 2005); Josh Sides, *L.A. City Limits: African American Los Angeles from the Great Depression to the Present* (Berkeley: University of California Press, 2006).

5. John Mollenkopf, *The Contested City* (Princeton, NJ: Princeton University Press, 1983), p. 28.

6. Douglas Massey and Nancy A. Denton, *American Apartheid: Segregation and the Making of the Underclass* (Cambridge, MA: Harvard University Press, 1993).

7. I am indebted here to Sean McCann, who has recently argued that hard-boiled detective literature provided a theater where the dilemmas and contradictions of New Deal liberalism could be staged. McCann, *Gumshoe America*.

8. The people who have contributed to the critical assessment of Himes's literature in recent years are too numerous to list. Some of the best early essays and reviews on Himes are collected in James Silet, ed., *The Critical Response to Chester Himes* (Westport, CT: Greenwood, 1999). Other important contributors to scholarship on Himes include Stephen Milliken, *Chester Himes: A Critical Appraisal* (Columbia: University of Missouri Press, 1976); Franklin, *Prison Literature in America*; Robert Skinner, *Two Guns from Harlem: The Detective Fiction of Chester Himes* (Bowling Green, OH: Bowling Green State University Popular Press, 1989); Soitos, *The Blues Detective*; Edward Margolies and Michael Fabre, *The Several Lives of Chester Himes* (Jackson: University Press of Mississippi, 1997); James Sallis, *Chester Himes: A Life* (New York: Walker, 2000); Megan E. Abbott, *The Street Was Mine: White Masculinity in Hard-Boiled Fiction and Film Noir* (New York: Palgrave Macmillan, 2002).

9. Chester Himes, "To What Red Hell" (1934), in *The Collected Stories of Chester Himes* (New York: Thunder's Mouth, 1990), pp. 280–289.

10. There are a few critics who do discuss *Run Man Run*. See, for instance, Soitos, *The Blues Detective*, pp. 164–167; Megan E. Abbott, "The Strict Domain of Whitey: Chester Himes's Coup," in *The Street Was Mine*, pp. 155–159; and Alice Mikal Craven, "A Victim in Need Is a Victim in Deed: The Ritual Consumer and Self-Fashioning in Himes's *Run Man Run*," in *Questions of Identity in Detective Fiction*, ed. Linda Martz and Anita Higgie (Newcastle, UK: Cambridge Scholars, 2007), pp. 37–55.

11. Michael Denning, "Topographies of Violence: Chester Himes's Harlem Domestic Novels," in Silet, *The Critical Response to Chester Himes*, p. 165.

12. William F. Nolan, *The Black Mask Boys: Masters in the Hard-Boiled School of Detective Fiction* (New York: Morrow, 1985), p. 13.

13. See Frankie Bailey, *Out of the Woodpile: Black Characters in Crime and Detective Fiction* (Westport, CT: Greenwood Pandarus, 1991); Dana Nelson, *The Word in Black and White: Reading "Race" in American Literature, 1638–1867* (New York: Oxford University Press, 1992); Eric Sundquist, *To Wake the Nations: Race and the Making of American Literature* (Cambridge, MA: Belknap, 1993); Smith, *Hard-Boiled*; McCann, *Gumshoe America*; Gerald Kennedy and Liliane Weissberg, eds., *Romancing the Shadow: Poe and Race* (New York: Oxford University Press, 2001); Abbott, *The Street Was Mine*; and Stanley Orr, *Darkly Perfect World: Colonial Adventure, Postmodernism, and American Noir* (Columbus: Ohio State University Press, 2010).

14. Raymond Chandler, "Noon Street Nemesis," in *Raymond Chandler: Collected Stories* (New York: Everyman's Library, 2002), pp. 431–432.

15. Harold Hersey, *Pulpwood Editor: The Fabulous World of Thriller Magazines Revealed by a Veteran Editor and Publisher* (New York: Stokes, 1937), pp. 8–9; Tony Goodstone, introduction to *The Pulps: Fifty Years of American Pop Culture*, ed. Tony Goodstone (New York: Chelsea House, 1970), p. xii; Michael Denning, *Mechanic Accents: Dime Novels and Working-Class Culture in America* (1987; reprint, London: Verso, 1998), pp. 45, 210; and Smith, *Hard-Boiled*, pp. 23–32.

16. Ron Goulart, *Cheap Thrills: An Informal History of Pulp Magazines* (New Rochelle, NY: Arlington House, 1972), p. 115.

17. Smith, *Hard-Boiled*, p. 32.

18. This territory has been well covered by Stephen Knight, *Form and Ideology in Crime Fiction* (Bloomington: Indiana University Press, 1980), p. 155; William Marling, *Raymond Chandler* (Boston: Twayne, 1986), p. 98; Bailey, *Out of the Woodpile*, pp.

47–48; McCann, *Gumshoe America*, pp. 160–163; and Abbott, *The Street Was Mine*, pp. 108–110.

19. Morrison is just one of the many important figures who helped establish the critical study of whiteness. See also David Roediger, *The Wages of Whiteness: Race and the Making of the American Working Class* (London: Verso, 1991); Shelley Fisher Fishkin, *Was Huck Black? Mark Twain and African-American Voices* (New York: Oxford University Press, 1994); Eric Lott, *Love and Theft: Blackface Minstrelsy and the American Working Class* (New York: Oxford University Press, 1995); Kenneth Warren, *Black and White Strangers: Race and American Literary Realism* (Chicago: University of Chicago Press, 1995); Richard Dyer, *White* (New York: Routledge, 1997).

20. Toni Morrison, *Playing in the Dark: Whiteness and the Literary Imagination* (Cambridge, MA: Harvard University Press, 1993), pp. 32–33.

21. Raymond Chandler, "The Simple Art of Murder: An Essay," in *The Simple Art of Murder* (New York: Vintage, 1988), p. 18.

22. Eric Lott makes a similar point about the film version of *Farewell, My Lovely*, titled *Murder, My Sweet*. Eric Lott, "The Whiteness of Film Noir," in *National Imaginaries, American Identities*, ed. Larry J. Reynolds and Gordon Hutner (Princeton, NJ: Princeton University Press, 2000), pp. 159–181.

23. Raymond Chandler, *Farewell, My Lovely* (1940; reprint, New York: Vintage, 1992), p. 5.

24. Davis, *City of Quartz*, p. 161.

25. Chandler, *Farewell, My Lovely*, p. 3.

26. Ibid., p. 6.

27. Ibid., pp. 4–5.

28. Ibid., p. 7.

29. Ibid., p. 15.

30. Himes, "To What Red Hell," p. 281.

31. Ibid., p. 284.

32. Himes's motivation for creating the figure of the runner is in part a reflection of his own relationship to a life of crime. In 1928, Himes had been sentenced to twenty to twenty-five years of hard labor for armed robbery after he tried to sell a four-carat diamond ring to a Chicago pawnshop dealer named Jew Sam. As Himes remembers it in his autobiography, "Sam said give him a few minutes to examine it and took it into the back room. I suspected he was calling the police. I should have let him keep the ring and escape. But I couldn't run; I never could run. I have always been afraid that that one mental block is going to get me killed." Chester Himes, *The Quality of Hurt* (New York: Thunder's Mouth, 1971), p. 56.

33. Abbott too notes that Himes was aware of Chandler's text, though she argues that Himes's creative revision of *Farewell, My Lovely* takes place in Himes's *The Real Cool Killers*. Abbott, *The Street Was Mine*, p. 168.

34. John A. Williams, "My Man Himes: An Interview with Chester Himes," in *Conversations with Chester Himes*, ed. Michel Fabre and Robert E. Skinner (Jackson: University Press of Mississippi, 1995), p. 55.

35. This statement is also a reflection of Himes's own vulnerable position within Los Angeles's racially segregated labor market. Although Himes only lived in Los Angeles between 1941 and 1944, the racism, urban segregation, and grueling labor conditions he experienced there caused him to reflect in his autobiography, "Los

Angeles hurt me racially as much as any city I have ever known—much more than any city I remember from the South. It was the lying hypocrisy that hurt me. Black people were treated much the same as they were in an industrial city of the South. They were Jim-Crowed in housing, in employment, in public accommodations, such as hotels and restaurants." Himes, *The Quality of Hurt*, p. 73.

36. Chester Himes, *Run Man Run* (1959; reprint, New York: Carroll and Graf, 1995), p. 7.

37. Ibid., p. 9.

38. Ibid., p. 13.

39. Ibid., p. 15.

40. Ibid., p. 17.

41. Himes famously drew on the existentialist philosophy of Sartre and Camus as a means of articulating black subjectivity in the modern world. At the opening of his second autobiography, *My Life of Absurdity*, Himes writes, "Albert Camus once said that racism is absurd. Racism introduces absurdity into the human condition. Not only does racism express the absurdity of the racists, but it generates absurdity in the victims. And the absurdity of the victims intensifies the absurdity of the racists, ad infinitum." Chester Himes, *My Life of Absurdity* (New York: Doubleday, 1976), p. 1.

42. Himes, *Run Man Run*, p. 18.

43. Richard Wright, *Native Son* (New York: Harper and Brothers, 1940); Chester Himes, *If He Hollers, Let Him Go* (New York: Doubleday, 1945); Chester Himes, *Lonely Crusade* (1947; reprint, New York: Thunder's Mouth, 1997).

44. Himes, *Run Man Run*, p. 111.

45. Marshall Berman, *All That Is Solid Melts into Air* (New York: Penguin, 1982).

46. Caro, *The Power Broker*, p. 20.

47. For an interesting updated assessment of Moses's legacy, see Hillary Ballon and Kenneth Jackson, ed., *Robert Moses and the Modern City: The Transformation of New York* (New York: Norton, 2007).

48. Himes, *Run Man Run*, p. 77.

49. Ibid., pp. 155–156.

50. Phillip Langdon, *Orange Roofs, Golden Arches: The Architecture of American Chain Restaurants* (New York: Knopf, 1986), pp. 16–24.

51. Himes, *Run Man Run*, p. 55.

52. Ibid., p. 156.

53. Ibid.

54. Ibid., p. 152.

55. Ibid., p. 177.

56. Quoted in Margolies and Fabre, *The Several Lives of Chester Himes*, p. 149.

57. When Himes did publish in the men's magazine *Esquire*, he made the principal characters of these stories white, and his own racial identity as the author was not disclosed. As Edward Margolies and Michel Fabre postulate, "Possibly Himes or Arnold Gingrich, the editor of *Esquire*, thought the magazine's readership would not be especially drawn to Negro characters different from the then popular Amos 'n' Andy stereotypes." Margolies and Fabre, *The Several Lives of Chester Himes*, p. 36.

58. Many recent works of secondary criticism on hard-boiled literature conclude with a chapter on Himes. See, for example, McCann, *Gumshoe America*; Smith, *Hard-Boiled*; and Abbott, *The Street Was Mine*.

59. Himes, *My Life of Absurdity*, p. 126.

2 / Pimping Fictions

1. Iceberg Slim, *Pimp: The Story of My Life* (Los Angeles: Holloway House, 1967), pp. 305–306.

2. Ibid., p. 306.

3. As William Andrews reminds us, "Perhaps more than any other literary form in black American letters, autobiography has been recognized and celebrated since its inception as a powerful means of addressing and altering sociopolitical as well as cultural realities in the United States." William Andrews, introduction to Andrews, *African American Autobiography*, p. 1.

4. In this chapter, when I refer to Robert Beck, I mean the historical person who wrote *Pimp: The Story of My Life*. When I refer to Iceberg Slim, I mean the narrator of the story.

5. Phil Patton, "Sold on Ice: Six Million Readers Can't Be Wrong," *Esquire* October 1992: 76.

6. For information on Beck's influence on blaxploitation films, see Darius James, "That's Blackpulpsploitation: Deeper Roots of the Baadasssss 'Tude," *NY Press Books and Publishing* November 1997: 10–11, as well as Ed Guerrero, *Framing Blackness: The African American Image in Film* (Philadelphia: Temple University Press, 1993), pp. 94, 225–226. For information on Beck's influence on hip hop, see Gwendolyn Osborn, "The Legacy of Ghetto Pulp Fiction," *Black Issues Book Review* September 2001: 50; Tracy Grant, "Why Hip-Hop Heads Love Donald Goines," *Black Issues Book Review* September 2001: 53; and Alan Light, ed., *The Vibe History of Hip Hop* (New York: Three Rivers, 1999), pp. 116–117.

7. Tracy "Ice-T" Marrow, introduction to *Pimp: The Story of My Life* (1967; reprint, Edinburgh, UK: Payback, 1996), pp. v–vi.

8. See Denning, *Mechanic Accents*; and Richard Slotkin, *Gunfighter Nation: The Myth of the Frontier in Twentieth-Century America* (1992; reprint, Norman: University of Oklahoma Press, 1998).

9. See Abdul JanMohamed, *The Death-Bound-Subject: Richard Wright's Archaeology of Death* (Durham, NC: Duke University Press, 2005).

10. Bob Moore, "The Inside Story of Black Pimps," *Sepia* February 1972: 56.

11. Helen Koblin, "The Portrait of an Ex-Pimp Philosopher, Iceberg Slim," *Los Angeles Free Press* 25 February 1972; Hollie I. West, "Sweet Talk, Hustle, and Muscle," *Washington Post* 20 March 1973; Kalamu ya Salaam, "The Psychology of the Pimp: Iceberg Slim Reveals the Reality," *Black Collegian* January–February 1975: 33–35, 55. Many of the interviews with Robert Beck have been recently reprinted in Ian Whittaker's *Iceberg Slim: The Lost Interviews* (Croydon, UK: Infinite Dreams, 2009).

12. Robert Beck does get mention in a few academic sources. See, for instance, D. B. Graham, "Negative Glamour: The Pimp Hero in the Fiction of Iceberg Slim," *Obsidian* 1 (Summer 1975): 5–17; John W. Roberts, *From Trickster to Badman: The Folk Hero in Slavery and Freedom* (Philadelphia: University of Pennsylvania Press, 1990); Peter A. Muckley, "Iceberg Slim: Robert Beck—A True Essay at a Bio-Criticism of an Ex-Outlaw Artist," *Black Scholar* 26.1 (1996): 18–25; Bryant, *Born in a Mighty Bad Land*; Suzanne B. Dietzel, "The African American Novel and Popular Culture,"

in *The Cambridge Companion to the African American Novel* (Cambridge: Cambridge University Press, 2004), pp. 161–163; and Munby, *Under a Bad Sign.*

13. Graham, "Negative Glamour," pp. 14, 16.

14. For an elaboration of this point in the field of music, see Eithne Quinn's analysis of the pimp figure in gangsta rap, "'Who's the Mack?': The Performativity and Politics of the Pimp Figure in Gangsta Rap," *Journal of American Studies* 34.1 (2000): 115–136.

15. Stuart Hall, "What Is This 'Black' in Black Popular Culture?," in *Black Popular Culture*, ed. Gina Dent (Seattle: Bay, 1992), p. 31.

16. Bentley Morriss, interview with author, June 2004.

17. Ibid.

18. For an account of Holloway House's history, see Peter Gilstrap, "The House That Blacks Built," in *The Misread City*, ed. Scott Timberg and Dana Gioia (Los Angeles: Red Hen, 2003), pp. 87–99.

19. Morriss interview.

20. Ibid.

21. Slim, *Pimp*, p. 17.

22. Nolan Davis, "Iceberg Slim: Pimping the Page," *Players* June 1977: 83.

23. I would like to thank both Diane Beck and Jorge Hinojosa for providing me access to Robert Beck's royalty statements and contracts.

24. Davis, "Iceberg Slim," p. 30.

25. Slim, *Pimp*, p. 163.

26. Ibid., p. 164.

27. Joel Dinerstein, "Lester Young and the Birth of Cool," in *Signifyin(g), Sanctifyin', and Slam Dunking: A Reader in African American Expressive Culture*, ed. Gena Dagel Caponi (Amherst: University of Massachusetts Press, 1999), p. 267.

28. Eric Lott, "Double V, Double Time: Bebop's Politics of Style," *Callaloo* 0.36 (Summer 1988): 603; see also Kobena Mercer, *Welcome to the Jungle: New Positions in Black Cultural Studies* (London: Routledge, 1994).

29. Robin Kelley, *Race Rebels: Culture, Politics, and the Black Working Class* (New York: Free Press, 1995).

30. Christina Milner and Richard Milner, *Black Players: The Secret World of Black Pimps* (London: Michael Joseph, 1972), p. 287. It should be noted that before Robert Beck, Harlem Renaissance writer Rudolph Fisher also included a glossary of street talk in his 1928 novel *The Walls of Jericho.*

31. Drake and Cayton, *Black Metropolis*, p. 174.

32. Ibid., p. 178.

33. Hirsch, *Making the Second Ghetto*, pp. 262–263.

34. Slim, *Pimp*, pp. 86, 117, 141, 146.

35. Ibid., p. 46.

36. Ibid., pp. 86–87.

37. As Robert Beck explained once in a letter to an aspiring young writer, he viewed these psychological traumas as a central literary device to structure his story: "Perhaps your story would have more impact written in the first person. In writing your story, use as much as possible those characters and situations which enhance excitement and interest for readers. Be brief with the pre-adult bio segments unless you have determined that certain of these experiences (parental failure) are causal in the later traumas of your life. Keep your sentences crisp and release as many ego restraints

and as you can. In a biographical work, to confess imperfection and vulnerability on the page is to charm and win the empathy of readers." Undated letter by Robert Beck, currently in author's private collection. Thanks to Diane Beck for providing this letter and others.

38. Slim, *Pimp*, p. 19.

39. According to Moynihan's infamous formulation, "Nonetheless, at the center of the tangle of pathology is the weakness of the family structure. Once or twice removed, it will be found to be the principal source of the most aberrant, inadequate, or anti-social behavior that did not establish, but now serves to perpetuate, the cycle of poverty and deprivation." Daniel Patrick Moynihan, *The Negro Family: The Case for National Action*, in *The Moynihan Report and the Politics of Controversy*, ed. Lee Rainwater and William L. Yancey (Cambridge, MA: MIT Press, 1967), p. 30.

40. Hortense Spillers, "Mama's Baby, Papa's Maybe: An American Grammar Book," *Diacritics* 17.2 (Summer 1987): 65–81; Michelle Wallace, *Black Macho and the Myth of the Superwoman* (London: Verso, 1990); Phillip Brian Harper, *Are We Not Men? Masculine Anxiety and the Problem of African American Identity* (New York: Oxford University Press, 1996).

41. Slim, *Pimp*, p. 31.

42. Patricia Hill Collins, *Black Feminist Thought: Knowledge, Consciousness, and the Politics of Empowerment* (1990; reprint, New York: Routledge, 1991), p. 77.

43. Slim, *Pimp*, p. 194–195.

44. Ibid., p. 215.

45. Ibid., p. 146.

46. Ibid., p. 150.

47. Ibid., pp. 176–177.

48. I would like to thank Jorge Hinojosa for providing access to interviews of Betty Mae Shue, Camille Beck, and many other people connected to Robert Beck.

49. Camille Beck, interview with Jorge Hinojosa.

50. Robert Beck, *Night Train to Sugar Hill*, p. 134. Thanks to Jorge Hinojosa for providing me access to this unpublished document.

3 / The Revolution Will Not Be Televised

1. With rare exception, Goines, much like his literary forbearer Robert Beck, is not studied much in literary circles. The few exceptions include Greg Goode, "From *Dopefiend* to *Kenyatta's Last Hit*: The Angry Black Crime Novels of Donald Goines," *MELUS* 11.3 (Fall 1984): 41–48; Michael Covino, "Motor City Breakdown" *Village Voice* August 1987; William Van Deburg, *Black Camelot: Black Cultural Heroes in Their Times, 1960–1980* (Chicago: University of Chicago Press, 1997); L. H. Stallings "'I'm Goin Pimp Whores!': The Goines Factor and the Theory of a Hip-Hop Neo-Slave Narrative," *New Centennial Review* 3.3 (2003): 175–203; Bryant, *Born in a Mighty Bad Land*; Eddie Allen, *Low Road: The Life and Legacy of Donald Goines* (New York: St. Martin's, 2004); Munby, *Under a Bad Sign*.

2. Donald Goines, *Whoreson: The Story of a Ghetto Pimp* (Los Angeles: Holloway House, 1972), p. 259.

3. Ibid., pp. 291–292.

4. Sugrue, *The Origins of the Urban Crisis*, p. 234.

5. Tupac Shakur calls Goines a "father figure" in the lyrics for "Tradin' War Stories."

Nas named a song "Black Girl Lost" as a tribute to Goines's novel of the same name. Other hip hop stars who have been influenced by Goines include the Wu-Tang Clan's Ghostface Killah and RZA, Kool G Rap, Ludicris, MF Grimm, and Grand Puba. See Munby, *Under a Bad Sign*, pp. 154–155. In the recent documentary on Goines, *Donnie's Story: The Life of Donald Goines*, rappers Ice Cube, E-40, Bowtie, DMX, Big B, and many others all cite Goines's literature as the source for modern hip hop.

6. Goode, "From *Dopefiend* to *Kenyatta's Last Hit*," pp. 42–43.

7. Ibid., p. 43.

8. My thinking here is influenced by Phillip Bryan Harper's analysis of Motown music in his *Are We Not Men?*. He writes, "The relevant question here, then, has to do not with what happens to the 'authenticity' of black music once it is subjected to the demands of the mass market, but, rather, with how the very idea of 'blackness' itself is constructed and manipulated within the industry in such a way as both to produce and meet those very demands" (85).

9. Donald Goines, *Dopefiend: The Story of a Black Junkie* (Los Angeles: Holloway House, 1971), back cover.

10. Ibid., p. 15.

11. Official numbers on Goines's book sales have been sketchy at best. It was reported that he sold about a million and a half copies by March 1975. According to Greg Goode, his novels had sold over five million copies by 1984. However, in my 2004 interview with Bentley Morriss, he claimed that Goines had sold ten million books. Greg Goode, "Donald Goines," *Dictionary of Literary Biography 33: Afro-American Fiction Writers after 1955* (Columbia, SC: Bruccoli-Clark, 1984), p. 99.

12. I would like to thank Goines's biographer, Eddie Allen, for providing me access to Goines's letters, diaries, and other documents.

13. Later in the letter, Goines writes, seemingly to his publisher, "Even if it cost you five thousand dollars out of your private account . . . send me somewhere that I can work uninterrupted for just four to six months—not on garbage—but on one book that might not be a number one best seller; but it would be the best that I ever do."

14. Wanda Coleman, interview with author, August 2009.

15. Ibid.

16. In another one of Goines's handwritten notes found in his briefcase, he seems aware that this practice of stealing other people's materials may be putting him in danger. It reads, "Finish the book. Hard to stay away from truth. Could get hurt. Know too much. Be careful in the life. If they read this [they] can tell who [the] story is about [by the] middle of the story. Called Marie for advise. Change story line. No brothers. One person. Change story and drug used. May not finish this one."

17. Emory Holmes, interview with author, August 2009.

18. Eddie Stone, *Donald Writes No More* (Los Angeles: Holloway House, 1974), p. 9.

19. Donald Goines's own background was in fact more complex than the advertisements created by Holloway House suggested. Donald Goines was not actually a product of the slums but grew up in a middle-class environment in the black suburbs of Detroit, miles away from the ghetto streets he immortalized in his fiction. Goines's father, Joe, owned a number of successful laundry businesses, which provided the Goines family with wealth relative to their neighbors. He attended Catholic school until the eighth grade, and his family was the first on the block to own a car and a television. During the summer months, Joe and his wife, Myrtle,

would take Donald and his sister, Marie, across the Canadian border to ride horses. See Allen, *Low Road.*

20. Quoted in Stallings, "I'm Goin Pimp Whores!," p. 190.

21. Allen, *Low Road*, p. 191.

22. Donald Goines, *Kenyatta's Last Hit* (Los Angeles: Holloway House, 1975), p. 212.

23. Donald Goines, *Crime Partners* (Los Angeles: Holloway House, 1974), p. 49.

24. Goines, *Kenyatta's Last Hit*, p. 14.

25. Goines, *Crime Partners*, p. 48.

26. Ibid., p. 69.

27. Franz Fanon, *The Wretched of the Earth* (1961; reprint, New York: Grove, 2004); Kenneth B. Clark, *Dark Ghetto: Dilemmas of Social Power* (New York: Harper and Row, 1965); Harold Cruse, *Rebellion or Revolution* (New York: Morrow, 1968); and Stokely Carmichael and Charles Hamilton, *Black Power* (New York: Random House, 1968).

28. Clark, *Dark Ghetto*, p. 11.

29. Goines, *Crime Partners*, pp. 125–126.

30. Goines, *Kenyatta's Last Hit*, pp. 86–87.

31. Adopting strategies previously used during the 1940s and 1950s against the Socialist Workers Party and the Communist Party in the United States, J. Edgar Hoover and the FBI sought to create dissent and internal strife within the Black Panther Party. In an internal memorandum Hoover sent to all FBI offices on 25 August 1967, he wrote, "The purpose of this new counterintelligence endeavor is to expose, disrupt, misdirect, discredit or otherwise neutralize the activities of black nationalist hate-type organizations and groupings, their leadership, spokesmen, membership, and supporters." Through various means, including fomenting conflict with rival political organizations, infiltrating the BPP ranks, and assassinating the BPP leaders, the FBI and local law enforcement agencies effectively undermined the Panthers by the early 1970s. See Ward Churchill and Jim Vander Wall's *Agents of Repression: The FBI's Secret War against the Black Panther Party and the American Indian Movement* (Cambridge, MA: South End, 2001).

32. Donald Goines, *Kenyatta's Escape* (Los Angeles: Holloway House, 1974), p. 45.

33. Donald Goines, *Never Die Alone* (Los Angeles: Holloway House, 1974), p. 9.

34. Ibid., p. 32.

35. Ibid.

36. Ibid., p. 36.

37. Ibid., pp. 84–85.

38. Ibid., p. 164.

39. Ibid., p. 87.

40. Ibid., p. 115.

41. Ibid., p. 156.

42. Ibid., p. 177.

43. Tom Rick, "The Fast Life and Violent Death of Donald Goines, Writer and Victim," *Detroit Free Press* 16 March 1975: 13.

4 / Black in a White Paradise

1. Roland Jefferson, *The School on 103rd Street* (1976; reprint, Los Angeles: Holloway House, 1982), p. 138.

2. Massey and Denton, *American Apartheid*, pp. 60–82.

3. Fredric Jameson, "Reification and Utopia in Mass Culture," *Social Text* 1 (Winter 1979): 144.

4. Dohra Ahmad, *Landscapes of Hope: Anti-Colonial Utopianism in America* (New York: Oxford University Press, 2009). For further discussion of utopias in African American literature, also see Charles Scruggs, *Invisible Cities in the Afro-American Novel* (Baltimore: Johns Hopkins University Press, 1993); Mark Christian Thompson, *Black Fascisms: African American Literature and Culture between the Wars* (Charlottesville: University of Virginia Press, 2007); and Adenike Marie Davidson, *The Black Nation Novel: Imagining Homeplace in Early African American Literature* (Chicago: Third World, 2008).

5. Bryant, *Born in a Mighty Bad Land*, p. 133.

6. Thank you to Diane Beck, who provided me with numerous letters written to her husband, Robert Beck, by inmates of various prisons who were looking for advice on how to write their own stories of criminal activity and redemption.

7. Andrew Stonewall Jackson, *Gentleman Pimp* (Los Angeles: Holloway House, 1973), pp. 8, 10.

8. Elroy Waters, *Stack A. Dollar* (Los Angeles: Holloway House, 1979), p. 95.

9. Radway, *Reading the Romance*, p. 63.

10. Charlie Avery Harris, *Con Man* (Los Angeles: Holloway House, 1978), p. 224.

11. Charlie Avery Harris, *Whoredaughter* (Los Angeles: Holloway House, 1976), p. 5.

12. Charlie Avery Harris, *Broad Players* (Los Angeles: Holloway House, 1977), pp. 98–99.

13. Harris, *Con Man*, pp. 133–134.

14. Harris, *Whoredaughter*, p. 138.

15. Amos Brooke, *Black in a White Paradise* (Los Angles: Holloway House, 1978).

16. Ibid., p. 142.

17. Ibid., p. 218.

18. Omar Fletcher, *Walking Black and Tall* (Los Angeles: Holloway House, 1977), p. 10.

19. Ibid., p. 9.

20. Omar Fletcher, *Black against the Mob* (Los Angeles: Holloway House, 1977), p. 224.

21. Ibid., p. 90.

22. Fletcher, *Walking Black and Tall*, p. 215.

23. Joseph Nazel, *Billion Dollar Death* (Los Angeles: Holloway House, 1974), p. 8.

24. Ibid., 11.

25. Joseph Nazel, *Iceman #7: The Shakedown* (Los Angeles: Holloway House, 1975), p. 17.

26. Joseph Nazel, *Iceman #2: The Golden Shaft* (Los Angeles: Holloway House, 1974), p. 68.

27. Ibid., pp. 81–82.

28. Ibid., p. 82.

29. Dom Gober (Joseph Nazel), *Black Cop* (Los Angeles: Holloway House, 1974), p. 7.

30. Ibid.

31. Ibid., p. 205.

32. Dom Gober (Joseph Nazel), *Doomsday Squad* (Los Angeles: Holloway House, 1975), p. 64.

33. Dom Gober (Joseph Nazel), *Killer Cop* (Los Angeles: Holloway House, 1975), p. 167–168.

34. Ibid., p. 13.

35. Odie Hawkins, *Ghetto Sketches* (Los Angeles: Holloway House, 1972), p. 9.

36. Odie Hawkins, interview with author, June 2009.

37. Roland Jefferson, interview with author, June 2009.

38. Ibid.

5 / "For He Who Is"

1. Jawara, "Letter to the Editor," *Players* August 1976: 16.

2. Abby Arthur Johnson and Ronald Mayberry, *Propaganda and Aesthetics: The Literary Politics of Afro-American Magazines in the Twentieth Century* (Amherst: University of Massachusetts Press, 1979), p. 10.

3. Robert Fanuzzi, "Frederick Douglass's 'Colored Newspaper,'" in *The Black Press*, ed. Todd Vogel (New Brunswick, NJ: Rutgers University Press, 2001), p. 56.

4. Tom Pendergast, *Creating the Modern Man: American Magazines and Consumer Culture, 1900–1950* (Columbia: University of Missouri Press, 2000), pp. 109, 179.

5. Jannette Dates, "Print News," in *Split Image: African Americans in the Mass Media*, ed. Jannette Dates and William Barlow (Washington, DC: Howard University Press, 1983), p. 353; Charles A. Simmons, *The African American Press: With Special Reference to Four Newspapers, 1827–1965* (Jefferson, NC: MacFarland, 1998), p. 34.

6. Pendergast, *Creating the Modern Man*, pp. 243, 251; James C. Hall, "On Sale at Your Favorite Newsstand: *Negro Digest/Black World* and the 1960s," in Vogel, *The Black Press*, p. 194.

7. Pendergast, *Creating the Modern Man*; Noliwe M. Rooks, *Ladies Pages: African American Women's Magazines and the Culture That Made Them* (New Brunswick, NJ: Rutgers University Press, 2004); and Elizabeth Fratterigo, *Playboy and the Making of the Good Life in Modern America* (New York: Oxford University Press, 2009).

8. "Hustlers' Cars," *Players* November 1973: 67.

9. Michele Kidd, "Raymond St. Jacques: A *Players* Interview," *Players* July 1974: 25.

10. Art Aveilhe, "New Dude on the Block," *Players* July 1976: 4.

11. Stanley Crouch, "Crouch on Jazz," *Players* July 1974: 75.

12. Stanley Crouch, "Crouch on Jazz," *Players* January 1975: 13.

13. "Hustlers' Cars," p. 69.

14. For more detailed information on this history, see my interview with Wanda Coleman, titled "'Harvard in Hell': Holloway House Publishing Company, *Players Magazine*, and the Invention of Black Mass-Market Erotica—Interviews with Wanda Coleman and Emory 'Butch' Holmes II," *MELUS* 35.4 (Winter 2010): 111–137.

15. According to critic Elizabeth Fraterrigo, in the early 1960s, *Playboy* had been the leading men's magazine among African American readers, who made up 11 percent of its paid circulation. Fraterrigo, *Playboy and the Making of the Good Life*, p. 249.

16. Ibid., 146.

17. "Pam Grier/Ms. Foxy Brown," *Players* March 1974: 68.

18. "Gaye," *Players* May 1975: 35.

19. Robert E. Foreman, "Black and Beautiful," *Players* March 1975: 37.

20. Bobbye Dones, "Conversin'," *Players* June 1976: 26.

21. Kathy Clark, "A Sister Raps," *Players* September 1975: 26.

22. Joseph Nazel, "Who It Is," *Players* June 1975: 5.

23. Gifford, "Harvard in Hell," p. 121.

24. Ibid., pp. 130–131.

25. Ibid., p. 131.

26. Ralph Weinstock, "Statement of Ownership, Management and Circulation," *Players* January 1975: 88; Ralph Weinstock, "Statement of Ownership, Management and Circulation," *Players* December 1984: 69.

27. B.W., "Letter to the Editor," *Players* June 1979: 18.

28. Ralph Weinstock, "Statement of Ownership, Management and Circulation," *Players* December 1984: 60.

29. John Slade, "Dis Shit Is Nasty," *Players Nasty* May 1997: 2.

6 / The Women of Street Literature

1. Vickie Stringer, *Dirty Red: A Novel* (New York: Atria, 2006), p. 20.

2. Ibid., p. 27.

3. Ibid., p. 202.

4. For two useful recent articles on the street literature reading culture in American prisons, see H. Bruce Franklin, "Can the Penitentiary Teach the Academy to Read?," *MLA* 123.3 (May 2008): 643–649, as well as Megan Sweeney, "Books as Bombs: Incendiary Reading Practices in Women's Prisons," *MLA* 123.3 (May 2008): 666–672.

5. Ta-Nehisi Paul Coats, "Hustle and Grow," *Time* 16 October 2006: 75–76.

6. Judith Rosen, "Street Lit: Readers Gotta Have It," *Publishers Weekly* 13 December 2004: 31–35; Earni Young, "Urban Lit Goes Legit," *Black Issues Book Review* September–October 2006: 20–23.

7. Nick Chiles, "Their Eyes Were Reading Smut," *New York Times* 4 January 2006.

8. For a useful guide to fan websites and street literature publishers, see David Wright, "Streetwise Urban Fiction," *Library Journal* 1 July 2006: 42–45.

9. Shannon Holmes, *Never Go Home Again* (New York: Atria, 2004), pp. 185–186.

10. Vickie Stringer, *Let That Be the Reason* (Brooklyn, NY: Upstream, 2001), p. viii. It is interesting to note that the later Atria reprinting of the novel does not feature this acknowledgment.

11. Vickie Stringer, *Let That Be the Reason* (2001; reprint, New York: Atria, 2009), p. 11.

12. Ibid., p. 12.

13. Ibid., p. 16.

14. Ibid., p. 15.

15. Ibid., p. 139.

16. Ibid., pp. 30–31.

17. Ibid., p. 91.

18. Ibid., p. 287.

19. As Turner put it in a recent interview with *Essence*, "I really connected with that book. I went to the bookstore after I finished it, looking for other books like it. There weren't any. I kept looking for similar stories. When I realized there weren't any, I decided to write my own." Imani Powell, "Hustle and Flow," *Essence* May 2007: 92.

20. Sister Souljah, *The Coldest Winter Ever* (1999; reprint, New York: Pocket Books, 2006), p. 1.

21. Ibid., p. 33.

22. Ibid., pp. 293–294.

23. Ibid., p. 274.

24. Ibid., p. 430.

25. Nikki Turner, *A Hustler's Wife* (Columbus, OH: Triple Crown, 2003), p. 96.

26. Ibid., p. 187.

27. Ibid., p. 192.

28. Ibid., p. 258.

29. Nikki Turner, "A Special Message from Nikki Turner," in *Forever a Hustler's Wife* (New York: Ballantine, 2007), pp. ix–x.

30. Nikki Turner, *Riding Dirty on I-95* (New York: Ballantine, 2006), p. 218.

31. Seth "Soul Man" Ferranti, "Hip Hop Fiction Beefs," *The Urban Book Source* Nov. 2006.

32. Zakiyyah El-Amin, "Queen of Hip-Hop Literature," *Black Enterprise* January 2006: 49.

33. Patrick J. Sauer, "How I Did It: Vickie Stringer, CEO Triple Crown Publications," *Inc.* May 2006: 108.

34. Anthony White, "Ghost Writing: When Free Ride Crosses the Bottom Line," *Street Literature Review* November 2008: 13.

35. Ferranti, "Hip Hop Beefs." When Teague refers to World War I here, he is talking about the conflict over royalties that emerged between himself and Woods following the success of the *Dutch* series.

36. Ellison, *Invisible Man*, p. 441.

37. Kwame Teague, *The Glory of My Demise* (New York: Teri Woods, 2003), p. 146.

38. Ibid., p. 203.

INDEX

About the Author

Justin Gifford is Assistant Professor of English at the University of Nevada, Reno.